THE TEACHING
ONLINE HANDBOOK

COURTNEY
OSTAFF

First Published 2020

by John Catt Educational Ltd,
15 Riduna Park, Station Road,
Melton, Woodbridge IP12 1QT

Tel: +44 (0) 1394 389850
Email: enquiries@johncatt.com
Website: www.johncatt.com

ISBN: 978 1 913622 38 1

Set and designed by John Catt Educational Limited

CONTENTS

ABOUT THE AUTHOR

Courtney Ostaff has been teaching online since 1999. With a wide variety of experience as a public school special education teacher, an in-home early intervention specialist, a community college algebra instructor, and a homeschooler, she has worked with students ranging from the very young to the elderly. Along the way, she has developed practices and techniques for making the most of the online classroom. Currently, she teaches math, science, and social studies at an online learning services provider, working with secondary students worldwide.

Follow Courtney on Twitter @StuckIn48403550 and at https://courtneyostaff.com

INTRODUCTION

In the winter of 1999/2000, I was a twenty-two-year-old graduate student at West Virginia University when I lucked into a graduate assistantship in the West Virginia University School of Social Work. The school shared a building with my degree program in public administration. My assistantship paid a few hundred dollars a month plus my tuition and fees for twenty hours of work per week. Little did I know that this job would shape my career.

At the time, it was an open secret (exposed by the *Washington Post* in 1992) that the Greenbrier, an exclusive luxury hotel in the mountains of West Virginia, was a back-up location for the US Congress in case of nuclear attack. As part of ensuring internet accessibility for Congress, one of the first dedicated high-speed internet lines was installed from northern Virginia through the mountains to the Greenbrier hotel. For reasons above my pay grade, that line went through the building I was working in, complete with a state-of-the-art videoconferencing center.

My boss, Dr. Karen Harper-Dorton, won a grant from the Department of Commerce to bridge the digital divide by using these videoconferencing facilities to teach basic computer skills to local nonprofit organizations and the public. I was assigned to do the actual teaching. I had had a side gig in undergraduate school as a mathematics tutor, but I'd never taught a large group, or taught online.

Honestly, I was terrible. I stood in front of the camera, held up a workbook I'd printed from the Microsoft website, and went through it, page by page. After I read the workbook, I took questions from an audience I couldn't see. If I remember correctly, each session lasted about forty-five minutes, and I did a whole series of them over the next couple of years.

After I graduated, I fell into teaching online for the University of Phoenix's community college, Axia. I have eighteen graduate hours in mathematics, which they felt qualified me to teach college algebra. At the time, the for-profit college industry was booming, and they had refined a process for training new adjunct instructors to teach college algebra via newsgroups. Newsgroups are an online discussion forum containing discussions about a specific topic, as if Reddit was created by email. As part of my professional development, I attended a series of valuable workshops and was held to a high standard.

By the time the community college upgraded their accreditation to require their instructors to have master's degrees in mathematics, I had learned a lot about teaching non-traditional, often low-income, students I never met, would never see, and with whom I had no prior relationship. These skills would serve me well later in my career.

While I taught at Axia, students switched from typing their math homework into Word documents to using MyMathLab. I later discovered MyMathLab had become one of the default pieces of software for teaching math in higher education. When I taught the college algebra at my local universities, they used MyMathLab for their face-to-face math programs. This quickly became invaluable to my professional practice.

It took me a decade to earn my second master's degree. In my twenties and thirties, I taught two nine-week classes at a time for Axia. At the same time, I attended graduate school at West Virginia University to earn the 140+ credits I needed for dual certifications in general social studies and science grades for grades five through twelve. During this time, my husband and I ended up with custody of his niece, who needed a great deal from us.

When I finished my master's in secondary education, I was student teaching. Student teaching at West Virginia University required students to work the full-time job of a teacher as well as take classes at night. On the side, I was teaching a full course load of college algebra online (four courses every eighteen weeks). In addition, I had a young child of my own in half-day preschool and my husband and I were still caring for his niece. Simultaneously, I was attending Marshall University part-time to earn a special education certification in teaching the visually impaired from birth to adult. Despite this multi-faceted experience in education, no one ever suggested that I could teach kindergarten through twelfth grade online.

After I became pregnant with my second child, I landed a great job as a special education teacher in my local public schools. At this job, I was itinerant, working in multiple schools across the district to teach students with visual impairments, mostly one on one. However, my first child was not adjusting well to the classroom environment. Looking back, dismissing her distress as normal issues with her first year of full-time school was not a wise decision.

Then my second child was born with a health condition that required my focused attention. Despite turning over all of my take-home salary to a nanny, in two weeks my youngest child lost fifty percentiles of her body weight. Anxiously, my husband and I discussed our options during my maternity leave. That summer, I happened to see a help-wanted ad on Facebook for a new online middle/high school, the Well-Trained Mind Academy, and sent in my resume.

I am forever grateful that the Well-Trained Mind Academy offered me a job that allowed me to stay home with my youngest child. As a result, I impulsively decided to homeschool my eldest child, just for a little while. Because I was quite sensibly terrified about messing her up, I did a lot of research about homeschooling. While my oldest child found her joy again, I was still stressed out. After all, I didn't want her to be behind when she went back to public school.

Eventually, I found *The Well-Trained Mind*. I liked it, but I wasn't convinced. Many things sound good in theory but are terrible in reality. Because I wanted to know if classical education would work, I went hunting for data. There is no modern research about the usefulness of classical education. But there is research about curricula.

What did the research say about what to learn and how we should learn it? My teaching classes hadn't recommended any particular course of instruction. Students were to construct their own meaning of the world, and we were to foster their interests while teaching the curriculum standards and objectives. Where did those come from? Education experts had decided what was important.

As a nervous homeschooler, I wanted to do my best for my daughter. That first year, I was focused on teaching her to read. In my local Barnes and Noble, I came across *Proust and the Squid* by Maryanne Wolf, a book about how we learn to read. It was fascinating! I went looking for more about the science of reading and bought *Reading in the Brain* by Stanislas Dehaene. I had never heard of the "visual word form area."[i]

After I'd bought that and rated it with five stars, Amazon thought I might also like *When Can You Trust the Experts?* by Dr. Willingham. It had never occurred to me not to trust the experts in education. I found this bit particularly interesting:

> There are some things that humans are primed to learn, especially how to walk, how to talk, and how to interact socially. Each represents a highly complex skill that most children learn without the benefit of instruction, simply by watching others; thus such learning can fairly be called natural and effortless. But most of what we want kids to learn in school is qualitatively different.[ii]

That had never occurred to me. Later in the book, Willingham asked,

> Does Amy Chua's method of parenting "work"? If you share her goals, that's an open question, and you could use methods of science to answer it.[iii]

What were my goals? I thought about it for a while, and then went back to my Willingham book and read,

> What it [education research] means for schooling depends on your goals for schooling. Suppose I think that children attend school for self-actualization. . . . But now suppose my goal for schooling is not self-actualization but preparation for the world of work.[iv]

I wanted my daughter to be able to study whatever she wanted in college. At age six, she was determined to be a paleontologist, which requires a lot of math and science. The dedicated teachers at my tiny, rural public high school had done their best, but when I got to college I found myself woefully unprepared compared to my new classmates. I didn't want that to happen to her, which gave me a focus for her homeschooling content.

I thought what Willingham had to say was interesting, so I picked up *Why Don't Students Like School?* The book was interesting because he made statements like "It is not possible to think well on a topic in the absence of factual knowledge about the topic" and "we understand new things in the context of things we already know" and "proficiency requires practice" and "cognition is fundamentally different early and late in training."[v] These all rang true, because these kinds of ideas were repeated in those books about how people learn to read—and *The Well-Trained Mind* supported them all in its prescribed practice.

I kept reading about how we learn. One of the high-powered homeschool moms on the Well-Trained Mind Forums recommended *A Mathematician's Lament* by Paul Lockhart, so I read it. I'd never felt like a good math student, and I wanted my daughter to be good at math so she could be a paleontologist. Hunting down more books about how people learn math, I read *The Number Sense* by Stanislas Dehaene. Surely, math proficiency was a matter of talent? "No," said Dehaene, and "No," said *The Math Gene* by Keith Devlin.

The Well-Trained Mind Forums were international in scope, which made me wonder: why were students in other countries so much better at math? From a link on the forums I read "Word Problems in Russia and America" by Andrei Toom. Ah, this was something I could work with. Trying to do a good job homeschooling, I sought out math curricula that matched as best I could. Eventually, I bought Singapore math for my young daughter.

Because my husband and I now had custody of his teenage niece, I read *The Teenage Brain*. I stopped and stared in wonder when I found its chart mapping students' ability to memorize and their ability to think abstractly, recognizing how it matched with the grammar stage, the logic stage, and the rhetoric stages in classical education.

Then, I read *The Knowledge Deficit* by E.D. Hirsch, Jr. I could see why this made so many people angry—it was anti-establishment at its best. Gently put, thoroughly cited, and relentless in its take down of modern education truisms.

> The Romantic idea that learning is natural, and that the motivation for academic achievement comes from within, is an illusion that forms one of the greatest barriers to social justice imaginable, since poor and disadvantaged students must be motivated to work even harder than advantaged students in order to achieve equality of educational opportunity. . . .
>
> once basic underlying skills have been automated, the almost universal feature of reliable higher-order thinking about any subject or problem is the possession of a broad, well-integrated base of background knowledge relevant to the subject. . . .
>
> There is no natural pace for gaining the nonnatural learnings of alphabetic literacy and base-ten mathematics. Moreover, it is impossible to conduct an effective classroom when there are attempts to accommodate twenty-five different "paces" of learning.[vi]

Hirsch's statement lined up neatly with James R. Delisle's opinion piece at EdWeek, "Differentiation Doesn't Work."[vii] Carol Ann Tomlinson's response[viii] was unconvincing—it works if you do it differently than it's been done? The empirical research that I could find that a) took place in the United States, and b) applied to elementary/middle school showed that differentiated instruction in kindergarten through eighth grade made students happier, but didn't actually increase their learning.[ix x]

Looking for more, I borrowed Hirsch's *Cultural Literacy* from the library and successfully managed to keep my infant from gnawing on the book. Why, this was exactly what *The Well-Trained Mind* prescribed, only seemingly random rather than *The Well-Trained Mind*'s coherent timeline! I felt like I was joining a cult. I went looking for contrary opinions, and found many people who hated Hirsch, but no one who contested him because his ideas didn't work. I discovered that his Core Knowledge program spawned a best selling series "What Your _____ Grader Needs to Know."

That summer, I dug deeper. Hirsch's Core Knowledge prescribes Frederick Douglass and King Arthur and so on for middle school students, in order to give them what he called cultural literacy. This was not unlike Susan Wise Bauer in *The Well-Trained Mind*, prescribing Shakespeare and Robinson Crusoe for elementary school to train the mind. Even Allan Bloom, for all his many faults, prescribed only one answer to his vast critique of the modern education system:

> the good old Great Books approach, in which a liberal education means reading certain generally recognized classic texts . . . wherever the Great Books make up a central part of the curriculum, the students . . . get . . . a fund of shared experiences and thoughts.[xi]

On the other end of the political spectrum, Deresiewicz wrote in *Excellent Sheep*,

> studying the most challenging works of art, literature, and philosophy— "being forced every day to think about the hardest things people have ever thought about," . . . is the best training you can give yourself in how to talk and think.[xii]

Even so, I still wanted good data. However, it is hard to find quality research on the effect of curriculum, because the types of parents who seek out private or charter schools tend to affect the data. One summer afternoon, I came across a report from the Center on Education Policy that noted:

> Only one type of school shows an advantage over comprehensive public high schools in student achievement across subjects: Catholic religious order schools.[xiii]

I don't know much about these schools. There aren't many independent Jesuit schools (not part of a diocese), so there are very few students who attend these schools. Thanks to the internet, I found one, Jesuit High School in New Orleans. On their website, the curriculum is definitely classical, with a classics department that teaches Latin and Greek.[xiv]

Because these schools are rare, how does this compare with homeschooling? Dr. Sandra Martin-Chang's research, "The Impact of Schooling on Academic Achievement," was the best research I could find on modern homeschooling. Structured homeschoolers outperformed public schoolers of matched socioeconomic status:

children who received structured homeschooling had superior test results compared to their peers: From a half-grade advantage in math to 2.2 grade levels in reading.[xv]

Then structured curriculum with tough books is the key to good education. That makes sense, after reading *Make It Stick* by Brown, Roediger, and McDaniel.

> Learning is deeper and more durable when it's effortful. Learning that's easy is like writing in sand, here today and gone tomorrow.[xvi]

I definitely want my child's knowledge to be here today and tomorrow. I kept reading *Make It Stick*, and found this gem:

> All new learning requires a foundation of prior knowledge. . . . Mastery in any field, from cooking to chess to brain surgery, is a gradual accretion of knowledge, conceptual understanding, judgment, and skill. These are the fruits of variety in the practice of new skills, and of striving, reflection, and mental rehearsal. Memorizing facts is like stocking a construction site with the supplies to put up a house. Building the house requires not only knowledge of countless different fittings and materials but conceptual understanding, too.[xvii]

After seven years of classical education at home, with many tough books adding to her cultural literacy, I worry less about comparing my eldest child to her peers. Every now and then, I can see a glimpse of the adult she'll become, with an increasingly furnished mental house.

All the while, I've been perfecting my skills in teaching ever-younger children online, using the principles of cognitive science, classical education, and online education. Over the last six years, I have planned and taught yearlong online courses in:

- ancient history (middle and high school)
- geometry
- algebra I
- pre-algebra
- preparation for pre-algebra
- world geography
- astronomy
- biology

Teaching middle and high school is both very different, and yet much the same as teaching busy community college students. I wrote this book to share what

11

I've learned over the years with you, the classroom teacher. I'm not an expert in online education, cognitive science, or even classical education. To paraphrase Liam Neeson's character in *Taken*, "But what I do have are a very particular set of skills, skills I have acquired over a very long career, skills that make me" helpful for the average classroom teacher moving to online instruction.

ACKNOWLEDGMENTS

One last thing, before we dive in. Is there a science of learning? Yes. Am I a scientist? No. While I have done my level best to interpret implications of research for the online classroom, I am sure that I have made mistakes. Therefore, please place responsibility for those mistakes where it belongs—on my shoulders.

On the other hand, much credit should be given to North Landesman, who first suggested that I write this book. When I gave an incredulous laugh, he reached out to John Catt Educational publishers, where Mark Combes graciously took a chance on a literal unknown—I was Tweeting under a pseudonym for privacy. Michelle Brake added her voice to North's, asking for a book, and I appreciate it. When I decided to write a book proposal, Cara Jackson read over my tentative table of contents and gave me great feedback.

When I felt overwhelmed by the idea of writing an entire book, Ruth Joy gave me unexpected support. Jasmine Lane offered feedback on various sections, and her writing always keeps me on my toes. Blake Harvard took time out of his busy schedule to read over sections I was unsure of, and I am thankful for his support. When I was feeling down during the middle portion of the book, Holly Korbey asked for a copy of the finished product, which offered me a big incentive to finish it. Kripa Sundar reached out with a phone call, and we had a fun discussion about the implications of cognitive science, learning, and parenting during this pandemic. Michael Pershan offered to read portions over at a time when I was feeling unsure about my worthiness as an author, and he offered excellent critiques.

Shout out to my some of my mom friends, who are experts in their own right, and who graciously read over portions with an eye toward keeping me from making egregious errors. Dr. Kimberly Meigh read over the portion on working with students with speech and language issues. Denise Tafen read over the section on working with students with autism spectrum disorder. Calla Rieger read over the words on working with students who are deaf and hard of hearing. I am grateful to have you all in my life. Any bad takes, insensitive phrasing, and outright mistakes are all mine.

Last, but definitely not least, I am appreciative of my husband, Jason D'Aprile, who has spent nearly every evening in the last three months handling nearly all of the housework and parenting the children after working all day. My mother, Elizabeth Hall, shares our home, and she has spent countless hours supervising her grandchildren while I wrote during this seemingly endless pandemic. Credit is due to my oldest, Gwendolyn D'Aprile, for tackling pre-algebra mostly independently while I wrote, and to my youngest, Elena D'Aprile, who followed the rule to not interrupt mommy when her office door is shut.

I hope I haven't forgotten anyone, but as I'm terribly absentminded, I almost certainly have. My apologies in advance. I sincerely thank all of you.

CHAPTER 1

WHAT IS TEACHING ONLINE?

When learning something new, we should always make sure we have a shared vocabulary. For the purposes of this book, *teaching online is a complete replacement for face-to-face instruction in a core content area.* This is fundamentally different from teaching a face-to-face class. In this chapter, I'm going to establish some definitions and make some observations about teaching online.

> **Teaching online is a complete replacement for face-to-face instruction in a core content area.**

While **blended courses**, in which some work is completed online but instruction takes place face to face, are a vital and engaging type of education, they are not the focus of this book. High-quality blended courses are structured differently because they have an opportunity to build a classroom culture that relies on face-to-face, nonverbal interactions, with the online portion of the course providing enrichment and extension.

This book is not about classroom enrichment with online supplements, apps, and extensions, for several reasons.

1. Digital extras are usually *meant for face-to-face classrooms*, so they are rarely useful for the all-online classroom. Their inputs and outputs are often designed to be displayed on digital whiteboards, in-class devices, and so on.
2. Just like in a face-to-face classroom, teachers must *consider the trade-offs*. Teachers will have to learn how to use the website or app, and because they only have so much time, they'll have to take that time away from the time they've currently devoted to doing assessment, doing feedback, and reaching out to students. So, when adding in "extras," the question is, "Is it really worth it?" Often, teachers are better off refining *teacher talk*[xviii] (extra important online[xix]), improving concept presentation, making connections with students, and so on.
3. *Overwhelming* students with the number of locations and gadgets and apps is easy to do. Teachers will spend significant time teaching students where to locate materials in the online classroom. Adding multiple websites? Students (and parents) would be overwhelmed.[xx]

4. Why would teachers use something that *doesn't directly improve student learning*? Very rarely do shiny new websites or apps have any evidence to support learning. If it's not directly useful in improving student learning, then it has no place in your classroom.

Academic success in a rigorous, content-focused online course is possible.[xxi] Reflective discussions,[xxii] enhanced focus on individual student-teacher relationships,[xxiii] automated retrieval practice,[xxiv] and quality group dynamics[xxv] are all possible in online classes. Because face-to-face courses are readily available in public schools, my expectation is that I must teach at least as well as a face-to-face course, and wherever possible, better. Otherwise, why would students sign up for my class?

Non-Academic Reasons for Online Courses

There are some non-academic reasons why parents and students choose online education. One is *flexibility*. In theory, online classes are available at any time of the day or night, any day of the week. Of course, this assumes students have high-speed internet access. Between 10% and 35% of students do not have high-speed internet access at home, depending on how you define the metric.[xxvi]

Many fans of online education praise its ability to *distribute content efficiently*. For example, collaborative games are wildly popular, with more than 73% of teenagers playing some kind of videogame. In non-pandemic times, more than 66% of students under the age of eighteen play at least once a week, mostly online with others.[xxvii] I'm sure these figures are higher today, given the need for social distancing.

Often, people see online education as online lectures, perhaps with a textbook. *Massive open online courses (MOOCs)* are one kind of online education, although I would argue that they're not particularly successful. They are mostly attractive to people who are already well educated,[xxviii] and they have abysmal completion rates.[xxix]

Self-paced courses are popular, but in my experience (I volunteered to run an experimental self-paced college algebra course while working for the University of Phoenix), they have terrible completion rates. This is borne out by the data that show that self-paced courses have about half the completion rates of instructor-paced courses.[xxx]

Another perception of online education is that it *allows teachers to reach more students*. In my experience, this is not always a good thing. For example, a teacher working for K12, Inc. could have as many as 275 students.[xxxi] As teachers found, this leaves little time for student interaction, much less direct instruction.[xxxii]

Good Reasons for Online Classes

As a West Virginian, I live in a rural state. My state has worked hard to bridge the digital divide, with hardwired high-speed internet at every school.[xxxiii] Our local libraries use federal funds[xxxiv] to provide free internet access to the public at a public library in every county.[xxxv] Because our state has *difficulty attracting and retaining teachers*, particularly in science and math,[xxxvi] online classes have been used by public schools here for the last twenty years.[xxxvii]

An *inability to meet special needs* in the face-to-face classroom is another reason students are enrolled in online classes. Some parents feel that their children need more education than is provided by their local school and sign their children up for online classes. Children with major health issues that require extensive hospitalization or children who are working professionals often opt for non-traditional education options. Homeschoolers often make use of online classes. Small private schools sometimes outsource entire departments to online instructors.

Public health mandates that shut down entire school systems force teachers to transition their classes to online education. In that case, public school teachers might feel forced to use online education and feel unprepared. **This book is designed to help schoolteachers transition to online teaching.**

Types of Online Interaction

When I began teaching online, I didn't have the words to talk about it. This section is designed to give us a common vocabulary. Throughout the rest of the book, we'll use these terms as they are defined here.

First, with more experience I learned that there are two kinds of online learning: *asynchronous* and *synchronous*.

- **Synchronous** means something that happens at the same time—teacher and students are working together at the same time, interacting with each other in real time. One strong argument for this type of education is that it creates a community of learners—students enjoy each other's company, and the teacher can direct the experience.
- **Asynchronous** interaction has a time delay built in. Like text messaging and voicemails, asynchronous education allows time for reflection before students respond. This can increase the quality of class discussions and allow introverted students, students who have trouble with audio processing, English language learners, and students who don't think as fast to participate more equally.

Asynchronous

- Email
- Threaded discussion boards
- Websites
- Blogs
- Text/voice messages

Synchronous

- Telephone calls
- Live interactive audio/videochats
- One-way audio/video with immediate response
- Text-based chat rooms

Email

I use email every day because email is probably the most valuable tool in the online teacher's toolbox. Most children who can read enjoy getting email. Parents can easily be copied on emails, to help communication between parent and teacher. Email doesn't take very much internet access, and it permits users to attach files. Recordkeeping can also be done via email—"I sent it on May 7, 2017, and you responded on May 9, 2017." One last benefit of email is that it is private, meaning that teachers can send some sensitive information or a request to meet for absolute privacy.

Discussion Boards

It's no accident that Reddit is mostly discussion boards and is one of the top websites in the United States.[xxxviii] Discussion boards have benefits, which we'll discuss later, but a good argument for discussion boards is that they let students who are not in the same place or time have discussions with each other. Students can insert links, attach files, and exchange information. I think discussion boards are an essential part of online classes.

Websites

Websites are common and are what most people think of when they think of the internet. Each page on a website is like a page in a book. Authors can "bind" webpages by arranging them in order, with a cover page on top. The hierarchical arrangement isn't always clear to website users because users can skip pages with hyperlinks. Like books, webpages are great tools to share text and photos. Most online classes will run through websites called Learning Management Systems (LMSs). Unlike books, authors can include audio and video components. I frequently link to useful videos and simulations for my students.

Blogs

Blogs are some of the oldest types of websites on the internet. Like a diary, they're blank, sequential pages that authors fill in. Blogs are good for writing and often have discussion boards (the "comment" section). Teachers can run a course using a blog. Once upon a time, I taught a high school civics class by using posts for the day's news article. During the face-to-face class, students responded to the day's news article by writing comments. Blogs are a great way to push information out to students and have them respond in writing.

Text/Voice Messages

Many people don't think of text messages or voice messages as classroom tools, and in a face-to-face class, phones are a distraction. However, in an asynchronous learning environment, they can be valuable tools for contacting students with limited internet access. Photos can also be exchanged, which can be helpful for assessment. I give my personal cell phone number to students and urge them to contact me if they have an emergency. Every semester, I get panicked text messages.

Telephone Calls

Telephones are an older form of technology, but sometimes nothing beats picking up the phone and reaching out to a student and their parent. Tone of voice, sensitivity to feedback, and willingness to listen to the parent or student can have an influence on whether a student finishes the course. Being available by phone signals that teachers care for the student, and building relationships helps in teaching. Often, students will reveal information during a phone call that they didn't feel was important enough to write down, like the fact that they're in the hospital.

Live Interactive Videochats

Live, interactive videochats such as FaceTime, Skype, and Zoom are popular. However, there are several issues. First, teachers often assume that students have the technology, reliable internet access, time, and space to make this software usable. Second, videochats require a different set of classroom management skills. Third, most teachers do not have the required materials. Fourth, privacy and security are worries. However, students like coming to class and being able to chat with each other, which is why I do this every day.

One-Way Audio/Video with Immediate Response

This type of communication is different from live, interactive videochats because the communication is one-way. Examples of this would be television or radio broadcasts that take callers on air, and Twitch or YouTube livestreams with live chats. These are good, but don't let students participate as much. These are less common in the online classroom.

Text-Based Chats

Like text messaging, these allow for delay; unlike text messaging, these are synchronous interactions. Early versions were more limited than current versions. Public forms include Ask Mes on Reddit, Twitter chats with hashtags, or group texts. There are privacy concerns when involving students on these types of public platforms. But most videochat software has text-based chat components. During videochats, most of my students prefer to use the chat box rather than the microphone.

⭐ Combine asynchronous and synchronous methods when teaching an online course.

Types of Online Pedagogy

This section gives an overview of the three most common ways that teachers structure their class. Lectures, hands-on activities, and collaborative activities happen in face-to-face classes and online. We'll look at these from the point of view of an online class. I'll review the advantages and disadvantages. All three of these can happen synchronously and asynchronously.

Lectures

Many teachers actively avoid lecturing in the face-to-face classroom. However, we all need to transmit information efficiently and effectively, and lectures have a long history in education. I took many excellent college classes where the professor simply stood in front of the class and talked for two or three hours. In terms of online education, there are two options:

Synchronous

live, interactive videochats, usually with a set curriculum

Synchronous lectures allow for easier checking for understanding, so teachers can adjust to what students know. Students enjoy the course more when they can interact with other students.[xxxix]

However, students need to have excellent internet access and high-quality gear for this to work well. Nearly 40% of school-age children have no internet access at home.[xl] Particularly in rural areas, high-speed internet can be hard to find.

Even high-speed internet and a new iPad do not guarantee an easy class. Other children or parents might be using up the internet or just creating distractions. I have had students attend class while hiding in the bathtub.

Approximately 80% of US children have a sibling (almost 40% have more than one sibling),[xli] and competing demands for device access, bandwidth access, and a quiet space in which to focus can make it hard for a student to attend class.

Getting students' attention is hard when teachers cannot control distractions. Physical presence and nonverbal expression are important ways to manage a classroom. Fully one-quarter of the techniques described in Lemov's *Teach Like a Champion* depend on the teacher's physical presence in the classroom.[xlii] Without the physical control of the student's space, engaging the student can be an uphill battle.

Asynchronous

> prerecorded lectures students use as they need

Asynchronous lectures are more convenient for students. Students can work at their own pace and on their own schedule. Paying attention to the teacher isn't important to the student, because the teacher isn't there. Teachers can use exit tickets and similar activities to insist that students engage with the material.

> A *blended class* is a face-to-face class with online pieces.

There is a difference between asynchronous teacher-directed courses and asynchronous self-paced courses.

- **Self-paced courses** have awful completion rates (self-paced MOOCs hover around the 10% mark).[xliii] Students don't learn as much. Research shows that only about 10% of students who complete a self-paced course can pass a proficiency test.[xliv]
- **Teacher-directed courses** have much better outcomes, with students learning as much as they would in a *blended* or face-to-face class.[xlv xlvi]

Asynchronous courses have the same problems as synchronous courses with high-speed internet access and tech access issues.

Therefore, recorded lectures work best when used as part of a course, not as the center.

 Conduct synchronous sessions, but record them for students with access issues. Force engagement with the material through assessment.

Hands-On Activities

Hands-on labs, games, interactive notebooks, and other activities are common in face-to-face classrooms.[xlvii] The danger is that students will remember the context more than the content. Another way to put this is as Willingham wrote, "Memory is as thinking does."[xlviii] This is true online too. There are two main options:

Synchronous

> hands-on labs guided by live chats (calling tech support for assistance with your computer)

Calling tech support is one of the most reviled activities of the modern age,[xlix] and there is no reason why students enjoy teachers guiding them through labs any more than an adult does calling tech support. Without what early childhood teachers call "joint attention," or shared focus on a task or object, this quickly becomes pointless.

Only when teachers and students look at the same thing at the same time does this work. Shared remote desktop screens for tech support and split-screen activity monitoring[l] are two ways for this to work. Some newer websites are better, but even the best require high-speed internet access and good gear.

Most of us do not have sophisticated technology to monitor hands-on activities like studio art, physical education, or sewing, and so these are usually not good for online classes. When college classes were moved online because of the pandemic, all the studio art majors I know withdrew from their courses.

Given the tech needed, how hard it is to teach students to do the activities, and the high-quality internet access needed, this is a limited activity for most classroom teachers. I do not include this in my online classes.

Asynchronous

step-by-step task lists (symptom checkers, DIY handbooks)

Most students can work through task lists on- and offline. Careful directions for activities ranging from using analemmatic sundials to tell time[li] to mummifying chickens[lii] are important in homeschooling. (I skipped the chicken mummification, but we did the sundial.) Entire high-quality curricula for use by individual students have been created with this in mind, and I own many of them.

> "Written to the student" means that a student is supposed to be able to read and follow the directions without help.

However, as I have experienced with my own children, you can't hand out curriculum "written to the student" and walk away. Daily teacher support is required for answering questions, scheduling, and assessing completed work. Creating these checklists is a key part of my job, and we'll discuss these in more detail later.

Older, more self-motivated students can work independently, but even adults don't like to teach themselves. A total of 70% of college students prefer to take face-to-face classes, although nearly half expressed a preference for classes with online learning components, a *blended class*.[liii]

 Limit synchronous hands-on activities to those that are well supported for joint attention. Favor asynchronous task lists.

Collaborative Activities

Collaborative learning is popular in constructivist pedagogy—in other words, the average classroom teacher does this a lot. Many teachers do what Lemov calls "Vegas"—singing the long division song, or charades.[liv] These are heavily performance oriented and sometimes off-the-cuff, and therefore hard to replicate in online education. However, there are strong alternatives.

Synchronous

multiple students interacting on web-based simulations

Massively multiplayer online role-playing games (MMORPGs) are popular. A total of 59% of teens and young adults ages fourteen to twenty-one play MMORPGs, and about the same proportion watch others play—with over half of those saying that they play to spend time with friends.[lv] It is popular but like football, it's hard to insert academics into "e-sports."

There are some web-based simulation pieces of software with high educational value, but be careful. Few are designed for group work in all-online courses. Teachers may have to piece together screen sharing—not always easy.

Asynchronous

threaded discussion boards (Reddit, blog comments)

Threaded discussion boards have been around for a long time, descended from text-based newsgroups. They are easy to use, even for my youngest students, the ten-year-olds. In fact, my youngest students seem to like being able to show off their work to their friends in the class.

Online, written discussion can help students build relationships with peers. For students who struggle with talking to other people, this can be a good way to help them feel like they're part of the class.[lvi] It's easy for students to "space out" of the course. By using online discussion boards and requiring students to attend to the course three days a week, teachers will increase student success. Online, written discussions build skills for engaging in Socratic discussion. Learning to write well begins with regular practice, and these discussion boards can help. I enjoy watching my students polish their writing over the course of a school year.

Most LMSs have discussion boards. Teachers often start with a prompt and have students respond. There are good ways to run a discussion board and bad ways, and we'll discuss these in more detail later.

Use synchronous group simulations wisely. Asynchronous discussion boards are a strong tool for online learning.

Areas of Concern

Location

We have already discussed how location affects student learning. Ideally, students have a quiet, safe place to work with decent internet and up-to-date technology. Problems include the following:

- About one-third of US households rely on cell phones for internet access.[lvii]
- Many students struggle with competition with siblings or parents for internet and gear.
- In schools, staff might not have knowledge of the academic content.[lviii]

These problems can hurt a student's ability to work, especially in a fast-paced, rigorous course. Teachers must design their courses to help students with these problems. Later in the book, we'll cover this in more detail.

Content

One-to-one tutoring is the most effective instruction, partially because students can be guided through avoiding errors. A skilled classroom teacher can conduct frequent checks for understanding and catch common mistakes by watching students work.[lix] It is hard for an online teacher to observe students working and provide feedback. Instead, teachers must resist the urge to stress declarative knowledge in easy-to-grade assignments. In other words, don't just assign easy reading and assess only with easy multiple-choice questions. Students gaining temporary fluency and regurgitating information is bad teaching, leading to poor learning.

Privacy matters. For example, Facebook originally started as a micro-blog. While many online teachers recommend commercial blogs for online classes, I am not comfortable with potentially violating Family Educational Rights and Privacy Act requirements by allowing the public to see student work. In addition, parents often won't consent to their child's work being shown in public. As a parent, I would not consent. Teachers are often responsible for creating usernames and passwords for students on commercial websites, which adds another unwelcome layer of complexity to student tracking. More cringe-worthy are the ads meant for adults on these websites, which can violate the Children's Online Privacy Protection Rule. For better teaching, avoid outside websites and social media altogether.

Vulnerable Populations

Many of our most vulnerable learners are also those with poor high-speed internet access and low-quality tech. Without this, students have limited access to better online learning. In addition, students with special learning needs, like hearing impairments, dyslexia, and so on, are often hurt by the limited communication available online. Without live signing, captions, audio tracks, Brailled worksheets, and so on, students can be left behind. English language learners and English as an additional language students can also be hurt by text-heavy class designs. Teachers must think about these issues when designing their courses.

In addition, successful online students tend to be organized, have time to devote to the class, have good reading and writing skills, and have adult support. Not all students are lucky enough to have those skills, time, or support. Teachers must compensate as much as possible.

Types of Online K-12 Courses

Online Public School

As I write this in the spring of 2020, public schools all across the United States are either shut down completely or moved to all online learning. The students of these schools are more representative of the nation than the typical online student is, and their teachers are rarely well prepared for the transition. Part of the reason I'm writing this book is to assist the classroom teacher with transitioning their course load to an online format.

Credit Recovery Programs

In my opinion, credit recovery programs are questionable at best and shuffling paperwork at worst. Sticking dozens of bored, previously unsuccessful students in front of a series of digital worksheets, supervised by a teaching assistant who knows nothing about the material, is ripe for academic dishonesty and failure.[lx] Unfortunately, many people conflate credit recovery programs with online education in general.

Online Charter Schools

Online charter schools have a history of questionable performance in the United States. For example, the Center for Research on Education Outcomes authored a study of online charter schools across seventeen states. Students fell behind nearly half a year in reading and essentially made no gains at all in mathematics, with lower scores than students in traditional schools in most states.[lxi] Essentially, we don't want to do this.

Boutique Online Course Programs

A handful of companies offer specific online courses to school-age children. Some of them have a well-deserved reputation for high quality, as measured by outside organizations. For example, at PA Homeschoolers AP Online Classes, about half of their students score a five on their AP exam, and about another quarter score a four. I work at one of these boutique operations, the Well-Trained Mind Academy. While these are not large organizations, clearly they're doing something right.

> Design flexible courses with an emphasis on concepts and procedures, and with consideration for vulnerable learners, using techniques learned from high-quality online course offerers.

Chapter Summary

- Combine asynchronous and synchronous methods when teaching an online course.
- Conduct synchronous sessions, but record them for students with access issues. Force engagement with the material through assessment.
- Limit synchronous hands-on activities to those that support joint attention. Favor asynchronous task lists.
- Use synchronous group simulations wisely. Asynchronous discussion boards are a strong tool for online learning.
- Design flexible courses with an emphasis on concepts and procedures, and with consideration for vulnerable learners, using techniques learned from high-quality online course providers.

CHAPTER 2

WHAT IS A GOOD CURRICULUM?

When planning to teach online, we should always make sure we have a good curriculum to support us. For the purposes of this book, a good curriculum blends declarative knowledge, procedural knowledge, and experience with a well-planned scope and sequence of facts and skills covered in a spiral pattern over a school year. This is true whether teaching happens in a face-to-face

> **A good curriculum blends declarative knowledge, procedural knowledge, and experience with a well-planned scope and sequence of facts and skills covered in a spiral pattern over a school year.**

class, in a blended class, or all online. This chapter discusses attributes of a good curriculum and some aspects that are particularly applicable to teaching online.

Knowing the content to be taught is critical in an online classroom. Because information has to be pushed out to students in advance, teachers need to know what they are doing in the future. Teachers must have a plan. The best plan begins at the end—what is the goal of the course?

 Determine your course goal first.

Class Goal Types

- *survey course*—skims over major content areas; requires vocabulary study

  ◻ western history from 1500 to present; fifth-grade biology

- *methods course*—mastery of facts, concepts, and procedures; requires rigorous practice

  ◻ algebra I; elements of art and composition; expository writing

- *remediation course*—must begin at first principles and work forward; designed to fill gaps

  ◻ preparation for pre-algebra; conceptual physics

If teachers are lucky, they are using a complete, high-quality, direct instruction curriculum that meets their goals and "combines a focus on content with an instructional method that fully exploits the potential of writing to build knowledge and critical thinking abilities."[lxii]

To paraphrase *The Well-Trained Mind*, these instructions are for the rest of us.[lxiii]

Getting Started

If I have been handed a curriculum that I don't think is adequate—or perhaps no curriculum at all—I will look for a better curriculum. Because I currently work at a private school, I can request that students purchase a different textbook, an encyclopedia, and perhaps another text. As a homeschool parent, I invest hundreds of dollars in books every year. As a public school teacher with a great boss, I requested and received permission to order a new curriculum.

If teachers have the freedom, they decide what to study. Part of the decision-making process should be an examination of values and objectives in education. One of my core values is that content knowledge is a central part of education.

Curriculum Components

- *declarative knowledge*—facts, good for memorizing, easy to assess
- *procedural knowledge*—skills, requires scaffolding, assess through tasks
- *experiential knowledge*—hands-on activities, good background knowledge, use wisely

When I am researching curriculum, I'm going to look for one that emphasizes declarative and procedural knowledge, as well as experience. A good curriculum will provide a well-planned scope and sequence of facts and skills to be covered over the course of the year, along with a lab manual.

> *scope and sequence*: chart of what and when specific items are covered in a curriculum

	Term 1	Term 2	Term 3	Term 4
procedure variant 1		•	•	•
procedure variant 2		•	•	•
procedure variant 3			•	•
procedure variant 4	•	•	•	•
procedure variant 5	•	•	•	•
New Concept				
concept variant 1	•	•	•	•
concept variant 2	•	•	•	•
concept variant 3	•	•	•	•
concept variant 4			•	•

	Term 1	Term 2	Term 3	Term 4
concept variant 5			•	•
concept variant 6				•
concept variant 8				•
concept variant 9	•	•	•	•
New Concept				
concept variant 1	•	•	•	•
concept variant 2				•
concept variant 3				•
concept variant 4			•	•
Mastering basic facts	•	•	•	•
Procedure	•	•	•	•
Procedure		•	•	•

Curriculum Designs

- *mastery*—each concept is taught only once, but thoroughly; students are not taught the concept again. Example: Math-U-See, many penmanship programs
- *spiral*—concepts are reviewed throughout the year; more depth of knowledge is added at each visit. Example: Saxon Math, many foreign language programs

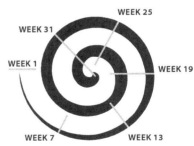

The merits of each type are debated, but given that cognitive science supports interleaved, interval spaced retrieval practice, a spiral design benefits most students.[lxiv] I choose spiral curriculum whenever possible.

 A spiraling series of exercises that cycle back to key skillsets in a seemingly random sequence that adds layers of context and meaning at each turn.[lxv]

Spiral Curriculum Challenges

Many US curricula combine the worst parts of mastery and spiral curricula. For example, most math textbooks have a chapter on fractions. Students learn one type of fraction per lesson, take a chapter test, and don't learn about fractions again until the next year. While technically this is a spiral, this is not a useful spiral—instead, as Willingham writes, "students don't stick with any topic long enough to develop a deep conceptual understanding."[lxvi] I call these *exposure* curricula.

In poor curricula:

- practice is not spaced—students have one or two days to learn
- practice isn't interleaved—homework has ten problems of type 1, ten of type 2, and ten of type 3, in that order.
- practice is not varied—homework is only on that day's concepts or procedures.

Teachers and students tend to dislike intensive spiral curricula because:

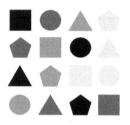

- spacing out practice means that students have to put forth more effort to remember
- interleaved practice feels more difficult than massed practice; it seems hard, chaotic, or boring
- varied practice loses the sense of mastery students get from successfully completing ten problems in a row

 Choose a curriculum with built-in interleaved, interval spaced retrieval practice whenever possible.

Procedural versus Conceptual

Most curricula emphasize procedures or concepts, but not both. While I appreciate conceptual understanding, what I'm regularly concerned with is, "Can my students do math, efficiently and on grade level?" Procedural emphasis curricula ensure that math gets done right, and they are my first choice.

Conceptual-emphasis curricula are also an equity issue. When I teach students with special education needs, fluency is a major goal. Students with working memory issues are helped by curricula that emphasize memorization of basic facts and procedures. Many students don't have the luxury of good working memory to re-derive procedures or good executive functioning to focus through lengthy procedures. They need to be able to just do it by combining memorized chunks of processes in limited working memory.

 Supplement a procedural curriculum with extra work on concepts, or supplement a conceptual curriculum with extra work on facts and procedures.

Other Curriculum Considerations

Expertise

When I search for a curriculum, I want one written by experts. Experts understand the "deep structure" in a content area.[lxvii] Because experts organize knowledge differently,[lxviii] we want their expertise when deciding what is important to include in class.

For example, a non-expert who writes curricula might wrongly interpret the Slave Narrative Collection at the Library of Congress as accurate, truthful memories about life under slavery—and then use this to argue for a white supremacist interpretation of slavery. An expert would have a deeper understanding about amateur interviews by government officials and be able to transfer that knowledge to correctly interpret the Slave Narrative Collection as a distorted view of the past.

Look for curricula where an expert has identified prerequisite pieces of knowledge and worked with an **instructional designer**. Instructional designers are experts in creating a useful sequence of instruction and assessment. Frequently, an instructional designer can produce a **knowledge organizer**, or "a concise table with all key vocabulary, concept knowledge, timelines, and maps."[lxix]

Experience

Teacher experience matters. The best curriculum in the world does not work if the teacher cannot adjust it for students who don't have the prerequisite knowledge, need extra practice, or already know the material.

For example, I became a better teacher when I realized that the distributive property was an obstacle for my pre-algebra students. I changed my lesson to include adding by place value. Then I taught several variations of the multiplication algorithm. Next, I taught the distributive property. Last, I assigned practice questions.

Recognizing prerequisite knowledge is key to good teaching—even given high-quality direct instruction curriculum. When I discovered what my students needed first (along with common mistakes), I layered complexity later. I thought about the ways I could explain it to them and decided how I wanted them to practice.

Hands-On Tasks

Look for curricula that include hands-on projects, even at the higher grades. For example, many math teachers discard hands-on manipulatives by fourth grade or so. But manipulatives are good through high school mathematics. Teachers can instruct students in multi-digit division and multiplication with Cuisenaire rods; demonstrate the Pythagorean theorem with scissors, tape, and squares of paper; and walk students through the derivation for the formula for the volume of a sphere with kinetic sand and hollow geometric solids.

A general rule of thumb for teaching is to start learning with concrete manipulatives, move to visual representations, and finally end with abstract representations.[lxx] While this sequence is helpful for all students, it's especially helpful for students who learn differently. A high-quality curriculum will "hook" students with concrete examples. In addition, high-quality curriculum identifies key vocabulary.

Assessments

Supporting divergent students can be hard when using a curriculum. Maybe the student hates all math classes. Maybe a student has an unidentified learning disability. Maybe a student has a stressful home situation. Teachers need to identify the minimum amount of work and their minimum standard. This depends on a curriculum that has frequent, high-quality assessments built into the course structure.

Choose a curriculum with assessments written by a professional. Professional test designers are called psychometricians, and they use high-level statistical analysis to create assessments. Bad assessments exist—I've written some. I have also purchased curricula with tests on material that wasn't explicitly reviewed in the curricula. Bad tests can have confusing questions, can be formatted badly, or can test trivia. Assessment is a science, and having an expert write questions is better for teachers and students.

Appropriate Difficulty

Does the curriculum look easy, with lots of word searches and fill-in-the-blank worksheets? Don't pick that one. Students will spend too much time on below-grade level tasks,[lxxi] and boredom leads to academic failure.[lxxii] Do not seek out a curriculum that promises to deepen conceptual understanding by teaching through critical thinking or problem solving—for most students, working to frustration level every day isn't sustainable. Instead, choose a curriculum with a manageable amount of work, with sufficient repetitions to cement understanding and at a high enough intensity to keep students focused on the topic.

Scaffolding for Differentiation

Ways to lure skeptical students into the content are good. Does the curriculum have connections to real life? Are non-standard problems or scenarios built into the curriculum? Is important vocabulary defined? Does it support literacy with background information and include reading and writing across the content area? Does it acknowledge the contributions of women, Blacks, and indigenous people of color?[lxxiii] Those are all signs of a promising curriculum.

- choose curriculum that emphasizes declarative and procedural knowledge and experience
- choose within-year spiral curriculum whenever possible
- choose curriculum written by experts working with instructional designers
- don't assume curriculum replaces your experience
- choose curriculum that has some hands-on projects
- choose curriculum that has frequent, high-quality, professionally designed assessments
- choose curriculum that's the right level of difficulty
- choose curriculum that has scaffolding for differentiation

Finding a Good Curriculum

Despite the popularity of Google and Pinterest,[lxxiv] don't just search online. Look for people who have experience in comparing curriculum. Make friends with an experienced teacher and ask them to be a mentor. Maybe a principal will assign a mentor teacher. Reach out online. Twitter is a good place to make teacher friends.

Useful websites for finding good curricula:

- *What Works Clearinghouse*—standards are so high they can leave out good curricula
- *EdReports*—measure compliance to Common Core standards and not effectiveness
- *Evidence for ESSA (Every Student Succeeds Act)*—not all good curricula has had high-quality research conducted on it

Teachers may find those websites intimidating. Not all administrators like teachers purchasing off-the-shelf curriculum. If so, teachers may wish to quietly purchase second-hand textbooks to help guide teaching. Note that it is a violation of copyright law to make copies of textbooks for distribution to students.

A **spine** is a text that teachers refer back to and expand on throughout the school year. Much like a spine holds the body together, a spine text is the organizing structure of a course. While not all spines are textbooks, all textbooks are spines. Ideally, all students would have a copy of the spine. Teachers cannot copy the spine and post it in the course, but they can use the organization of the spine for their own reference when creating materials.

 Ask for help finding high-quality curricula backed by research; find a spine text.

Why Use a Textbook or Booklet?

Without the ability to hand information to students during class on an as-needed basis, teachers and students need some way to share content. Online teachers can't easily photocopy sheets and hand them out in class. Even if teachers send out PDFs, many students cannot print them out; most people prefer to read on paper.[lxxv] In the end, giving students textbooks increases equity for poorer students.

Instructional design is a science, with its own best practices. I rely on experts to do hard work in the form of a high-quality textbook with clear learning goals, clear concept summaries, worked examples, model answers, concept extensions, and tons of independent practice. Sherrington notes that a good textbook has "a broad overview of the subject . . . helpful for schema-building."[lxxvi] Over time, a high-quality textbook can have a big impact. For example, four consecutive years of a high-quality math textbook series can add an *extra* four years of learning.[lxxvii]

Teaching is hard work. Online teaching is difficult and takes a lot of time. Teachers need to make efficient use of their resources by not duplicating the work of experts. Therefore, textbooks save time.

Many people have horror stories about teachers who assign the textbook reading, have students answer the questions at the back of the chapter, and do nothing else. I've had those teachers, too. You don't have to be that teacher—it's a resource, not a limitation. At the same time, it is important to ask students to read across their content areas, and textbooks and booklets provide reading material.

 Teachers can choose how they want students to use a textbook or booklet. Online teachers are not there most of the time. Students need support, and they need it to be offline, because computers break, internet access costs money, and students in front of screens all day is not healthy.

Some people object to textbooks because they tend to present facts as static, with a single point of view. But a textbook is only a resource. Good teaching will bring in many points of view. Having a single, basic resource is helpful when teachers are not there to help students sort through stacks of paper.

Teachers want to assess students frequently. Online, one frequent objection is "How was Tommy supposed to know this?" It is helpful to be able to reply, "Everything the student needed to know was in the book." Because students are frequently distracted during video lessons, reviewing material during live or recorded videos is *much less helpful* than information written in a textbook or booklet.

Textbooks make classrooms more equitable for students with less background knowledge. Because a high-quality textbook clearly identifies key vocabulary, has flow charts and diagrams of important concepts, embeds background knowledge and photographs, and has well-designed self-checks, students from all backgrounds have a solid base of what they need to succeed.

Textbooks and booklets help teachers plan better lessons, offer literacy practice across the curriculum, and come with built-in questions and problems. Textbooks and booklets make teaching easier because the focus of instruction is now reviewing information in the textbook, giving explanations, having students elaborate, and checking for understanding. Because online teaching generally has a good whiteboard built-in, teachers can easily illustrate concepts from the textbook and model good work from the textbook.

 Use a high-quality textbook.

Planning for the Year by Standards

As I'll discuss in later chapters, planning is critical for a successful online class. Teaching a high-quality course requires weeks of planning before school starts and significant amounts of dedicated planning time during the school years. This planning time is separate from grading, following up with students outside of class, answering student questions, modeling good practice within the course, and other important pieces of online teaching.

I have met first-year teachers who told me that their only instructions were to cover the standards. If so, I would count the number of standards, and then divide them by the number of instructional days. For example, in West Virginia, where I live, there are twenty-eight standards for eighth-grade mathematics. West Virginia has 180 instructional days,[lxxviii] so that would mean approximately six days per standard. Given interruptions for snow days, testing, and holiday programs, it's safest to assume five days of instructional time per standard, or 140 days of on-task instruction.

There are five strands of eighth-grade mathematics in West Virginia, organized into ten clusters, so I would make those clusters my ten units. Each unit contains different numbers of standards—the smallest contains one standard and the biggest contains five standards.

Over the years, I have used many ways to schedule daily work, everything from paper planners to spreadsheets to web-based software (my current favorite), but the best planner is the one that you will use. With luck, your school has already posted the calendar, but if not, take your best guess based on last year's calendar.

For best teaching practices, now would be the time to double-check that you've scheduled in interleaved, interval-spaced review for students. I schedule review as part of the Friday assessments, but teachers should do it at least weekly, and preferably some kind of review every day.

 Divide the number of instructional days by the number of standards. Use that number for units and daily scheduling. Make sure teachers have built in interleaved, interval-spaced review.

Designing Your Own Curriculum

When I designed my Preparation for Pre-Algebra course, I used a spiral design. Students circle back to concepts over time. Preparation for Pre-Algebra is for students who have completed a K-6 math curriculum but have gaps or math learning issues.

Identifying main concepts is key for planning. Before I started, I realized that there were difficult concepts for my incoming pre-algebra students, like fractions and decimals. Other K-6 math concepts I omitted because most students understand them. I reviewed algebra entry tests and gathered tested skills. (In some school systems, students must pass a prerequisite skill test before being allowed to take algebra courses, even though students must pass algebra in order to graduate from high school.)

When I had my concept list, I combed through an entire K-6 math curriculum and traced how the tested topics are revisited every year, book by book and page by page. After I had created a spreadsheet listing the concept, page number, and book, I created a one-year spiral for my concepts. In my course, we revisit ideas every three to five weeks, going deeper every time. I "decorated" the spiral with a simultaneous fraction curriculum for extra reinforcement. Because we circle back around, students have time to see how connections are made between seemingly disparate topics, like decimals and fractions.

 **Note:** Designing your own curriculum is not recommended. This takes a great deal of time, experience, and planning. From concept to execution, planning this course took me about two years—and I didn't create my own practice problems. Instead, I worked with a textbook publisher to rearrange their problems sets in a custom textbook, as well as requiring my students to purchase a separate fraction curriculum.

Using Third-Party Supplements in Your Instructional Design

I do not recommend the regular use of materials from third-party (for-profit or not-for-profit) lesson-sharing websites. While teachers may sometimes run across a good supplement for an individual unit, using these sources as a major part of a course has several issues.

Copyright

Many public school teachers are accustomed to the expansive fair use policy that applies to in-classroom use of copyrighted material. However, that fair use does not apply to materials they create and sell on lesson sharing websites—and so copyright infringement is rampant on these websites.[lxxix] Even when teachers create materials from scratch and sell it online, they may be violating copyright laws.[lxxx]

In addition, copyright law for face-to-face classes does not automatically translate to their online classes. Teachers may be held liable for posting materials that violate copyright, even when purchased in good faith.[lxxxi] Fair use online means that the material must be "integral" to the class—not a cute supplementary worksheet or fun activity.[lxxxii] Last, teachers cannot allow students to download the copyrighted material, and teachers must keep copyrighted material password protected.[lxxxiii] These requirements make it difficult for an online teacher to use materials from third-party (for-profit or not-for-profit) lesson-sharing websites.

Differentiation

Good teachers differentiate their instruction. When teachers purchase lessons from third-party (for-profit or not-for-profit) lesson-sharing websites, the lessons have been made as to be as generic as possible for sale to the widest possible market. Products are rarely aimed at more than the average student.[lxxxiv] Online teachers have to differentiate in ways that classroom teachers don't, so this is an added burden. Differentiation will be discussed in another chapter.

Quality

Completing a random worksheet because it is what a teacher can find the night before doesn't lead to the same educational result as a carefully designed worksheet that's part of coordinated plan of instruction. Curriculum design is a science, and most lessons from third-party (for-profit or not-for-profit) lesson-sharing websites are poor, with bad directions, bad assignments, bad assessments, bad depth of knowledge, bad knowledge-building, and little support for diverse learners—and they're often boring.[lxxxv]

Generic content from these websites is designed to produce paper products, because a document is what is sold. Learning happens in the mind, not on adorable papers that parents can hang on the refrigerator. In addition, online teachers cannot assume their students have working printers.

Opportunity Cost

Content-specific courses require big investments of teacher time and expertise in differentiating the off-the-shelf content for their students. Online teachers cannot easily differentiate on the fly, ("Tommy, only do every other question"), and so by the time the teacher finishes customizing their purchase, they might as well have created the material from scratch. High-quality online instruction means these materials don't save time.

Don't spend money on lessons from third-party (for-profit or not-for-profit) lesson-sharing websites.

Chapter Summary

- Determine the course goal first.
- Choose a curriculum with built-in interleaved, interval spaced retrieval practice whenever possible.
- Choose curriculum that emphasizes declarative and procedural knowledge and experience.
- Choose spiral curriculum whenever possible.
- Choose curriculum written by experts working with instructional designers.
- Don't assume curriculum replaces teacher experience.
- Choose curriculum that has some hands-on projects.
- Choose curriculum that has frequent, high-quality, professionally designed assessments.
- Choose curriculum that's the right level of difficulty.
- Choose curriculum that has scaffolding for differentiation.
- Ask for help finding high-quality curricula backed by research; find a spine text.
- Use a textbook.
- Divide the number of instructional days by the number of standards. Use that for units and daily scheduling. Make sure teachers have built in interleaved, interval-spaced review.
- Do not design your own curriculum.
- Do not purchase materials from third-party (for-profit or not-for-profit) lesson-sharing websites.

CHAPTER 3

HOW DO YOU SCHEDULE THE WORK?

When planning to teach online, we should always make sure our students know what we want them to do. When teaching online, provide a written, posted schedule weeks in advance. My standard of practice is to post upcoming work a minimum of two weeks in advance. I also

> **When teaching online, provide a written, posted schedule of repetitive assignments two weeks in advance.**

repeatedly assign the same *types* of assignments. This is true whether I'm teaching in a blended class or all online. In this chapter, I will argue that teacher should post work two weeks in advance and counter common objections to doing so.

I am not afraid to tell students what I want them to do and when I want them to do it. Research supports this: instructor-directed online learning has a greater effect on student learning (+0.39) than collaborative instruction (+0.25) or independent work (+0.05).[lxxxvi]

Why Post Schedules so Far in Advance?

Offering students a schedule well in advance increases equity in education because it gives low-income parents, who are often subject to severe time constraints,[lxxxvii] forewarning to plan for their child's device access, internet access, and quiet space to work, as well as time to seek assistance for concepts their child doesn't understand.

Why do Online Students Need Extra Activities Outside of Live Classes?

Parents do their best, but the home environment is often distracting. Because students are part of an active household, often in apartment buildings, when students turn on their microphones teachers can sometimes hear musical instrument practice, crying infants, arguing siblings, and loud televisions.

Because teachers are not in a face-to-face classroom, they cannot easily tell how well students understand the topic and adapt their teaching. Even when students seem to understand the topic, students are not going to remember what was said during a synchronous session without reinforcement. Most students will pay attention, but many will not be able to recall and use the information.[lxxxviii]

Instead, teachers must provide materials and activities outside of lecture, on a schedule given to students and parents in advance.

Why Does Assigning Work during Synchronous Lectures Create an Undue Burden for Parents?

In a face-to-face classroom, teachers often reserve the last part of the class for monitoring newly assigned student work. But online, teachers cannot see students struggle and assist them. Instead, teachers who assign work at the last minute have made more work for parents, who must now teach the topic.

Online teachers do not control the learning environment—during a live session, they cannot pull students into completing the work. Who can? The adult in the room with the student.

When a teacher assigns work during a live session and makes it due that night, the adult in the room with the student is responsible for making sure the work gets done. The teacher has now subjected the parent to just-in-time scheduling.

Just-in-time scheduling, when businesses call in people to work short shifts at the last minute, is one of the most despised modern labor practices.[lxxxix]

Why Does Assigning Work during Synchronous Lectures Create Chaos for Family Schedules?

As a parent myself, I have a deep respect for those parents who have worked hard to make sure that their child is online and logged into my class. Those parents have often moved mountains to make sure their child is available, has a device, and has internet access for a live class. If a student attends a synchronous session, many parents will have arranged a special trip outside the home just so the student can attend the online class.

When a teacher creates a last-minute assignment, they've thrown a wrench into the family's plans. Unlike homework assignments that might be completed at an afterschool care center and tucked in a backpack to be turned in the next day, online assignments must be completed at home and then uploaded into the learning management system (LMS). This requires internet access, which is not always available at home. Nearly 40% of school-age children have no broadband internet access at home.[xc] Particularly in rural areas, high-speed internet can be hard to find and expensive.

 Even high-speed internet at home and a new device do not guarantee easy internet access. For example, students with good broadband often swap devices between siblings for synchronous sessions. About 80% of US children have a sibling (almost 40% have more than one sibling).[xci] In addition, I often hear that a student has swapped the mobile hotspot with their parent for the synchronous session, or that they've walked to another household to obtain internet access.

Most families have some kind of evening routine, but with a last-minute assignment, a parent must change the routine for the family to provide internet access, a device, and space for the child to work.

Why is Posting Work in Advance Sensitive Teaching?

Although face-to-face classroom teachers may refer to their students as "my kids," in the online learning environment teachers are not *in loco parentis*. Instead, teachers must work closely with the parents or other caregivers as partners in the student's education. In this case, being sensitive to the student's needs also means being sensitive to the family's needs by posting work in advance.

When families have their schedules in advance, they can plan to make sure that the work gets done. This is as true for small, ungraded assignments as it is for big, multi-week research projects. In my most recent astronomy class, 96% of students completed a science fair project despite being in the middle of pandemic.

 Assign all work two weeks in advance.

Repetitive Assignment Types

"We are what we repeatedly do. Excellence, then, is not an act, but a habit."

—*Will Durant, paraphrasing Aristotle*

Teaching Habits

One of my favorite parts of Doug Lemov's *Teach Like a Champion* is the introduction. "Consider one unmistakable driver of student achievement:

carefully built and practiced routines for the distribution and collection of classroom materials."[xcii] By limiting the number and types of assignments, teachers can invest time teaching the expectations and routines for those assignments and benefit from that familiarity all year long.

One of the challenges of an online classroom is limited contact time with students. Teachers can't walk students through an assignment by giving verbal directions. "Alright class, everyone pull out your book and turn to page 42. Yes, that book. Yes, page 42." Instead, teachers must demonstrate in a synchronous (or asynchronous) class session. Because students are working by themselves at home, there is no peer reinforcement, so students learn the routines more slowly.

Harry Fletcher-Wood has identified three keys to create a habit.[xciii]

1. **Repetition.** Research suggests it takes about six weeks to form a habit.[xciv] All my students have an assignment due on Monday, Wednesday, and Friday—every week, all year long. By the third or fourth week, students have practiced enough that they're not quite so confused. Six weeks into the school year, I rarely get questions about when or how an assignment is due.
2. **Context.** Giving students context clues of dates and situations (the assignments are always located in the same place in the LMS) helps reinforce the habit.[xcv] In my courses, Monday and Wednesday's assignments are always the same, whereas Friday's assignments change.
3. **Rewards.** Irregular, explicit rewards are most effective.[xcvi] Because I want my students to work for intrinsic motivation, rather than stickers on behavioral charts or artificial bribes, I almost never offer rewards or extra credit. Instead, my students get weekly feedback on assignment completion via grades and, if earned, my praise.

 Use assignment routines and feedback to create the habit of completing assignments.

Reduced Workload

A teacher buckling under fifty emails a day benefits by having fewer confused students. The more habitual the routine, the fewer questions students ask.

Sorting the flood of student assignments is difficult when teaching online. Add in chasing down missing work, and sorting online homework becomes a large part of the job. When students have had assignments for two or more weeks, the teacher can be firm about deadlines and reduce the workload.

Work Written to the Student

Online teachers must consider that parents are the supervisors of task completion. Teachers must create work written to the student.

Written to the student is a specialized term. This is curriculum meant to be read by the student so that the student can understand the presented concept and complete the work independently, without needing assistance from the teacher or parent. When teachers assign work that can be completed without direct supervision, it's more likely to be completed.

In the online classroom, setting tasks written to the student means that teachers don't assume a student has constant access to a device or the internet, design work to be completed without peers, and assign work that doesn't require significant background knowledge or assistance from the parent. Everything that the student needs to know or have to complete the work is included in the lesson, including how long it should take, the criteria for success, and an example of good work.[xcvii] In the United Kingdom, school- or teacher-created booklets are often written to the student.

For example, one of my common assignments is an online written discussion question. I review the concept during my orientation session, teaching students where to find it. These slides are provided to the student in PDF format, so they can download it and print it out as they wish. I have another slide repeating the routine for due dates. Yet another slide gives examples of possible discussion question response topics. The next slide gives a model and explains exactly how I grade it. I mark this up during the synchronous session, detailing criteria for the rubric. Afterwards, when students go to complete the work independently, the directions are repeated in the relevant portion of the LMS. Finally, in the assignment itself, I have modeled and provided directions again.

At this point in the course, the vast majority of students can complete the work independently, without asking a teacher for assistance and without needing to be online for most of the assignment. They only need to be online long enough to copy and paste their work in the correct box, and submit it.

 Make all assignments written to the student.

Students Benefit from Repetitive Assignments

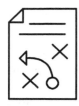 While all students benefit from structured classrooms with set routines, these are especially critical for students with special education needs.

For example, students with autism often do better with clear guidelines and expectations. By giving them a daily and weekly calendar along with a list of familiar assignments to be completed (complete with time expectations), teachers are increasing their chances of success.

Students with ADHD often have difficulty with executive functioning, making plans, and goals.[xcviii] Giving them a systematic plan with repetitive daily, weekly, and monthly goals and showing them how to mark work as completed—and then circling back around to check for completion—helps them succeed.[xcix]

As many as one in five students suffer from anxiety, especially given recent world events.[c] "Predictability is very important for anxious children,"[ci] and creating a predictable routine helps them be successful.

Another benefit is that by limiting the number of assignment types, students focus on the content, not the context. For students who are new to learning online, figuring out how to do a task may take up more of their attention than the content of the task itself: "What's the password? Where should I click? How does this program work?" Students learn better when they're thinking about the meaning of the information, not how to use software.[cii]

Provide:

- **daily calendar**
- **weekly calendar**
- **list of assignments**
- **estimated time for assignment completion**
- **monthly goals with checkups**
- **limited assignment types**

Repetitive Assignments Force Good Planning and Effective Teaching

Knowing that a limited set of tasks is available makes it more likely that the teacher will think carefully about which tasks they will choose to use throughout the year. Different content areas lend themselves to different tasks—problem sets in math, map work in geography, etc. Tasks should be carefully chosen for specific learning goals.

Students benefit because long- to medium-term planning forces teachers to be explicit about goals and expectations. When teachers create explicit planning, they may use a **scope and sequence**, brief lists of the knowledge and skills students are expected to master at each part of the school year or course. A scope and sequence can often be used to estimate how long a particular concept should take to learn. Teachers plan effectively when they can estimate how long teaching something should take.[ciii]

When teachers make sure each task is written to the student, they must consider what students need to know to complete the work.[civ] Therefore, foundation skills are more likely to be covered, leaving fewer students behind. Strong curriculum will assist with this design requirement because an instructional designer will have mapped a good path for students to build knowledge with strong mental organization.

- **Carefully choose a limited number of tasks for your course.**
- **Select explicit goals and expectations for student learning.**
- **Make assignments *written* to the student.**

Objections to Repetitive Assignment Types

Many teachers feel that they cannot be sensitive to student needs without tailoring assignments to what they think students learned in that day's synchronous session.[cv] However, online teachers have limited data about how students have responded to the lesson when compared to a face-to-face classroom. Teachers may ask students to self-assess during the lesson, but, as any parent of a young elementary-age student knows, students are often bad at self-assessment.[cvi] In addition, students frequently don't remember the point of a single day's lesson.[cvii] Therefore, adjusting lessons based on teacher perception of student learning during a synchronous session doesn't necessarily imply sensitivity to student needs.

Often educators believe they don't know where they'll be in two weeks. In my experience, this often leads to a teacher who doesn't cover all the standards, or who crams content in before annual testing. Crucially, this laissez-faire attitude often leads to students with knowledge and skills gaps in later years, so that kindergartners who enter school a full year behind their peers[cviii] end up three years or more behind at the end of elementary school.[cix] In other words, students' learning rates actually drop the longer they're in school.[cx] Rather than closing the gap by supplying content, poor planning omits knowledge critical to long-term success for students. In the words of Li, Klahr, and Siler, "60% of the [science] test gap can be attributed not to the quality of teaching in the urban schools, but merely to the breadth of coverage or opportunity to learn."[cxi]

Even though most teachers learn how to construct units as part of their teacher education programs, many practicing teachers are not required to write them or turn them in. Planning instruction helps ensure students don't have gaps[cxii] because their teachers cover the entire curriculum. Large-scale planning means teachers are sensitive to long-term student needs. Building in regular response time for poorly understood content—based on student work, rather than perceptions of that day's class—ensures sensitivity to current student needs.

Repetitive Assignment Challenges and Solutions

Challenge

Assignments are written. In the online classroom, writing is on display—writing from the teacher and writing from students. Writing directions for students never had higher stakes because teachers are not there to explain poorly written assignments, to clarify poorly written questions, or to deal with badly worded answer options. Frequently, parents will see these issues, become frustrated with the class, and negatively affect student achievement.

Solution

Be explicit, concise, and intuitive in written explanations and directions. If possible, test the assignment with an actual student. Optionally, do it yourself and pretend that you're ten. It is common to accidentally write bad directions, add a zero to the word count, etc. Online teachers must get the assignment right the first time, every time. Consider swapping assignments with a co-worker for review. Optionally, if there are several teachers who cover the same area, consider splitting up the preparation for online teaching and making the best writer responsible for writing all assignment directions in exchange for picking up a portion of their workload.

Bonus: An advantage of having only a handful of the same assignments is that once students are accustomed to the assignment, the directions become less important, because students already know what is expected.

Choosing assignment types before the class begins. Speaking from experience, while it is possible to change the types of assignments in the middle of the course, it is difficult. Students are comfortable with the pattern and routine and may reasonably object to an assignment they perceive as unnecessary or more difficult. "Begin as you mean to go on" is an aphorism for a reason.

Examine past assignments. Even if teachers are new to the course, they've probably had some experience as a student in the content area. For example, problem sets are a common feature of math courses, and should probably feature in a future math course. Texts are common in English language arts, primary sources in history, maps in geography, etc. When in doubt, ask for help from an experienced teacher.

Challenge

Write instructions in a positive, upbeat tone. Written instructions are an important way teachers connect with students.[cxiii] It can be difficult to consistently frame assignments—and requests for revision of assignments—from a positive point of view. As a parent, "because I said so" has featured in conversations more than once.

No face-to-face, in-depth class discussions. In an online class, teachers cannot rely on the ability to guide students through a Socratic discussion through subtle body language, gestures, and immediate responses. Many teachers rely on these discussions as the backbone of their classes.

No group work. Many teachers rely heavily on small group work in their face-to-face classroom. Synchronous small group work can only take place in under certain carefully managed situations that relies heavily on high-quality software, devices, and internet access. Asynchronous group work can be difficult to manage.

Solution

Work to develop warmth. Consistently reframing perceptions of student work (or lack thereof) as an honest mistake or failure to understand directions can be useful. For example: "Please resubmit—I can't wait to see what you've come up with!" By providing instructions in a cheerful, encouraging manner, teachers create an affirmative association with the class, which increases student engagement and task completion.[cxiv]

Use synchronous discussions and a variety of asynchronous methods. In an online class, arranging high-quality class discussions requires a different skill set. Briefly, alternatives include synchronous class discussions, written discussion boards, text-based chat groups, informal student meetings via videochat, email lists, and so on.

When possible, use an LMS that includes breakout rooms and course groups. Breakout rooms are subgroups in a synchronous class session, much like changing the channel and having only a few people in the "room" with you. Teachers must visit each of the breakout rooms in succession. Course groups in an LMS give each group their own private page with links to asynchronous collaborative tools, such as blogs, wikis, journals, tests, live sessions, etc. For a low-tech method, set up a group text chat.

Challenge

Creating consistent assignments across multiple concepts and ideas. Some concepts lend themselves to blank diagrams; others are a stretch. Some topics are the subject of numerous student-appropriate videos; others might require significant research before teachers find publicly accessible high-quality videos. Creating guided notes for mathematics classes can be challenging, for example.

Creating weekly student interaction. Opportunities for off-topic student interaction can feel unnecessary. Adding this into the weekly preparation checklist adds extra work. Not all students will take advantage.

Solution

Test whether chosen assignments lend themselves to the content. As far in advance as possible, create all assignments for a unit. Mismatch? Throw it out and substitute another. Then do another unit and check again. Use periodic assignments (monthly, quarterly, and annually) for less common tasks.

Build low-prep student interaction into the course. Show up to the synchronous session ten or fifteen minutes early so that students can chat. Start off-topic discussion threads in a special area to encourage students to interact outside of academic assignments. Require students to respond to each other in academic discussion threads. This can create equity in the online classroom by focusing "on the social elements of learning."[cxv] These weekly opportunities are essential in creating a sense of community and combating the isolation that students often feel in online courses.[cxvi]

Chapter Summary

- Assign all work two weeks in advance, with a checklist and a calendar.
- help students create the habit of completing assignments.
- Make all assignments written to the student.
- Carefully choose a limited number of tasks for your course.
- Select explicit goals and expectations for student learning.
- Be explicit, concise, and intuitive in written explanations and directions.
- Work to develop warmth.
- Use synchronous discussions and a variety of asynchronous methods.
- When possible, use software that includes breakout rooms and course groups.
- Test whether chosen assignments lend themselves to the content.
- Build low-prep student interaction into the course.
- Provide:
  - daily calendar
  - weekly calendar
  - list of assignments
  - estimated time for assignment completion
  - monthly goals with checkups
  - limited assignment types

CHAPTER 4

WHAT IS A LEARNING MANAGEMENT SYSTEM AND WHY DO I WANT ONE?

When planning to teach online, we should make sure that we have a quality **learning management system (LMS)** to support teacher-student communication. When teaching online, use an LMS that offers a wide range of features. My standard of practice is to use modules to organize the course. I also use

> **When teaching online, use a full featured learning management system to support teacher-student communication and teacher assigned work.**

the LMS to create the schedule of work for students. This is true whether I'm teaching in a blended class or all online. In this chapter, the parts of an LMS relevant to the online teacher are reviewed.

A complete analysis of LMSs is beyond the scope of this book. However, if a teacher is in the position to offer an opinion about an LMS, they might want to think about some key points. The most common LMSs are Blackboard, D2L (Brightspace), Instructure (Canvas), and Moodle.[cxvii] I have used Blackboard, Canvas, Moodle, and several other systems, such as newsgroups.

Goals

Not all students and teachers are open to the idea of taking and teaching an online class, so decide whether it's appropriate for your class and your school before investing in an LMS. Teachers need the LMS to be a user-friendly platform to interact with students, a virtual classroom. Students need it to be reliable and easy to use on a variety of devices with varying internet access.

Just like buying a car, check out the ratings. As of 2018, Canvas and Blackboard each have nearly a third of the market, and Moodle follows close behind with nearly a quarter—I'll call them **the Big 3**.[cxviii] The Big 3 are all going to be sound choices. Google Classroom is popular, but it lacks many vital features of a full-fledged LMS.[cxix]

Investing in an LMS is a major decision. As a teacher, responsibility for the LMS falls on someone else—we are users, not administrators. Therefore, while teachers should be consulted, someone else should take charge. A teacher's job description does not include being a software administrator.

Course Delivery

The most important element is whether the LMS is easy to use. Just as driving a sports car takes a little extra training, Blackboard has a steep learning curve and offers the most functions. In comparison, Canvas and Moodle are easy to use, but their basic models don't offer as many choices.

In the Big 3, students can see which courses they're taking and an integrated calendar across those courses. Many parents suddenly switching to online schooling in the spring of 2020 found the multiplicity of websites and apps to be difficult to navigate.[cxx] A **central single sign-on** across grade levels, subjects, and schools in a single website is much easier for parents and students. This website must be optimized for mobile viewing, not just accessible on a phone.

A single central website should also be accessible in multiple languages and give public information about alternate methods of contacting the school, including email, phone, web-based forms, postal mail, and text messages. Students and families should be able to log into the website and easily reach a live human via telephone, videochat, or text chat.

 The teacher should not be the students' information technology support or the primary source of information about school district policies, available services, contact information, closing, etc.

Students and teachers should be able to upload files from computers, devices, and cloud services like Google Drive or Dropbox. A good LMS will work with all kinds of files, from slides to documents to audio to video. Likewise, a good LMS will work on all kinds of devices, including those with limited internet access. For students who do not have regular internet access, the LMS should allow students to efficiently download work to print and complete offline.

In a good LMS, teachers will be able to contact students directly from within the LMS. In other words, it contains an email client that allows teachers to email one or more students directly from the online grade book. This is useful and timesaving.

One of the best parts about teaching online is that teachers can re-use classes, with version control. For example, I have taught world geography for the Well-Trained Mind Academy since 2015. Every year, I tweak the course a little bit—but I can also copy last year's course into this year's slot with only a few clicks. Another couple of clicks allow me to adjust the assignment dates for the entire course. In less than thirty minutes, everything is ready to go.

Easy content creation is important when choosing an LMS. When I teach a class, I create extensive content for the course, both within the course and as uploaded files. All of the items that I have created are saved and available for re-use in future classes in the LMS. In the LMS I currently use, I can organize this support material by type, by course, by date, and by learning module. For example, I have created and therefore need to organize:

- discussion questions
- web links to useful videos
- PDFs of skeleton notes
- customized problem sets
- journal writing assignments
- recordings of synchronous class sessions
- surveys
- assignment lists
- calendars
- flash cards
- sketches
- diagrams
- timeline assignments
- summarization and outline assignments
- primary source analyses
- lab assignments and assessments
- months-long units for essay writing
- months-long units for science fair projects
- memory work assignments
- comprehensive final exams
- unit tests
- reading assignments
- extensive lecture notes
- slide decks

Course Modules

One of the major differences between an LMS and other systems is the course module. While teachers often think in terms of units and lessons, a module is different.

Lesson plans are plans for the teacher—what students are supposed to learn, how teachers will instruct students (the hook, the direct instruction, the check for understanding, the guided and independent practice, the wrap-up), and how students will be assessed. Lesson plans are typically parts of units of instruction, which have overarching themes and goals—human body systems, modern poetry, or statistics models, for example. Typically, units of instruction cover at least one and often several weeks of instruction.

This is fine, but this kind of organization does not translate directly to online teaching. Instead, **the basic element in an online course is a module**. If your course is a file cabinet, the module is the individual file folder. The Big 3 help teachers organize their course in modules. The number of modules depends on the length of the course.

In my experience, the module is best organized on a weekly basis. Our world organizes things by weeks, so all but the youngest students have an idea of how long a week is. Students and parents can plan by the week. Weeks do not automatically correspond to lessons or units, so teachers must change the way they approach planning.

Modules contain all of the course content for students. Files, notes, discussions, videos, class recordings, assignments, tests, quizzes, links—all of those components are organized within a module. Just like a file folder, modules are labeled for students.

 Google Classroom topics are not equivalent to modules because the organizational flow is that of a social media feed, rather than a file folder. Finding a particular piece of information on a social media site is hard because they are designed to show new material. Old material needs to be readily available for students, which makes Google Classroom a bad choice for online classrooms.

Interaction

Accessibility. A good LMS will have a built-in provision for screen readers, including an accessibility checker for instructors.

 Two main rules guide accessibility for an LMS: Section 508 of the Rehabilitation Act issued from the US federal government and the Web Content Accessibility Guidelines (WCAG 2.1) issued by the World Wide Web Consortium (W3C). According to both the US Department of Education and the US Department of Justice,[cxxi] it is illegal to use public funds to purchase technology (such as e-books) that supplies inaccessible content, both at the collegiate and K-12 level.[cxxii]

Ease of access. A good LMS will be available on a wide variety of devices, including via apps optimized for phones and tablets. It should be intuitive, with clear paths and easy-to-read font. Students should not have a steep learning curve when finding assignments or when turning them in. Ease of use is often overlooked when thinking about other features, but it should be a primary concern.

Social media integration. Teachers often have morals clauses in their contract,[cxxiii] which makes them extra vulnerable to flashpoints on social media.[cxxiv]

While many LMS include social media integration as a feature, I see it as a bug. Often, schools, counties, and states have clear policies about teachers and social media use. Learning how to block students, scrubbing past photos for anything controversial (including politics, religion, finances, alcohol, and drug use), limiting school affiliations and mentions, and avoiding geo-tagging posts are all good ways to stay employed. Teachers should also avoid publicly complaining about their job and avoid posting photos of students on social media—both students' faces and their schoolwork are subject to Family Educational Rights and Privacy Act (FERPA) regulations.

Teacher-student contact. An LMS should have an easy method for students to contact instructors and other students from within the LMS. Typically, this is via email, although teachers may choose to set up within-course mail.

 Instructor availability is crucial for student engagement and course retention.[cxxv] Students without their own email address pose a problem for teacher-student interaction. Mediating all interaction through the parent creates a translation issue that cannot always be easily remedied, which means that an LMS that has easy-to-use within-course mail is superior.

Videoconferencing

A quality LMS has videoconferencing built into the system. While teachers may be tempted to use generic videoconferencing software, LMS videoconferencing has invaluable tools for teachers to fine-tune synchronous instruction.

Accessibility. In a good LMS, screen reader users can access text from optical character recognition–capable PowerPoint and PDF files shared in the session.[cxxvi] Slides should not be crowded, with a goal of no more than five lines of text per slide, and no more than five words per line. Slides should be high contrast (preferably black and white). Headings and text should be used for maximum legibility. To optimize for use with screen readers, assign titles to slides, and ensure that the text order works.

Alt text. This is text attached to an image for screen readers. Every link should be described for the student. For example, "Google Search." Use an accessibility checker when possible—PowerPoint has one built in.

Captions. Videos should be captioned, and audio files should include a transcript. Most LMS videoconferencing software includes the capability for live closed captioning for students who are deaf or hard of hearing as well as those learning English. Generally, one of the attendees must be designated as the captioner, who transcribes what is said during the session. Rarely, a teacher can use an automatic transcription—this is not recommended due to common transcription errors, especially for technical content. Good software will permit multiple simultaneous captioning. These captions should then be accessible during the recording.

Custom polls. These allow teachers to demand participation, keeping students engaged in the course. For example, teachers can have students take on meta-cognition to improve the accuracy of their self-assessments[cxxvii] by repeatedly polling students to self-assess their understanding, and then assigning the work so students can contrast their self-assessment with experience.[cxxviii] Other custom polls can include multiple-choice answers to pre-built problems on slide decks for retrieval practice[cxxix] with immediate feedback[cxxx] within the lesson. These techniques are also useful in an asynchronous session when students attempt to answer for themselves while watching the recording.

File sharing. Teachers need to be able to prepare files and share them with students. The most common files are slides and PDF files, although teachers and students can often use image files. This is useful during synchronous sessions because the slides are uploaded to the LMS server so that when bandwidth is clogged, priority is given to the slides. Slides can be saved from one session to the next. The teacher and the students can both mark up the slides.[cxxxi]

Interactive slide decks. Common on third-party websites, links to the websites are posted within a learning module in the LMS. For example, students see a Jeopardy screen on their device in a synchronous session, and tap it to play a game with other students.

 Gamification runs the risk that students engage with the context more than the content, distracting already distracted students.[cxxxii] Second, multitasking (switching between two or more screens) reduces academic performance.[cxxxiii] Third, because online teaching generally means that teachers have significantly less time with students[cxxxiv] (I have two, fifty-minute periods a week, for thirty-two weeks, to teach algebra I), using class time for unnecessary activities is prohibitively time-expensive.

Muting capabilities. Muting one or more students at a time is invaluable. While most adults will wait for their turn to talk, most students have difficulty with this, particularly without body language cues. Sometimes it is useful to allow more than one student to speak at a time.

Teach videoconferencing etiquette and set up a rota system for speakers to ensure equity in discipline.[cxxxv]

Picture-in-picture. Displaying a smaller video image while the main video screen is still on is a feature to be used with caution. Students have better engagement with recordings when they can see the instructor,[cxxxvi] but this does not necessarily translate into increased learning, possibly due to distraction.[cxxxvii] In addition, because live picture-in-picture adds additional video streams, it requires extra bandwidth for students in synchronous sessions.[cxxxviii] Therefore, limit this mode to the beginning of each synchronous session.

Recording access. Recordings are vital for asynchronous students. Good LMS videoconferencing software will save the synchronous session as a movie file that students can download and watch offline. Another useful option is the audio-only file for downloading and listening offline. Making recordings easily accessible in the LMS makes them more likely to be used. Recordings can be available for a short time, or permanently, depending on the LMS.

Recording use. Captions and text chats are saved with recordings and can be seen in the downloadable file. Students will often watch recordings of their synchronous classes to review content. Asynchronous students need specialized types of recordings.

 Approximately two-thirds of students watch recordings with captions on, and one in five use transcripts when available.[cxxxix] Research is firm that captions help students learn to read, help English language learners, boost vocabulary in good readers, and help students attend to videos.[cxl]

Screen sharing. Essentially, teachers can choose whether to show their entire screen to the class, just a portion, or just one application running on their computer. If a teacher insists on using animation in their presentation, this is a method for sharing the animations.

 Screen sharing strains bandwidth and should be used with caution.

Server-side file projection. Uploading simple files to the server and having them distributed to the students' computers from there is the best use of a student's limited internet access. While a teacher should ensure that they have hardwired broadband to conduct synchronous classes, students often attend with poor internet access. Good LMS videoconferencing software will check student bandwidth and provide instructors with data about student bandwidth. Frequently, the first sign of trouble is poor audio connection and student response delays.

Teachers should use video and application sharing during a class only when necessary. Teachers should also mute attendees and stop them from sharing their video.

Setting permissions. In the spring of 2020, many teachers switched to a variety of software and quickly realized that without the ability to set permissions for sharing screens and with automatic tracking when a student turned on their camera, synchronous classes became chaotic. Good videoconferencing software within an LMS typically sets the teacher as the moderator. A moderator can turn off the ability to chat, share video, share audio, draw on shared files, or draw on the board. Other useful permissions include whether students can arrive early to class, share their screens, upload images or presentation files, arrive via a guest link, or use the phone to dial in and listen.

Status updates. Students can set themselves as being "away," which is helpful so teachers don't stop the class and wait for students who have stepped away from the screen. Other options include green check marks for understanding, red stop signs for confusion, a clock for speeding up, and so on. These help compensate for the lack of body language during synchronous sessions.

Text chats. An LMS should allow instructors to anonymize the recorded chat stream so that shared recordings don't violate FERPA guidelines. Other LMS-specific text chat options include the ability to remove one or more students from the text chat, the ability to keep a student from participating in the text chat, the ability for students to turn visual and auditory chat notifications on and off, visual and auditory notifications that only appear for the instructor, and so on. These text chat options allow teachers to have better synchronous classroom management.

Video display. As most teachers can attest, playing a short video can be an effective part of a lesson, and that is true online as well. For students with limited access, watching the video during a synchronous class session may be their only opportunity to do so. Therefore, having the ability to show a video through application sharing, screen sharing, or uploading and playing the video is a minimum requirement.

Virtual hand raising. Enforcing the wait-your-turn-to-talk rule in a synchronous classroom can be difficult, but having students raise their hand is one way to make it happen. Another useful effect is that the system automatically keeps track of who raised their hand first, so teachers can have students "line up" to take turns at onscreen activities. This is particularly helpful when tracking participation in a course. My students frequently "run around" and get back in line to do "board work" on screen.

Whiteboard. Just like a dry-erase board, a whiteboard is a virtual blank space. All LMS videoconferencing software has a blank space with digital markers in a handful of colors. Depending on the particular software, teachers may be able place and resize shapes, move objects, add text, and erase all or a portion of the whiteboard. Some have the ability to save drawings (content annotation) for later reference. Others might display several whiteboards at once, so a teacher can monitor several students' work at the same time.

Assessment

Teachers should be able to easily create a wide variety of assessments and push them out to students in the LMS. Typically, creating an assignment automatically creates a space in the grade book for that assignment—although teachers can turn this option off or just hide grades from students. Teachers can see who has submitted their work and when, and contact students directly from the grade book.

Anonymous grading. The Big 3 allow teachers to grade work without seeing who turned it in. This can be useful for those with teaching assistants, or those who prefer to mark up work without seeing who completed it. Often this can be enabled by hiding the results from the teacher and/or students.

Assignment availability. Teachers can work ahead to make assignments and then release them to students when they are ready, with or without an announcement for a new assignment. This can be automated with a "display after" setting or a "display until" setting. Teachers can make exceptions to this for a single student or a group of students.

Auto-grading. Marking work takes longer online, but online teachers can set auto-graded assignments more easily. Canvas, Blackboard, and Moodle all have sophisticated auto-grading systems for test questions.

Automated attendance. Many LMSs permit automated attendance checking for synchronous sessions and have features that permit it to be a percentage of the final grade. This also applies to tardy students. Seating charts can be created as well.

 Automated attendance tracking is often buggy and not recommended.

Automatically schedule student meetings. Synchronizing self-scheduling appointments with an instructor's office hours calendar is a feature that promotes student engagement.[cxli] I have scheduled them in fifteen-minute increments, allowing students to choose as many blocks as needed.

Chat. Allowing online students and instructors to run a group text chat can have several benefits, such as increasing instructor presence.

 Without a constant monitor, this can also be a source for bullying and inappropriate behavior, so this feature should be used with care.

Cheating. An LMS might permit a teacher to filter IP addresses, only permitting a given set of IP addresses to access a quiz or test (requiring students to take it from a given computer lab, for example). Alternatively, an LMS might work with a *lock down browser*, software that does not allow other windows to be opened during the quiz or test. Teachers might require students to use an access code or password to complete a quiz or test.

Complex assignments. Teachers can add links, files, text, and so on to create complex, multi-stage, and multi-source assignments. Most LMSs offer an option for teachers to save an unfinished assignment and work on it later.

Copying assignments. If teachers create repetitive assignments, it is often useful to copy single assignments or groups of assignments. Copied assignments usually require the teacher to tweak due dates, peer reviewers, and students to whom it is assigned.

Deleting assignments. Teachers need to be able to delete assignments and replace them. Most LMSs permit this.

Discussions. Online, written discussions are a good tool for increasing student learning[cxlii] and engagement.[cxliii] In an LMS, teachers can create a discussion for the class or for groups. They can copy the discussion within the course, among sections and groups, and between courses. Teachers can grade discussion with and without rubrics. Discussions can be posted on a time delay, be marked read/unread, be pinned, be deleted, incorporate outside media (like podcasts and videos), and be subjected to peer review. Teachers can choose to require students to write their reply before reading other students' work and make the students' work editable. Discussions can be closed to late submissions, and grades exported to the school's *student information system* (SIS).

Download/upload student submissions. Teachers might want to download all student work for a given assignment, and the Big 3 allow teachers to do that in bulk for some submissions, like essays. Teachers may wish to mark them up on their tablet with a digital pen, for example, and then bulk upload the assignments to the LMS.

Due dates. Optimally, assignments with due dates automatically show in the single central sign-on website calendar for each student, as well as push out to a customized to-do list for each student. Teachers can have assignments automatically marked late or not allow late assignments to be submitted. Dates can include times, but generally only one time zone. Because assignments can be issued to one student at a time, due dates can be customized per student or class section.

Edit multiple assignments. Being able to edit due and availability dates for multiple assignments is useful when copying a course from one term to the next. Typically, teachers can either set a given due date at the beginning of the course and let the clock run out, or add/subtract a given number of days to move all dates equally.

Editing quizzes and tests. In an LMS, teachers can remove a question from a quiz or test, have the assignment be automatically re-graded, and have the new grades pushed out to students. Adding a question is slightly more complex and not always available once students have started the quiz or test. Instructors might want to give new attempts or add extra points to scores, instead.

External tools. All the LMSs permit teachers to add in bits of software from outside websites. Often, major textbook publishers allow their textbooks, assessments, and supporting materials to be integrated into the Big 3. Teachers may choose to use non-standard outside materials like YouTube, math editors, and homegrown videos.

 Integration is good because students don't need to go to multiple websites or use multiple apps to complete work.

Extra credit. The easiest method is to create an assignment with zero points and then give points when grading. Another option is to add points to a graded assignment. Yet another option is to make an assignment worth more than the total number of possible points. A teacher might also choose to add extra credit as an option within a rubric or make the rubric worth more than the assignment.

Feedback. Many options can limit how students see feedback, including "after submission," "only once," "on a given date," "after due date," "after availability end date," and "after attempts are graded." Teachers can permit students to see the score for a given question. Alternatively, students can see all the answers, only the correct answers, or only the answers that students have submitted. Teachers can choose whether to permit students to see individualized feedback and whether students can see if a given question is incorrect.

Force completion. I almost never use this, as it requires students to complete work in one, uninterrupted sitting. Students frequently have internet hiccups that disconnect them from the server and require my intervention to re-enable access or supply them with a new assignment. If one-third of my students have hiccups, then that is easily forty manual assignment interventions.

 Often this feature is not worth implementing.

Grade book. One of the best parts of teaching online is the auto-populated grade book. When a student completes an auto-graded assignment, or the teacher grades work, the grade is automatically placed into the online grade book, and the student's overall course average is recalculated. These grades can be overridden, and external grades can be imported from outside websites or exported to other software. Percentage grades are the default, but teachers can also opt for completion grades, points, and letter grades. Teachers can decide what parts of the grade book are available to a student and add student-by-student feedback within the grade book. Some LMSs have built-in curving programs for grades. Grade books make it easy for teachers to track who has turned in an assignment, whether it was late, and whether it has been graded. A well-done grade book allows a teacher to email a student from the grade book.

Grade distribution. Teachers may choose to allow students to see the grade distribution as graphs of grades for a given assignment.

 Use with caution, as clever students can use this to figure out each other's grades and violate FERPA.

Group work. Teachers can create a single assignment and push it to multiple groups, or assign different work to different groups. All students in the group receive the same grade. Class sections can be groups and receive different due dates per class section or group.

Ignoring scores. Teachers can choose to automatically drop a student's lowest score for a given grade book category or drop the highest score for a given category—or to never drop a specific assignment. Teachers can also choose to use *only* the highest score in a given category.

Mark-up tools. All of the big three LMSs allow teachers to mark up work submitted as a file with a digital red pen, as well as insert text snippets at appropriate points. Common file types include MS Office, PDF, Open Office, and most image files, such as .jpg and .png files. Work can also be graded with a reusable rubric that the teacher creates in the system.

Moderated grading. If multiple graders are desired, this feature permits temporary grades for an assignment. Teachers may choose to use this to sample assignments for consistent grading and allow secondary grade reviews. Moderated grades can also be done anonymously, though they can often read each other's comments.

Moving assignments. Assignment scores orders can be moved within the grade book, the entire assignment can be moved within a learning module, or different types of assignments can be moved, copied, or hidden within the course or between courses. This is useful when helping students decide what to do first. Teachers can move assignments from one type to another (from quizzes to tests, for example).

Multiple attempts. Allowing multiple attempts is helpful when assigning work that comes in separate files, such as a project with a presentation, data file, and report. Teachers can allow a given number of attempts or unlimited attempts.

Non-graded LMS assignments. Teachers can choose to exclude an assignment from the grade calculation and choose whether to show the feedback to students.

 This option is useful when assigning secondary work, like scratch work in math classes.

Non-LMS assignments. Teachers may wish to assign work that isn't for a grade or doesn't require students to upload anything to the LMS.

 This is useful for adding non-graded work, like reading assignments, to the calendar.

Password. Password-protecting assignments can be useful when teachers want to force students to work through assignments in a given order or meet an external requirement, like texting the teacher to check in.

Peer review. Some types of classes lean heavily on peer review of student work. Peer review can be required, and teachers can either manually assign peer reviews or have the system assign a peer review. Each user can be required to complete a certain number of reviews, before or after a given date. Peer reviews can be required within a given student group, or across the class. Peer reviews can also be anonymous.

Plagiarism. Built-in plagiarism detectors are a common feature, with originality reports and automatic calculations of how similar a given written assignment is to other writing in the database.

Points. Teachers can customize how much each assignment is worth and have that automatically calculated by assignment type in the grade book.

Portfolios. Teachers can help students collect their best work for presentation in a digital portfolio, with normal grading, rubrics, and feedback separate from portfolio comments. Student can type in their work directly, embed content from other sites, add previous submissions from within the course, and upload images and files.

Presentation. Teachers can choose to show an entire test at once or just one question at a time. Some teachers like to prohibit backtracking, preventing students from changing an answer to question that a student has already submitted. Randomizing questions for each test attempt is another popular option.

Printing. Depending on the LMS, formatting assignments for printing is a common option. This helps students who cannot be online all the time, as well as those who wish to keep copies of their work.

Report cards. While generating traditional report cards isn't often done within an LMS, each student has a record of work created within the LMS, complete with grades. Teachers can view these, as can students and parents. Work can be automatically tagged as late or missing, and rubrics and comments are directly accessible. Students can click through for assignment details.

Question banks. Teachers may want to reuse questions within a class or across classes. They can do that by creating questions and then adding them to *question banks*. Questions can be tagged by standard, difficulty, assessment type, or outcome for maximum utility. Questions can be copied from one question bank to another, wholesale or individually. Depending on the course settings, teachers can import whole question banks from textbook publishers. Teachers may also want to use groups—for example, any three of the eight questions about DNA. The LMS will randomly select the questions and insert them into the quiz when the student takes the quiz. Depending on the LMS, these questions can be set so that students never see the same question twice.

Quiz/test question options. Individual questions within an assignment can also be weighted differently, either automatically or manually. Partial credit by question is a common feature. Some teachers may wish to add optional hints by question.

Rubrics. Rubrics are an enormous time-saver when teaching online, and teachers can create complex rubrics with sophisticated criteria and grade types. Rubrics can be associated with different kinds of assignments, such files, essays, short-answer essays, blogs, journals, wikis, and discussions. Teachers can show rubrics to students, or not, or only after grading.

Set timer. Teachers can time students, allowing students to see how long they have been working on an assignment. Teachers can also set timers and force submission of the work when the timer goes off; alternatively, teachers can give the student the option to continue after the timer marks their spot.

 Students with special education needs often require extra time on assignments, which this feature should permit.

Single student assignments. Teachers can create an assignment for a single student or a handful of students, with all the associated features of a "regular" assignment.

SIS integration. The Big 3 offer various options for administrators to synchronize assignment data with online student record systems. Sometimes, depending on the LMS settings, teachers may choose whether to synchronize a given assignment with the SIS.

Submission types. Teachers may allow students to enter text, add files (included linked cloud databases, like Google Docs), or even link to outside websites for their assignment.

Unavailable to students. Frequently, teachers will want to add content to a course that is unavailable to students, much like adding files to cabinet. This is a simple checkbox option found many places in the LMS.

Weighted grades. For courses with weighted grades (essays are worth 10%, for example), teachers can easily create custom assignment types and a custom grade formula. Different weights can be applied in different grading periods (50% of the course grade earned in the first semester, for example). Typically, the grade formula is based on percentages (for example, 30% for homework, 30% for discussions, 20% for quizzes, 5% for extra credit, 15% for exams).

Question types. Common built-in test question types include:

multiple choice	surveys
fill-in-the-blank	peer assessments
matching	opinion scale/Likert
drag-and-drop	jumbled sentence
ranking/ordering	multiple answer
image selection	true/false
"hot spot" selection	"quiz bowl" style
calculated formula	fill in multiple blanks
calculated numeric	multiple drop-down
file uploads	computer code
short answer essays	pattern matching

Student Tracking and Reporting

Perhaps the most common question is, "How can students track their grades and progress?" The Big 3 provide that information either when students log in or within a couple of obvious clicks from the front page.

Parent observer accounts are an option in the Big 3. These are limited accounts that allow parents to see a list of assignments and their child's submissions, scores, course progression, teacher contact, and so on.

> Do not assume that parents are tracking their child's progress. Email, call, or text about missing assignments, poor grades, etc.

Teachers may want to track individual student proficiency. In that case, the Big 3 allow teachers to add outcomes or standards to assessments so that as teachers grade assignments, students receive a proficiency rating. A good LMS will automatically collect and compile data on student progress for the outcomes, and then flag students calculated to be at risk.

Another way that teachers may wish to track student progress is by task completion. The Big 3 track this, allowing an instructor to see who has completed what and when. My personal preference is for an LMS to make this obvious in the grade book.

All three of the major LMS providers permit teachers to choose certain criteria (like completing a series of assignments) to issue certificates and/or badges in a pathway toward a specific goal, which can then be shared in or outside of the class.

Often, an LMS will allow a teacher to import their state's standards directly and then designate a given assignment as matching their state's standards. Then a teacher can track their teaching progress toward covering standards as they go through the year.

Teachers need to see who hasn't been logging in, track student engagement in the course (reading, writing, watching, taking assessments, tracking and commenting on discussions, reading feedback on an assignment, re-submitting work), etc. The Big 3 all offer course reports and built-in alerts for these types of indicators. Sometimes, teachers may want to zoom in and see an individual student's level of activity, and the Big 3 allow them to do that as well.

 One way teachers can improve their own teaching is to run and analyze course reports on student progress.

Question analysis lets teachers review how well students did on a given question, and rates the question as good, bad, or ugly. Question design is a science called psychometrics that uses complex statistics. Built-in statistical analysis is an option in the Big 3.

 While most teachers do write their own assessments, when possible it is always best to use a psychometrician's expertise in pre-built assessments and double-check student performance. If 95% of the class missed a question, a teacher may decide that it is a bad question and throw it out (easy to do in a good LMS), or go back and reteach.

Because schools track more than just a student's academics, they typically maintain an SIS. Often, these are legacy systems, run on newer computers in older programming languages. Essential for K-12 school systems to meet recordkeeping and reporting requirements, these systems cannot be easily upgraded. Therefore, an LMS should offer an easy way to integrate with an SIS and a human resources database.

The Big 3 allow a variety of summative reports to be generated. One common report is the grade export report, which creates a spreadsheet with the final grade for all students in a course. Someone proficient in an office suite can easily take that spreadsheet and create certificates of completion, add it to transcripts, import it into databases, etc. Another common report is user activity and/or access, which is simply a record of what a student did in the course and when they did it, including their most recent access. An outcome or competency report shows student proficiency, often by standard.

Purchase Options

When thinking about purchasing an LMS, is the school going to purchase a service or a piece of software? Canvas and Moodle are open source, meaning that in theory a school could DIY it. However, that takes significant technical expertise, and most schools are going to end up purchasing a service. One advantage of a service is the service provider is then responsible for maintenance and upgrades. If a programmer is required to add features, then the LMS might not be a good choice.

Each LMS has its own quirks. Teachers need to be taught how to use it, preferably via live instruction from the service provider. When something goes wrong—and something will go wrong—the service provider should offer technical support from a real person, not just a documentation database.

 Teachers should be able to walk through an LMS and do a dry run before the software or service is purchased.

Security

If a teacher keeps a record of student information or work on their home computer, or on a cloud-based system, teachers are responsible for ensuring data security, much like student records should only be in a locked filing cabinet.

Student data must be protected. The FERPA protects personally identifiable information (PII) from students' education records from unauthorized disclosure. FERPA defines education records as "records that are: (1) directly related to a student; and (2) maintained by an educational agency or institution or by a party acting for the agency or institution." FERPA also defines PII, which includes direct identifiers (such as a student's or other family member's name) and indirect identifiers (such as a student's date of birth, place of birth, or mother's maiden name).[cxliv]

An LMS that requires students (and their parents) to log in and access class materials almost certainly requires the students' names and contact information from the students' education records, which are protected by FERPA. Therefore, a parent or guardian must given written consent to a student's use of an LMS—or the public school must prevent the provider from using the PII for unauthorized (non-instructional, outside of the school's direct control) purposes in the terms of service. Under FERPA, parents must have access to all the records from the LMS.[cxlv]

 Security requirements include, but are not limited to, photos and recordings of students made during synchronous class sessions, work that students upload, typed responses that students submit in the LMS, and so on. All of these should be locked securely within the LMS.

Registration

While a principal might usher a new student into your face-to-face classroom as long as a chair is available, online classes work differently. Good online teaching requires teachers to give detailed feedback and support to every student, and over-large class sizes create poor conditions for teaching and learning.[cxlvi]

 It is relatively easy to add students to an online class, but teachers should be on the lookout for an administrator who assumes that an extra student doesn't create extra work.

A good LMS will allow a student to be withdrawn from the course—and no longer have access. Having a withdrawn student enter the online classroom and rampage through your carefully designed environment is not good. "Zoom bombing" made international headlines in the spring of 2020.[cxlvii]

Students should be able to find their classes through a single, central login for the school. Some mechanism for adding and dropping courses for both students and teachers should be readily available for the LMS administrators.

Chapter Summary

When reviewing an LMS, teachers should consider their goals, the ease of course delivery, whether an LMS is one of the Big 3, central single sign-ons, course modules, student interaction, videoconferencing, assessment, student tracking and reporting, purchase options, security, and registration.

CHAPTER 5
DIFFERENTIATION IN THE ONLINE CLASSROOM

When planning to teach online, teachers should support all students by providing background information and a variety of ways to access the content. This chapter discusses non-special-education-related differentiation and applies it to the most critical differentiation needed in an online setting.

> **When teaching online, provide students with material in each module that covers the same content in different ways.**

This type of differentiation is not the same thing as meeting special education requirements, although the two may overlap. Meeting special education requirements is a legal obligation, unique to each student with an Individualized Education Program.

In this chapter, differentiation is directed toward students with a wide variety of background knowledge, skills, and abilities—outside of special education requirements. While this is a complex and difficult topic, differentiation must be built into online classrooms at the planning stage. Skills for differentiation are not the same as those needed for classroom management, deep content knowledge, K-12 instructional design, or special education. Differentiation that includes adapting instruction on the fly in the online classroom is an advanced skill, one that I am still learning.

When teaching online, provide students with content in each module that aims to cover the same material in different ways. My standard of practice is to assign readings from the textbook, readings from a course spine, videos, written discussions, hands-on activities, and practice problems that cover the same concept from different angles. This is true whether I'm teaching in a blended class or all online.

Goals

Some basics are useful when planning for online teaching. First, teachers should consider their goals. There are two main approaches, each with philosophical differences:[cxlviii]

- convergent—all students should reach a minimum standard
- divergent—all students should reach their highest potential

Real life is always more complicated but thinking about these two goals can help a teacher plan instruction. Professionally, I lean toward the convergent goals, as reflected in the course design in this text. I "dedicate additional time and effort to low-achieving students in order to help them reach a minimum performance level."[cxlix] For example, I designed and currently teach a course whose goal is to remediate elementary math gaps.

Rationale

One argument for the convergent approach is that deliberately including assignments that honor students' diversity while teaching the same skills to all students helps create equity in the classroom.[cl] For example, when I assigned a biographical essay to my middle school biology students, I began with a limited number of individuals from whom they could choose. When making the list, I decided to include equal numbers of famous men and women. Some were US citizens who identified as being East Asian, African American, and white, and some were citizens of other countries, such as the United Kingdom, Prussia, and India. In addition, I made sure to include individuals of multiple faiths and individuals who did not always identify as being straight. As a result, more than one of my students felt safe enough to privately ask if I was of their particular ethnic group, belief system, or sexual orientation.

Another reason for my preference for the convergent approach is that teachers are often poor judges of student ability. Years ago, I read a study indicating kindergarten teachers frequently placed students in ability groups based on the child's perceived socio-economic status.[cli] When my oldest daughter started kindergarten, I made sure she wore the nicest outfits I could afford.

When I was taught about differentiation (I took an online, three-credit-hour graduate course from the West Virginia Department of Education in 2018), the class required teachers to plan for low-ability, moderate-ability, and high-ability students. Creating these kinds of groups for instructional purposes is a common practice, especially when teaching reading or math.

From the teacher's point of view, grouping students for instruction makes perfect sense: teachers don't want bored students goofing off in class and distracting other people. Either students don't understand what teachers are talking about and tune out, or students know it already and tune out. How can teachers avoid this problem? Group students by what they already know and assign them different tasks based on what they know. In a bigger school, administrators could create whole class grouping, with an advanced math class or reading class. Some teachers may live in a district with magnet schools.

 Online, judging student ability is difficult because teachers have few nonverbal cues, like confused looks and spitballs from the back of the classroom. All we have is the completed work, not a view of the effort it took to get there.

At first glance, the "neutral" online results-only orientation may seem more equitable, but allowing some students to skate by isn't equitable to them, because in due course they will become bored, disengage, and never learn how to work hard. Allowing other students to flail without assistance means that eventually they'll become overwhelmed and tap out. Online, keeping close track of student effort is important so that teachers can offer interest-led extensions for students that are more skilled and (arguably more difficult as a teacher) offer scaffolding for lesser-skilled students.

While these grouping practices are often good for gifted students, the impact is limited. Worse, these grouping practices often negatively affect overall student learning.[clii] If this result seems odd, let us take a detour.

Gifted Students versus High-Achieving Students versus Learning Disabilities versus Socio-economic Status

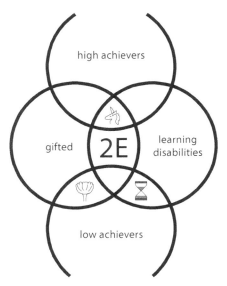

Although schools often sort students by classroom performance, high-performing students are not always the **gifted students** identified by screening (IQ tests).[cliii]

Experienced elementary educators know **high-achieving students** who are not gifted. These students have often been hothoused at an intense preschool or by eager parents. They are well-behaved students and they will do well in school, but these students are not gifted. When their peers catch up with their prior knowledge, usually by about third or fourth grade, these students are often not significantly different from their peers.

There is an overlap between high achievers and gifted students. Some gifted students perform well in school, and they are then tapped for testing. They test as gifted and continue to perform well in school. Others test as gifted and fall victim to **"tall poppy syndrome,"** or crushing self-esteem in the name of modesty or equality.[cliv] In addition, a large and important subgroup of gifted students is never tapped for screening because they do not perform well in the classroom.[clv] Many gifted children tune out early, cut down before their schools begin academic work on their competency level.[clvi]

Then there are students who are standard deviations above the average student in some areas, but who *also* have a learning disability. Frequently, these students fall through the cracks in our education establishment. Because they are gifted, they figure out how to somewhat compensate for their learning disability, but they are not achieving high enough to be tapped for the advanced classes. Nor are they performing badly enough to receive special education services for their learning disability. Mental health issues are often significant for these students.[clvii] These students are often referred to as **2E, or twice exceptional—** once for a learning disability and once for giftedness.

Students can have **learning disabilities**, such as dyslexia, and be high achievers in schools, with proper support and accommodations in the classroom. However, for most students a substantial test score gap appears over time— somewhere on the order of 30% to 40%.[clviii] Many attribute this test score gap to teacher expectations of student ability.[clix]

Socio-economic status also matters. Teachers tend to have low expectations of students who live in poverty,[clx] and an opportunity gap has long existed for students who live in poverty.[clxi] **Black students, indigenous students, and students of color** are more likely to live in poverty.[clxii] They are also overrepresented in special education programs.[clxiii] One might argue that this leads to what former President George W. Bush memorably coined as "the soft bigotry of low expectations."[clxiv]

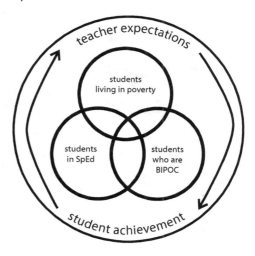

Students who identify as LGBT also experience an opportunity gap.[clxv]

The idea that teachers are not always the best judges of student ability is supported by a policy change in Broward County schools in 2015:

> universal screening raised the percentage of black students receiving gifted services by 80 percent, and Hispanic students by 130 percent. The percentage of economically disadvantaged students in the gifted program went up by 180 percent.[clxvi]

Are there students who are gifted, who have a learning disability, who grew up in poverty, identify as LGBT, who are an ethnic minority—and who are high achievers? Yes, but they are statistically unlikely[clxvii] —one might even say that they are a unicorn. However, good differentiation will support all of these complicated aspects of students' identities.

In my experience, 2E students and students with learning disabilities are overrepresented in online education because online courses have traditionally existed as an alternate education route.

Impact on Learning

One finding from education research is that within-class ability grouping often has negative effects for low-ability students, or, at the least, benefits them much less than it benefits high-ability students. As the authors of one meta-analysis put it, "just grouping students and putting them together physically does not ensure differentiated teaching."[clxviii]

According to that same meta-analysis, sorting children into different classrooms based on ability showed no overall difference when compared with equivalent classrooms with children of mixed ability groups. Sometimes this sorting practice is great for gifted students, but it often has a "significant negative effort for low-ability students."[clxix] The pattern is repeated for teacher-created groupings within a given classroom.

According to the meta-analysis, successful differentiation works in two ways.

First, differentiation is successful when it involves computer-adaptive teaching, in which a computer program offers suggestions for individual student instruction based on student performance as assessed by the software, or computer adaptive instruction in which instruction differs by student scores on performance-based assessments.

Computer-adaptive instruction works well in the online classroom.

Professionally, I use MathXLforSchool software in the online classroom, which offers supplemental per problem instruction based on student performance. I have good things to say about this software, and I would agree that it is preferable to "normal" classroom mathematics instruction—even if I went back to face-to-face instruction, I would continue to use this software. Given my experience with these computer-adaptive teaching systems, I am not surprised to learn that they "positively affect student performance (d = +.290; 95% CI [0.206, 0.373])."[clxx]

The second way differentiation has a positive impact is in the context of a broad reform program or school reform. That impact is beyond the scope of this book, but I suspect that the divergent effect of the general US curriculum on student achievement[clxxi] contributes to the positive effects for high-ability students and the negative effects for low-ability students.

Differentiation

Recall that for the purposes of this book, **teaching online** *is a complete replacement for face-to-face instruction in a core content area.* This is fundamentally different from teaching a face-to-face class. For example, an online teacher cannot give one-to-one handwriting lessons online, correcting grip as the student writes.

While **blended courses**, in which some work is completed online but instruction takes place face to face, are a vital and engaging type of education, they are not the focus of this book. High-quality blended courses are structured differently because they have an opportunity to build a classroom culture and provide differentiation that relies on face-to-face, nonverbal interactions, with the online portion of the course providing enrichment and extension.

 Online classes rely heavily on print instruction, due to limited instructor availability.

Teachers can structure an online class in a way that is more easily accessible to students with some learning issues—and use that structure for all students. Teachers don't have to do the work twice, if they do it for everyone in the first place. It is a simple, but important concept as articulated by Rosalind Walker in 2018:

If a lesson isn't bang on, some students will make up for that deficit, through prior knowledge, independent study, or some other means. But some other students won't.[clxxii]

Students with Print Issues

Students with print issues could be English language learners, be learning English as an additional language, have dyslexia, have poor reading comprehension skills, or perhaps be visually impaired in some way.

Nationwide in the United States, about one in ten students are learning English[clxxiii] while they attend school. Between one in twenty and one in nine have dyslexia.[clxxiv] Overall, two-thirds of fourth graders are not proficient readers.[clxxv] This means that in a typical US class of twenty-four students,[clxxvi] two are learning English, one or two have dyslexia, and the majority of them are not good readers.

To help students with print issues and other learning issues, teachers can **post visual schedules**. Decades of research supports the use of visual schedules.[clxxvii] Color coding these is also useful. Every day, the student with print issues can find the item that they're supposed to do that day. In my experience, some parents print these out and stick them on the refrigerator, while others export the learning management system calendar to their personal digital calendars and use that for scheduling.

Week 2

1) At the end of Week 2, students will have:

- Attended the videoconferenced session
- Answered the Discussion Question (ten minutes)
- Responded to two other students (fifteen minutes)
- Completed the Sedimentary Rock diagram (fifteen minutes)
- Read and summarized the *Origin of the Species* excerpt (twenty minutes)
- Completed the *Galapagos Islands* lab (twenty minutes per day/sixty minutes)
- Read Chapter 7 and completed the Guided Notes (twenty minutes per day/sixty minutes)
- Added *adaptation, evolution, natural selection* to your Leitner box (five minutes)
- Added dates to your timeline (ten minutes)

- Completed the quiz in the learning management system (thirty minutes)

2) Your calendar for Week 2 is below.

Monday	Tuesday	Wednesday	Thursday	Friday
Day 1	**Day 2**	**Day 3**	**Day 4**	**Day 5**
Aug 26	**Aug 27**	**Aug 28**	**Aug 29**	**Aug 30**
DQ Due (ten minutes)	Lecture 1 pm	**Two DQ** **Responses Due (fifteen minutes)**	Lecture 1 pm	**Quiz (thirty minutes)**
Read Chapter 7, Section 1 and completed the Guided Notes (twenty minutes)	Read Chapter 7, Section 2 and complete the Guided Notes (twenty minutes)	Read Chapter 7, Section 3 and complete the Guided Notes (twenty minutes)	**Read and summarize the *Origin of the Species* excerpt (twenty minutes)**	
Add *adaptation, evolution, natural selection* to your Leitner box (five minutes)	Complete Part A of the *Galapagos Islands* lab (twenty minutes)	Complete Part B of the *Galapagos Islands* lab (twenty minutes)	Complete Part C of the *Galapagos Islands* lab (twenty minutes)	
Complete the Sedimentary Rock diagram (twenty minutes) **fifty-five minutes**	Review Memory Work (five minutes) Complete the Sedimentary Rock diagram (fifteen minutes) sixty minutes + class session	Review Memory Work (five minutes) sixty minutes	Add dates to your timeline (ten minutes) Review Memory Work (five minutes) fifty-five minutes + class session	

Use OCR-capable text.[clxxviii] OCR stands for optical character recognition, and it is what lets computers recognize text in documents. Have you ever tried to use your mouse to copy something from a PDF, only to realize that someone had scanned a photo and inserted it instead? If you're a dyslexic student or have visual impairments and you need to make the text bigger or have your device read the text to you, photos of text are disastrous. Text-to-speech technology only works for OCR text. Therefore, when teachers scan files for students to read, they should always scan as text.

Allow students to use speech-to-text software. Most students can listen and speak many grade levels above their reading level.[clxxix] Allow them to use Siri, Cortana, or whatever they have to dictate assignments. They still have to use correct punctuation and grammar, but teachers will find that they get far more out of their students when they facilitate their writing.

 Learn what devices your students are using and figure out how to turn on the accessibility features.

Provide the slide deck to students before class. This is helpful for all students—students who have the slide deck score higher than students who do not.[clxxx] Counterintuitively, having the slide deck ahead of time leads to better attendance and participation.[clxxxi, clxxxii] The slide deck should contain slides with vocabulary highlighted, their definitions prominent, with an example (visual, wherever appropriate). A good rule of thumb is no more than five words per line and no more than five lines per slide. A good slide deck is a linear outline of the lesson—and so when teachers provide that slide deck to their students, they are providing students with typed notes that students can easily transform into flash cards for retrieval practice.

> **equation** - a sentence that states that two mathematical expressions are equal
>
> $2x - 16 = 18 + x$

 While a teacher should never just read the slides, teachers should read the slides for students with print issues.[clxxxiii]

Train students to complete assignments.[clxxxiv, clxxxv] Give step-by-step instructions and visually share the videoconferencing screen, using a student view of the material, to review the written instructions during a live lecture.

If this isn't possible, make a recording students can watch. If recordings aren't possible, make a phone call and go over the steps together, checking that the student is looking at the same thing during the conversation. Even a voicemail is better than handing off written instructions.

Have students tell it back.[clxxxvi] Students rarely attend well enough to be able to tell it back. Students with dyslexia often have attention deficit/hyperactivity disorder or other issues when make it difficult for them to repeat something in the right order, much less understand what they're saying.[clxxxvii] When students can't tell it back, go over the procedure until they have it—and make sure students also have the directions in writing for later reference.

Make sure students know the standard to which they're being held. Are you disappointed by shoddy work? Did teachers explicitly tell them what they wanted?[clxxxviii] Were they given a sample of a good, completed assignment?[clxxxix] Were they provided with a rubric or checklist with a grade break down?[cxc] Did the teacher review the rubric and identify the key parts of a good assignment for students?[cxci]

Do not overload students. Break assignments into small steps.[cxcii] For example, here is a set of instructions on how to complete skeleton notes:

1. Download notes.
2. Open notes in Microsoft Word/Google Docs.
3. Open your textbook.
4. In notes, read the first word that needs to be defined.
5. Read your textbook until you find that word.
6. Copy the definition from your textbook into your notes page.
7. Repeat from step 4.

Make sure that grading standards reflect teacher priorities.[cxciii] Because I don't teach English or literature, I don't take off significant numbers of points for spelling. "Pythagorum" theorem is fine, as long as they can use it. Grading written assignments online is more tedious and time consuming than in a face-to-face classroom, so teachers would be wise to readily accept alternative assignments[cxciv] and make as many assignments auto-grading as possible.[cxcv] Point and click is best when a student can't easily hold a pencil.

Use assignments with visual elements. Every week, teachers should create slide decks with labeled diagrams. Every week, teachers should assign diagrams for students to label. Every week, teachers should assign skeleton notes that involve labeling things. Every week, teachers should have students add dates to a visual timeline. Using these visual elements helps students learn.[cxcvi]

Link to videos and simulations on websites.[cxcvii] When creating a week's worth of assignments, carefully select videos/simulations that cover all of the key information for the week. Many students with print issues can use the captions to increase their reading ability[cxcviii] —and access the information in an audiovisual format when it is convenient for them. Because students can hear and understand content far above their reading level, this is also a good opportunity to provide access to higher-level content than the class entails. I do not require students to watch the videos, but I do provide this alternative access to the content.

Create flash card decks with visuals.[cxcix] There are several good websites/apps that use interval spaced, interleaved retrieval practice, such as Anki or TinyCards, but they can be expensive, and not all students are able to access them. Nearly all students can cut up pieces of paper and draw pictures on one side.

 Help students by providing the basis for flashcard pictures in your slide deck.

Use online discussion boards to prepare for short-answer essays. Using the discussion boards for retrieval practice is a two-for-one move anyway, but students with print issues also often have issues with writing. Give them a leg up by preparing them to support their answers in ways teachers want them to write on your essay exams.[cc]

Give students skeleton notes to complete.[cci] This tells students exactly what is important, allows for a little retrieval practice as they fill in the notes, and helps them organize the information in their own minds—because a teacher has done the organization for them in the notes. Then, review those notes together, when possible.

Assign consistent types of assignments. Students do better when they can focus on the content instead of the context.[ccii] Always want their low-stakes weekly quizzes to be matching and multiple choice? Good idea—do it every time, and if teachers are going to switch it up, let students know in advance. Consider teaching them the new question types so that they spend less time on figuring out what the question means and more time on the answer to the question. This is particularly important for students with limited working memory.

Scheduling Assignments

While all students benefit from structured classrooms with set routines, these routines are especially critical for students with special education needs.

For example, students with autism often do better with clear guidelines and expectations. By giving them a daily and weekly calendar along with a list of familiar assignments to be completed (complete with time expectations), teachers are increasing their chances of success. Students with attention deficit/hyperactivity disorder often have difficulty with executive functioning, making plans and goals.[cciii] Giving them a systematic plan with repetitive daily, weekly, and monthly goals and showing them how to mark work as completed—and then circling back around to check for completion—helps them succeed.[cciv] As many as one in five students suffer from anxiety, especially given recent world events.[ccv] "Predictability is very important for anxious children,"[ccvi] and creating a predictable routine helps them be successful.

First, create your assignments at least a week in advance and post them to the learning management system. My preferred practice is to post two weeks in advance and sometimes more. This allows the parent to plan for students' device and internet access. I frequently receive questions about assignments over religious holidays and family vacations, which I can answer because my assignments are scheduled and posted in advance.

Second, assign the same types of assignment to be due on the same days every week. Want to have a weekly quiz in your classes? Great, set it up and assign it every Friday. Or Monday. Or Wednesday—the day and particular type of assignment doesn't matter so much as the routine. Parents tell me that part of the reason they sign their children up for my classes is the reliability of the posted routine.

Teachers should not make the live video sessions the central axis of their course. As a classroom teacher, your presence is the center of the classroom—but in the online classroom, teachers are not there most of time, and when teachers are there, students are distracted.[ccvii] Instead, while I attempt to make the video sessions engaging and thorough, every piece of necessary information I offer in live class sessions is available elsewhere in writing.

Instead, repeat yourself. Have you ever watched reality TV? At least one-fourth of the time is devoted to recaps, presumably because watchers are distracted. That design is worth imitating in the online classroom. I repeat information in my syllabus, in weekly auto-posted announcements, in weekly calendars, in weekly lists, inside weekly assignment folders, and so on.

Chapter Summary

- Consider convergent and divergent goals when planning.
- Teachers are often poor judges of student ability.
- Ability grouping has minimal positive impact on student performance.
- Gifted students are not always easily identified.
- Students with learning disabilities are capable of being high achievers.
- Students can be both gifted and have a learning disability.
- Judgment about a student's socio-economic status might negatively affect perception of a student's ability.
- Sorting by ability groups has a strong negative impact for low-ability students.
- Using computer-adaptive software to aid instruction works for all students.
- Online classes rely heavily on print instruction.

Tips for Differentiation in the Online Classroom

- Use OCR-capable text.
- Allow students to use speech-to-text software.
- Provide the slide deck to students before class.
- Train students to complete assignments.
- Have students tell it back.
- Make sure students know the standard to which they're being held.
- Do not overload students.
- Make sure that grading standards reflect teacher priorities.
- Use assignments with visual elements.
- Link to videos and simulations on websites.
- Create flash card decks with visuals.
- Use online discussion boards to prepare for short-answer essays.
- Give students skeleton notes to complete.
- Assign consistent types of assignments.
- Post regular, repetitive assignments two weeks in advance.

CHAPTER 6

COMMON ONLINE ASSIGNMENTS

When planning to teach online, ensure that all tasks explicitly support the goal of the unit by reviewing the same information in different formats, such as discussion board questions and guided notes. Teachers should create assignments that promote content-specific background knowledge, skills, and abilities. This is true whether they are teaching in a blended class or all online. This chapter argues for several specific online assignments.

> When planning to teach online, ensure that all tasks explicitly support the goal of the unit by reviewing the same information in different formats.

Research supports providing a consistent structure and scaffolding to reduce cognitive load,[ccviii] freeing the student to learn the material. This is not "discovery learning," in which students search for solutions to problems—and which "imposes an extraneous cognitive load," thus reducing learning.[ccix] Particularly important online, "a checklist and incremental deadlines" with "meaningful feedback" helps improve student learning.[ccx]

Some subjects lend themselves to different kinds of assessments—for example, problem sets are normal in math, whereas essays are common in history. By thinking of instruction in weekly units, with repetitive assignment types, teachers can offer a variety of ways to attack the information and make the content more appealing to students.

Make sure that each assignment includes the instructions and requirements, the criteria for assessment, the due date, where it's found in the class, and how to find feedback. Generally speaking, a learning management system (LMS) has a designated place to write instructions for assignments, and an easy way to include a rubric or other assessment criteria for students to view before completing the assignment. The due date is typically a setting when creating an assignment. Assignments should always be located within the weekly content module. Feedback should be located within the rubric and assessment criteria in an LMS.

While it may be tempting to organize each weekly module around a central project, there are several problems with that approach.

- When teachers are not physically present with the student, they cannot engage in the kind of joint attention required for a Socratic discussion that enables students to make good, independent sense of the content—also known as "essential overload."[ccxi]
- Students are often distracted by a novel task and not focused on the content itself.[ccxii]
- Big projects are often a form of massed practice—"This week is all about titration!" Massed practice is inferior to distributed practice for long-term mastery.[ccxiii]
- By assigning several smaller tasks (also known as "segmenting"), students are more likely to be independently successful at the tasks.[ccxiv]
- When teachers don't use a variety of tasks all focused on the same goal, students don't extract the underlying principles of the concept. This means they have difficulty differentiating the key ideas.[ccxv]
- Performing big tasks in isolation means that students don't center the content into a larger historical or conceptual network.[ccxvi]
- Students with special education needs often require more practice or alternative approaches to content[ccxvii] —this is not about learning styles[ccxviii]; rather, it is a diagnosed physiological difference such as a visual impairment, an attention deficit disorder, etc.

Instead, in a given week teachers should ensure that students access the same content multiple times but in different ways, strengthening learning. Reading, writing, taking notes, completing diagrams, practicing problems, memorizing critical vocabulary, doing hands-on projects, participating in class discussions, taking quizzes—all of these work together to help etch the content into the student's brain. Teachers can ask students to:

- answer discussion questions about the concepts in the textbook

  - *"Discussion, collaboration, and extensive practice promote situational cognition and learning."*[ccxix]

- read the textbook and complete notes based on the textbook

  - *"introducing knowledge organizers at the beginning of a topic of study is likely to be very beneficial for learning"*[ccxx]

- complete diagrams based on the concept in the book

  - *"Studying with words and pictures together was found to better learning."*[ccxxi]

- watch and discuss videos about the concept in the textbook

  - *"Students who had been given pre-questions did much better . . . than those who didn't."*[cxxii]

- complete problem sets about the concept(s) in the textbook

  - *"Include activities that focus on application."*[cxxiii]

- memorize vocabulary/processes from the textbook

  - *"Memorizing facts is like stocking a construction site with the supplies to put up a house."*[cxxiv]

- play games or complete hands-on activities that illustrate the concepts in the textbook

  - *"Assignments that demand creativity may also be motivating."*[cxxv]

- participate in highly structured, live class discussions about the concepts in the textbook

  - *"Not only do the most effective teachers plan their activities, often minute by minute, but they script their questions in advance."*[cxxvi]

- take weekly quizzes about the concepts in the textbook

  - *"at the end of each week—or on the Monday of the new week—you should review in the form of a quiz the most important things that were handled the previous week and the same goes for each month."*[cxxvii]

When teachers assess students, they should favor auto-graded assignments. While many teachers may see multiple-choice questions as inferior because the answer is included, Bjork, Little, and Angelo say that "properly constructed multiple-choice tests can indeed trigger productive retrieval processes."[cxxviii] Students like getting specific, immediate feedback, and the immediacy increases their learning.[cxxix] Because it is private and neutral—either they got it right or they got it wrong—these types of assessments create less conflict in the class. Because we have weekly quizzes, each quiz is a small portion of their grade, which creates less stress for the students and less incentive to cheat.[cxxx]

A meta-analysis of different types of interactions in online classes concluded that stronger course design with high-quality, frequent interactions "makes a substantial difference in terms of achievement."[cxxxi] Sweating the details of these small, frequent assignments makes a big difference in student learning.

Written, Online Discussion Questions

"It's not enough for students to work with your content. It's not even enough for students to work with you. They must work with each other, too, to learn and succeed in our online classes."

–Flower Darby

Written discussion is one of the ways in which teachers can assist students in building camaraderie within the course. Shy students, students with low processing speed, students with facial recognition issues, students with high anxiety levels, students with speech delays, and so on can feel especially isolated. Having written discussions helps give students a low-key way to get to know each other, gradually, over the course of the year. This is especially important for students with social anxiety or learning issues who "freeze" when put on the spot in a live discussion. In fact, by the end of the year, many students say the written discussion questions are a favorite part of the course.

Students should discuss academic content as it relates to the student and our wider society. Giving structured feedback increases student learning.[ccxxxii] Therefore, in these discussions, teachers can introduce topics, attempt to create some reflection about the material, and try to provoke some deep thinking. Writing is a natural way to include elaboration and recitation in the class, which is one of the main ways that students can learn material.[ccxxxiii] However, I do not ask students to assess peers because they often reinforce wrong ideas and bad habits. Disagreement is fine, as long as it's polite.

One of the hardest parts of teaching is focusing a student's attention while online. It is very easy for students who are taking online courses to "space out" of the course. Students often have very busy schedules, with multiple competing demands. By requiring them to attend to the course at least three days a week, teachers increase student success because students have less opportunity to put the course on the back burner.

These online, written discussions build skills for engaging in Socratic discussion, or collaborative learning.[ccxxxiv] Every day, adults are fired for displaying poor manners on the internet. Throughout the class, teachers can ask students to be polite and respectful of one another. Teachers can require students to ask thoughtful questions and collaboratively engage in a search for reflective answers. Even in content area classes, teachers can help create an engaged citizenry, who as Robert Pondiscio puts it, "are able to advocate thoughtfully and passionately for their ideas without demonizing those they disagree with."[ccxxxv] Finally, by creating assignments that incorporate effective discipline through teaching skills and helping students take responsibility for their actions, teachers can increase equity in the online classroom.[ccxxxvi]

The online, written discussions are not meant to be difficult assignments. At the middle school level, teachers should be looking for perhaps fifteen minutes' worth of work on Monday, and another ten to fifteen minutes on Wednesday. The rewards of those twenty to thirty minutes outweigh the inconvenience.

 Resist the urge to use only synchronous discussions. Research shows that face-to-face, synchronous, or asynchronous students learn the same amount using "structured controversy" discussions.[ccxxxvii]

How to Use Written, Online Discussion Questions

Key to the success of online, written discussions is teaching students how to do it. In my classes, I create one single thread for students to reply to, because I think it's less difficult for students to navigate. In addition, if I require students to post before reading other students' work, then there are as many threads as there are students in the class, and only a few of these are read by most students. In order to have everyone's writing have a fair chance at being read, I keep one single thread per week.

During the orientation session, teach students:

- where to find the written discussion question
- when the written discussion answers are due
- how to find examples of possible written discussion questions
- what makes a good written discussion answer, using a model
- how written discussion will be graded, marking up the model and assigning points in the rubric

In addition, include a mini lesson on communication standards and meaningful participation. The official course policy, reviewed during the orientation and posted within the course, could include:

Your communication skills are on display in this class. A positive attitude and tone are keys to success. Read your messages before you send them—especially if you disagree. We can't see your expression or hear your voice. The written word is much harsher than the spoken one. Always respond with tact and eliminate any sarcasm.

No personal attacks, forms of harassment, discrimination, or threatening messages will be tolerated. I take electronic communication seriously—so should you. Never send a message you composed while you were angry or upset. Wait until you cool down. By now you should know that all messages are retained either on the server or on a backup. Just because you deleted it on your PC doesn't mean it's gone.

We do not discuss (or vent about) other instructors, other classes, students, etc. Always keep your posts "clean" and respectful. If it isn't something you would tell your parent or guardian, don't post it.

Criticizing without offering support is not considered worthwhile participation, and you will not receive credit.

Structure and appropriate levels of difficulty are also important for successful collaborative learning.[ccxxxviii] I do not set up debates, because the object of the class is not winning, it's everybody learning. I'm not a Roman emperor pitting my students against each other for my amusement, giving a thumbs up or down. Nor am I foolish enough to think that students win because they have the better argument, or that arguing does anything but refine one's ability to argue. To keep students accountable for their words, I do not permit students to edit or delete their discussion board posts.

Encouraging community in the online class can be difficult. In most classes, I set up "for fun" discussion boards, where students are allowed to discuss anything. To warm students to the idea, I tend to post starter threads of jokes, favorite books or movies, and "Continue the Story" threads. One of my middle school classes wrote thousands of words of a story over the course of a school year. There were some talented writers in that class, and it was a pleasure to read every time I checked the posts. Teachers should always read every post in the "for fun" boards, because students can be unsafe, they could be disclosing personal information, and they can be rude to each other.

Here are some examples of meaningful participation that I include examples within the course syllabus:

- *Sharing a related experience*
- *Commenting on others' experiences*
- *Asking others questions about their ideas and/or experiences*
- *Offering a different perspective about an idea that is being discussed*
- *Describing an interesting idea from the week's reading and explaining what you learned*
- *Asking the group a question about something in the course*
- *Disagreeing (respectfully)*
- *Describing a problem and asking for help*
- *Describing how you've used something you've learned in the course*

- *Sharing a relevant resource*
- *Describing relevant research and sharing information on how to find it*
- *Noting, briefly, the content and/or purpose of a useful website and providing a link (it is a violation of copyright law to copy the actual page)*

Every week, students have three choices of written discussion questions provided by the teacher. They may choose any of the three options. Their first choice is usually watching and discussing a video, their second choice is usually reading and discussing a written article, and their third choice is usually completing and discussing a more hands-on type of assignment. Offering choices fosters autonomy, which in turn helps invest students in the discussion questions.[ccxxxix]

Consider using discussions as a basis for later assignments. For example, in my world geography class, students compare and contrast the topics of discussions from two separate weeks.

All of these choices are meant to be equally challenging and help link the course to everyday life, answering "Why are we learning this?!" Teaching students how the content extends beyond the class helps students make connections and expand their schemas.[ccxl] These questions can also be a more complex task than standard problem sets; as such, they are ideal for distributed cognition.[ccxli]

Online environments—especially asynchronous environments—require extra attention by the instructor or team leader to establish and maintain social presence.

–Clark and Mayer

Initially, students respond to the teacher's questions. Next, the teacher should go through and write written responses to all students, keeping them on track, correcting misconceptions, and modeling good responses. Always ask a question of students—don't dominate the discussion by having the final word. This is where teachers project warmth within the course, using students' names and adding in outside information (and personal information, if relevant). Student engagement in an online course reflects teacher engagement in the written discussion board.

Best practice is to read discussion questions daily and respond to any questions within forty-eight hours.

Then, students must write two substantive responses to other students, in complete sentences. As they get older, teachers should require answers that are more detailed.

Capable high school students might be expected to cite their textbook, and younger students can simply list three key ideas. This set-up creates an optimally sized group of four—the teacher, the initial responder, and the two students who respond further—with "team interdependence" and clear success criteria.[ccxlii]

Here is a sample discussion question format for middle school.

Choose one:

- Watch this video. Write a one-paragraph summary.
- Read this article. What real-life situation can apply to _____. Draw up the situation and either post your image or type your answer.
- Do _____ hands-on project. Show your work! Analyze the results for cause and effect.

Rosenshine's Principles of Instruction include the idea that teachers should engage in weekly and monthly review.[ccxliii] Discussion questions offer a perfect opportunity to use the "Last week, last month, term" format. That way, no matter which item students choose, they're engaged in retrieval practice.

In addition, Kirschner and Hendrick point out that "depth of processing," asking students to elaborate on a concept, noting how it is the same and different from another concept, aids in retention.[ccxliv] Using discussion question formats to review concepts in a slightly different viewpoint from the way they were taught last week, last month, or last term helps students remember information better by providing desirable difficulties. Even better, find a news article or video that applies the concept in everyday life, and ask students to paraphrase or summarize before applying it to their own lives.

In *The Writing Revolution*, Hochman and Wexler begin with sentence-level activities like asking students to write the four types of sentences (question, statement, exclamation, command) using a given vocabulary word or set of vocabulary words.[ccxlv] These types of exercises lend themselves beautifully to written discussion questions across the curriculum. One of my favorites for reinforcing math vocabulary is to use the famous "because, but, so" with a sentence stem like "When multiplying decimals, students should count the number of places behind the decimal because . . ." Then change "because" to "but," and then change it again to "so."

In the same vein, Beck, McKeown, and Kucan offer a series of excellent stems on page 91 of *Bringing Words to Life*.[ccxlvi] In addition, the appendix in *Bringing Words to Life* has three separate variations for using writing to reinforce vocabulary.[ccxlvii]

In *Reading Reconsidered*, the authors discuss a technique called Open Response, which are slightly longer prompts that "usually ask students to refer directly to the text and use specific evidence or details. Although they can be used to CFU, they also frequently assume that students have literal comprehension of the story and are now ready to analyze a character or event more deeply."[ccxlviii] These are perfect for discussion boards, because the teacher can assign reading on Monday and read over students' answers on Monday evening or Tuesday morning. Then teachers can use students' answers to form their instruction during a synchronous session or asynchronous video on Tuesday, sending students back to follow-up on their discussion questions on Tuesday night. This schedule can repeat on Wednesday and Thursday. If teachers establish a Monday read/write, Tuesday watch/write schedule, and use it every week, then the assignment is not just-in-time and should not impinge on a family's schedules too much.

While some teachers like to create a class question and answer discussion board, I prefer to have students email me with questions. Many students are self-conscious about needing help and prefer to ask without the pressure of being in front of peers. In addition, I believe that teaching is my job, and therefore, if students have questions, it is my obligation to answer them, not to pass that responsibility off onto the students in my class. If a student asks a question that other students might need to know the answer to, I will use the opportunity for formative assessment, adjusting my teaching.

For example, I will often post an announcement clarifying the issue. If it's more urgent, I might email the whole class. Often, I will review a question at the beginning of a synchronous session without identifying the student who asked the question. Alternatively, teachers could record a brief video in which they answer the question and post the video in that week's content module. These are all more personal and help build engagement far more than a class question and answer discussion board.

Because most teachers have multiple sections, and students from all sections should interact as much as possible in the discussion questions, teachers should use a rigid schedule. Keep it the same every week, regardless of synchronous lecture dates and times. My standard schedule looks like this:

- Monday: discussion question response due
- Wednesday: two discussion question replies to other students due
- Friday: content area assessment

Students are welcome to work ahead and customize how they get the work done. They don't need to ask for permission to plan their personal schedule. Work is posted at least two weeks in advance. This routine changes only at the holidays or during final exam weeks. Students do not need to work over the weekend.

 Making the discussion question due on Monday and carefully designing questions can help students activate prior knowledge about the content to be covered that week.

Modeling Written, Online Discussion Questions

When students respond to each other, "I agree" or "You're wrong" are not adequate answers. When prepping students for the assignment, teachers should remind students that if they were having a discussion with a friend, if everyone responded, "I agree!" to a statement that discussion wouldn't last very long.

Every student response requires two parts:

- The student must say something in response that is distinctive enough for me to read in isolation from the discussion thread and still know what they are responding to, because my LMS shows me responses by student when I'm grading. For example, "I also went camping in the Rockies."
- The student must bring in new information, disagree politely, or ask a question. "Did you know that the Rockies have an outbreak of Lyme disease?"

By responding to students every week, teachers model high-quality discussion responses. Teachers can also help struggling students by guiding their understanding of the topic at hand, correcting misconceptions, and just letting them know that teachers see them—they matter to someone. Demonstrating empathy and caring for students helps their course engagement and eventual success.

 Success with online, written discussion forums requires intensive teacher participation—for the entire course, not just the first couple of weeks.

Feedback for Written, Online Discussion Questions

Every student should receive discussion question feedback every week. Teachers should select a day of the week and grade all the work for a given class on that day, every week. This way, teachers have a standard extension deadline ("OK, if you don't get it in by this Saturday, you can have until next Saturday, since that's the next day I'll grade work for this class"). Students never have to wonder when their work will be assessed—they know that they can rely on their teacher and that they can trust their teacher to consistently follow through.

 Because teachers are working with students in elementary, middle, and high school, teachers should not assign work to be due on the weekend. Respect families by recognizing the importance of family time. Instead, make discussion questions due Wednesday by midnight. This way, students can easily email teachers on Monday (for the initial response) or Wednesday (for the two responses to other students) and receive a quick reply. Then, teachers can set aside Saturdays to grade work. This way, students receive their feedback within seventy-two hours.

In the LMS, the rubric also has an individual response area that teachers can use to assist struggling students by providing more specific, tailored feedback—including feedback about tone and "culturally sensitive language and behaviors."[ccxlix] In my experience, the most successful discussion feedback gives suggestions for what to do next time—formative feedback, instead of summative.

 If written feedback isn't going to cut it, and it's not particularly time-sensitive (in which case teachers should pick up the phone), teachers might consider making a quick audio or video recording. Teachers can use the LMS to record a screen capture of the discussion question and mark it up during the recording while giving specific feedback aloud. This helps convey instructor warmth and caring in a way that written text cannot. While it is more time consuming, it might be worth it for a struggling student or a critical misunderstanding.

If this is intimidating, teachers might consider just making a recording with their phone and emailing it to the student—never text it using a teacher's private number. Teachers always want a record of when and what was sent in the LMS in case a student or parent complains. In addition, the Family Educational Rights and Privacy Act (FERPA) applies to student feedback, and the LMS keeps it secure.

If teachers receive several responses that indicate a need for whole-class feedback, post an announcement that is automatically emailed to all the students. Save this, and teachers can schedule announcements in advance for next year's class, to help clear up the confusion ahead of time. Teachers might also consider adapting the materials that caused the confusion the next time they teach the course.

If teachers want to call out good work as a way of praising a student (the carrot is often more effective than the stick), there are several options.

- Use a "gold star" image as a virtual sticker in the teacher's response to students who went above and beyond.
- Take note of interesting questions or responses and address them in the next synchronous class session or recording. "Sally mentioned ____ on Tuesday . . ."
- Screenshot a particularly good piece and incorporate the image into the slide deck for the next lesson, which helps serve as a study guide.
- Send a note to the parent asking for written permission to display the student's work on social media as an example of the good work done at the school.
- Write a personal note to the student in that week's discussion feedback.

Teachers should use a standard rubric so that expectations are always clear. Because a learning management system integrates the rubric—it automatically totals the points awarded and posts results to the students—teachers can quickly sort through the responses every week and give clear feedback. Here is a discussion question rubric:

Assignment Part	Novice	Competent	Proficient
Initial Answer	Attempts to answer question.	Answers question. Uses incorrect spelling, grammar, and/or mechanics. Might not completely answer question, or answer does not correspond to question.	Completely addresses all points of the question, using excellent spelling, grammar, and mechanics.
Response 1	Attempts to meaningfully respond.	Responds to other student, but uses incorrect spelling, grammar, and/or mechanics. Does not completely address other student, or answer is not meaningful.	Meaningfully addresses other student, using excellent spelling, grammar, and mechanics.
Response 2	Attempts to meaningfully respond.	Responds to other student, but uses incorrect spelling, grammar, and/or mechanics. Does not completely address other student, or answer is not meaningful.	Meaningfully addresses other student, using excellent spelling, grammar, and mechanics.

Common Problems When Using Written, Online Discussion Questions

Problem: Students are rude to each other.

Solution: Depending on the severity of the rudeness, a teacher might wish to screenshot the comment *in situ*, and then delete the comment. If peers have called the student to task, the teacher will need to decide whether the "public" reprimand by peers is appropriate. If not, then those posts might need to be deleted. If a series of angry back and forth comments has ensued, then the teacher might wish to close and hide the discussion entirely, giving all the participants a chance to cool down. If the comment has seemingly gone unrecognized, the teacher must balance the need for a public reprimand (showing that this sort of behavior will not be tolerated in the course) versus the possibility that the statement was unintentional (and thus better handled as a private learning opportunity.)

 Before contacting the student, the teacher should take a moment to review their perception of the situation to identify possible biases in student discipline.[cl] If the rudeness is centered on race, class, or culture, then the teacher might wish to consult with a supervisor for assistance before contacting the student and their parent or guardian.

N.B. Students are less likely to be rude to each other when the teacher is visible in the online discussion every day.

Problem: Students are simply parroting "Good job."

Solution: Take time in a live class session to review a model set of answers. Don't use a student as a shining example but instead create your own model answer. Show them what the teacher is looking for, "These words show me that the student read the original question. This part shows me where they brought in new information." Remind them that mimicking "Good job" will not give them full credit for their work. No live session? Make a video. No videos? Make a PDF handout with a sample answer marked up in red pen with written explanations of why it was graded as it was.

Problem: Students are not using good mechanics when they write. Sentences are not capitalized, etc.

Solution: Take time in a live class session to show students how to use a word processor, like Google Docs or Microsoft Word, with the grammar check system on. Copy and paste a badly written answer (not one from a student) in the word processor and show students how to use the automatic correction.

No live session? Make a video. No videos? Make a PDF handout with a sample answer marked up in red pen with written explanations of why it was graded as it was.

Problem: Students are copying each other.

Solution: This is a two-part issue. Teachers will need to address the person being copied and the copier. This may take several rounds before it "sticks." Here are some sample responses:

- Round 1:
  - To the person who brought the complaint: "I'm sure you understand we can't discuss other individual students due to privacy concerns, but you may rest assured that I have taken appropriate measures."
  - To the student who copied (with attached screenshot): "I know that you're working hard in this class, but I'm sure you can see how similar this is. I realize that there are only so many right answers, but I would like to encourage you to write your answers in a separate word processor before even looking at the discussion board."

- Round 2:
  - To the person who brought the complaint, with a BCC to a supervisor: "I understand your frustration. I have looped others in on this situation so that we may handle it with grace for all involved."
  - To the student who copied (with attached screenshot, and copy and paste of the suggested models from the course policy): "I know we've talked about this before, but we need to sit down and discuss how you can structure your independent responses. Below is a list of models. I would encourage you to choose one of these in the future."

- Round 3:
  - To the person who brought the complaint, with a BCC to a supervisor: "You're absolutely right, and while I cannot discuss other students, the school administration is handling this."
  - To the student who copied (with attached screenshot): "From now on, I would like you to submit your written discussion responses individually to me via email so that I can offer you structured feedback to better support your writing."

Note that a general online classroom with these kinds of discussions and prior training meets many guidelines for successful constructive discussions, such including mixed-ability groups, providing access to relevant information, ensuring adequate social skills, and focusing group interactions.[ccli]

For more information on creating and using written, online discussion questions, Flower Darby's *Small Teaching Online* has an excellent overview, albeit aimed at higher education.

Guided Notes

Converting text or speech to notes is one of the most valuable skills you can teach your students. . . . It's a way of forcing students to process and understand what they've read, heard, and learned.

–Hochman and Wexler

While often overlooked as a formal assignment, teacher-prepared handouts with carefully designed blank spaces for students to write information have been found to improve student learning, particularly in school-age children.[cclii] A student with special education needs benefits from guided notes as well.[ccliii] Although most teachers assign these to be completed during lecture, younger students can also benefit from using guided notes to read a textbook.[ccliv] Including diagrams is also very useful—don't be afraid to assign extensive notes. My lower middle school/upper elementary age biology students were perfectly capable of completing five to eight pages of skeleton notes per week.

"Writing to learn" is an old idea. With guided notes, students are asked to restate concepts in their own words ("List the steps in long division") and create examples ("List three mammals kept as household pets"). Asking students to relate two different topics is another great way to have students reflect on the content and learn ("Complete this chart explaining how Assyrian kings were caught in the prisoner's dilemma").[cclv] Limit instructions in skeleton notes to short, clear items like "define," "list," and "label." These are not the places for critical thinking or answering complex questions.

Vocabulary is important in content courses, but having students copy definitions out of the textbook does not lead to strong learning by itself.[cclvi] Instead, refine students' understanding in the synchronous lecture, ask them to use the word in context during written discussions, and expose them to the word in context through outside readings. Finally, students will need these words for their weekly assessment, either by directly identifying the definition or by retrieving the meaning as part of understanding a related question.

 Each week, identify a handful of words or concepts and ask students to add these words to their memory work. Assess these in the weekly quiz.

One key point is that by assigning teacher-created skeleton notes, the teacher can explicitly teach note-taking strategies, such as adding drawings. One way to do this is to review the notes as part of the synchronous lecture—"Everybody completed their notes? Great, let's pull them out and see what your answers are. See how I put this bolded vocabulary word in the notes? That's because vocabulary is important."

Teachers should emphasize color coding and drawing as mathematics skills during synchronous lectures.

If this set of directions seems vague, Chapter 2 of *The Writing Revolution* has an excellent, lengthy description of how to teach note-taking skills in the context of writing across the curriculum—good for all teachers.

How to do it:

- Take your own notes.
- Use those notes to identify key vocabulary, rules, and concepts.
- Create an outline of the material with blank spaces for students to fill in with their own notes.
- Post as an editable document and as a PDF in the weekly module.
- Review content with students during synchronous class sessions or short recordings.

Diagrams, Flow-Charts, Infographics, and Sketchnotes

For the recall of facts, there were no differences between any of the groups. But when their understanding of the concepts involved was tested, the graphic organizer groups were more successful. And of those, the partially completed ones were better than the fully completed ones.

–Caviglioli

Using words and pictures together, dual coding, has been extensively studied. Dual coding has particular relevance to the online classroom, as teachers must create significant quantities of material for individual use by students. Completing graphic organizers seems to increase learning (whereas having students draw one from scratch is not effective),[cclvii] so go the extra mile and make one for every module.

If a teacher and their students all have textbooks, teachers can use the sketch or diagram from the textbook and not violate copyright law. Teachers should center the overarching concept for the weekly module as the main idea in the sketch. Then teachers should review the sketch during that week's synchronous lecture.

From the student side, teachers can ask students to work with the main ideas. For example, if you're covering Australia that week, ask students to copy and label a map of Australia. Factoring trinomials? Have them complete a flow chart of the process. Learning clades in biology? Have students fill in a concept map. History lends itself to a timeline, and indeed, students in my science and history classes keep timelines as an ongoing assignment throughout the school year.

Some non-academically inclined students view themselves as artistic, so an artistic-type assignment every week, across the content areas, builds their engagement and offers them a chance to shine. Even in subjects like math, art and music are tightly intertwined. In social studies, studying the art (including architecture) of the culture under discussion is a common task. Art and literature have been intertwined for centuries, and nearly every major piece of literature has art associated with it. Drawing the natural world has a long, storied history often associated with women such as Charlotte Mason. For example, phenology wheels are a lovely way to incorporate drawing and nature study into the science classroom for even the youngest students.

 While students often love to share their work online, be wary of overloading students and parents with too much uploading of student work. Instead, use the weekly assessment and the problem sets to gauge progress.

How to do it:

- Take your own notes.
- Use those notes to identify key vocabulary, rules, and concepts.
- Create a diagram or sketch for the students to complete.
- Post as an editable document and as a PDF in the weekly module.

For more information, *Dual Coding with Teachers* by Oliver Caviglioli offers a wealth of information.

Videos

The multimedia principle applies to video examples, in which students learned better from reading a lesson on teaching techniques followed by viewing video examples rather than reading a lesson followed by reading text-based descriptions of examples

–Clark and Mayer

 One underrated problem with online courses is the sheer amount of text involved. Carefully curated videos can help. While the understandable first inclination is simply to record standard classroom content, resist this impulse (see Chapter 11 for an explanation of why). Also, resist presenting any information to students with only text. Students learn better from reading a lesson and then viewing videos.[cclviii]

If teachers are making their own videos, the better way to do it is to invest a little money (less than fifty dollars) in a headset with a microphone. This way, extraneous background noise is reduced. Yes, a gamer headset works just fine. (NB—many students already own gamer headsets. Ask them to use their headsets for synchronous classes.) Oddly enough, audio quality is very important, whereas "pretty" graphics or unnecessary illustrations do not help learning and can even hurt learning.[cclix] Digital natives have no advantages here—much like excess sugar, excess pretty videos and complex pictures may be pleasurable, but they are not good for students.[cclx]

It's important that the audio narration (and captions) be about what's on the screen. Separating words and graphics even by a few seconds substantially impairs student learning.[cclxi] In accordance with dual coding theory, teachers should not place all the text on the screen. Just use a few key words, at most. Save the text for notes and captions that students can turn off. Fancy video editing software is unnecessary. Teachers need not worry about making artistic videos—make them plain and functional instead.

 Think about the potential consequences before asking students to record themselves in a video.

Privacy issues abound (not just FERPA) when students are visible in their homes, particularly if they have undocumented family members, fear for their safety in a domestic violence situation, or are just embarrassed by their home life. Student-made videos are an equity issue because not all students will have the devices and sufficient internet access to make a recording and upload it. In addition, teachers will have to take time away from content to teach them how to do it—is that instructional time loss really worth the student-made video?

How to Do It

When teachers make their own videos for asynchronous use, make them short (six to ten minutes), make them about one single topic, use a Q&A format with worked examples, draw students' attention to key points, and ask questions. Narrating the slide deck is fine—but offer a text option for the audio (captions, a transcript, a script, etc.).

 If selecting videos from outside sources, always watch the whole thing, make sure it is from a reputable source, and consider having students take notes or answer specific questions about the content. Don't assign videos because you find them amusing. Make sure every video is relevant. As part of offering content for students with print issues, teachers should offer a video link for each main idea in the weekly content module. (Don't upload the outside video to the LMS, as this usually violates copyright.)

If teachers want to require that students watch the videos, instead of offering them as optional tasks, assess students with a short (five to ten questions) auto-grading quiz afterwards. As per Flower Darby's suggestion in *Small Teaching Online*, consider embedding timestamps in the feedback for incorrect answers (e.g., "Chromosomes in meiosis are different from mitosis because meiosis ends with half the chromosomes while mitosis ends with cells that have the same number of chromosomes as the parent cell. See 1:17 in the video for more detail"). Correct answers can also include feedback such as links and references to more detailed videos.

Because teachers can embed videos in written discussion questions, students can be assessed about whether and how well they attended to the video when they choose that option.

 Vocabulary can be reinforced with carefully selected videos from outside websites.

If vocabulary instruction is important to a teacher's classroom, teachers might adapt a technique from *Bringing Words to Life* by Beck, McKeown, and Kucan by tracking when students find vocabulary words in a video and using it as a reward system (homework passes, etc.). Create a form where students can submit a link for the video, the name of the video, and the minute and second when the vocabulary word can be found, and after so many identifications, they can earn a reward. A variation is to have students find when a word should fit in the video.

Problem Sets

> *Only if we continuously work to develop and use our complex analogical and inferential skills will the neural networks underlying them sustain our capacity to be thoughtful, critical analysts of knowledge, rather than passive consumers of information.*

–Maryanne Wolf

Many content areas have problem sets—translations, math sets, comprehension questions, and so on. Fortunately, an LMS typically allows teachers to create daily problem sets. Note that directions should be on the same screen as the task to avoid the split-attention effect.[cclxii] Common built-in LMS question types include:

multiple choice	surveys
fill-in-the-blank	peer assessments
matching	opinion scale/Likert
drag-and-drop	jumbled sentence
ranking/ordering	multiple answer
image selection	true/false
"hot spot" selection	"quiz bowl" style
calculated formula	fill in multiple blanks
calculated numeric	multiple drop-down
file uploads	computer code
short answer essays	pattern matching

As much as possible, stick to the kind of problems that a teacher would use in a face-to-face class—don't get distracted by shiny new apps or websites. Very rarely do these websites or apps have any evidence to support learning. If the technology is not directly useful in improving student learning, then it has no place in the online classroom. Remember that problem sets should not include a distracting context, like a Jeopardy game—it might be fun, but without context, students are more likely to forget the retrieved information.[cclxiii]

Blake Harvard has some interesting variations on multiple-choice questions that would work well for retrieval practice.[cclxiv] In his template, teachers write the question as usual, and students select the correct answers as usual. These can be auto-graded by the LMS, and they autopopulate to the grade book.

But students must rank the wrong answers from most correct to least correct. Ranking and ordering can also be autograded, although students may have varying responses depending on their rationales. Teachers might consider assigning the ranking exercise as extra credit or partial credit for completion.

Finally, Harvard asks students to explain why they chose the ranking of the "best" wrong answer, rewrite the question to make an incorrect answer correct, relate a wrong answer to a student's daily life, and relate the most-wrong answer to a previous lesson or class. These are all short-answer essays that a teacher could include on a weekly quiz.

Consider including practice exercises for parts-to-whole instruction of complicated concepts—for example, when studying the digestive system, ask students to define and label each part individually, from beginning to end, *before* showing an animation of the digestive system process. This is called the "pre-training principle," and it helps make best use of a student's limited working memory by reducing the amount of work they need to do when understanding a complex topic.[cclxv]

Ensure that students have time to review faded, worked examples with the teacher before assigning independent practice via problem sets. A faded, worked example is just what it sounds like—a completely worked out model for the problem teachers want students to solve with follow-up examples missing key pieces that students can fill in with teacher support.[cclxvi] Another way to structure guided practice is "I do/We do/You do," or explicit instruction, and research shows it to be effective for all students in content areas as varied as art, law, and communication.[cclxvii, cclxviii]

In my experience, students tend to forge ahead without studying worked examples with the teacher, which makes an 80/20 ratio of old/new content in problem sets particularly helpful for online teaching. Provide sufficient practice for students to master and retain the knowledge, skills, and abilities, keeping in mind that students will work less efficiently at home than they would under the eagle eye of a face-to-face classroom instructor.

A Carnegie Unit is 120 hours of contact time and is the original basis for a high-school credit.[cclxix] Divided by the thirty-six weeks of the typical school year, that is 3 1/3 hours per week, or two hundred minutes per week. Divided by five, that is forty minutes per day that teachers can reasonably expect a student to focus on course content. By age nine, most students can focus for up to fifty minutes at a time,[cclxx] albeit with a supervising adult in the room. An experienced teacher can estimate how much work to assign for forty to forty-five minutes of on-task work—thirty math problems, read and take notes for a chapter, a dozen map questions, etc.

In addition, teachers need to design problem sets with hints for more difficult problems to ensure that students aren't wildly groping for random solutions, but instead discriminating among a limited set of options. All problems should be checked for all students, with systematic feedback and corrections.[cclxxi]

If this sounds like an overwhelming task, Daisy Christodoulou notes in *Teachers vs. Tech* that computer-adaptive learning technology is ideally suited to provide this kind of scaffolded support for students.[cclxxii] Particularly in mathematics and science, this software already exists, allowing teachers to focus on class management and instruction. MathXL, ALEKS, iReady, Redbird, and Reflex are all well-known computer-based adaptive math instruction tools.

Remember to use interleaved, interval-spaced varied practice sets. A useful rule of thumb is to assign 20% new content and 80% old content. That might mean ten problems on the new concept and twenty problems on old material—from the past week, the past month, or the past semester.[cclxxiii] Students will protest, but remind them that the objective is mastery, not fluency—they don't want to be familiar with it; they want to own it and have it etched into their neurons.

Memorization

Memorizing facts is like stocking a construction site with the supplies to put up a house.

–Brown, Roediger, and McDaniel

When I was taking classes for my special education certification, one of my professors said that the fundamental unit of learning was being able to reliably tell "same" and "different." In order to make this happen, students need to memorize facts, procedures, and concepts. In fact, cognitive scientists such as

Kirschner and Hendrick view learning as "a change made in one's long-term memory."[cclxxiv]

If this seems obvious, think about working memory—the part of the brain where people temporarily store information and work with it. Scientists know that working memory is limited and brief. How limited? Between four and seven items at a time. How brief? About thirty seconds. [cclxxv] Gifted students can often hold more in short-term memory and think longer,[cclxxvi] whereas students with attention and memory problems tend to have less holding capacity and less time on task.[cclxxvii]

We can "chunk" little pieces of information together to make it easier to remember. For example, when I was a little girl, our answering machine code was 1397, the four corners of the phone touch pad. Rather than remember the numbers, I remembered to use the corners. Each chunk occupies one part of working memory. In other words, rather than remember the telephone number 263-464-1397, I can easily hold the word CODING and then the idea of four corners in my limited working memory while I dial the number—only two bits of information instead of ten.

We can use chunks in "schemas," or the organization of how information is related. For example, most of us remember that all email addresses have an initial part, the "@" symbol, a domain name, and then an end code. For example, *example@test.com*. If someone gave you their email address, but simply said "at Gmail," your memorized chunks of common email address endings would cause you to recall that Gmail addresses end with .com and thus satisfy the schema for how email addresses should be arranged.

How many bits of information can our brains store in long-term memory? How many bits can our brains store in chunks? How many chunks? How many schemas? Humans have not reached the limit of long-term memory. Functionally, our long-term memory is unlimited.[cclxxviii]

This means that memorizing things expands students' long-term memories and expands their schemas, making better use of their limited short-term memory. For students on the lower end of working memory scale, memorizing vast swathes of knowledge is critical for problem solving,[cclxxix] because they can't afford to figure it out as they go—their working memory doesn't permit them the time or space. To quote the shoe giant Nike, these students need to be able to "just do it," or they'll forget what they're doing in the middle of a lengthy question.

Deliberate memorization helps students by chunking information in long-term memory to help compensate for limited working memory.

Many an early elementary teacher has dealt with a student straining their working memory as they carefully sound out words in a sentence—and are then unable to tell the teacher what the sentence was. Only when these students chunk all the graphemes in their long-term memory ("-ar" is pronounced "are") for quick recall can they easily read a sentence aloud. Likewise, students who have not memorized their multiplication tables are frustrated in learning long division, because by the time they stop and figure out 8 × 7, they have lost their place in the problem.

All of this is to say that a teacher must make students memorize facts, procedures, and concepts—one might even say that teaching is leading students through memorization. However, some things are harder to memorize than others. Sheer exposure means that the average three-year-old knows the McDonald's logo.[cclxxx] Alternatively, the French neuroscientist Stanislas Dehaene uses these excellent examples of address books to illustrate the difficulty in memorizing addition (lives on) and multiplication (works on) tables. (Zoe is 0, Albert is 1, etc.)[cclxxxi]

- *Charlie David lives on George Avenue*
- *Charlie George lives on Albert Zoe Avenue*
- *George Ernie lives on Albert Bruno Avenue*
- *Charlie David works on Albert Bruno Avenue*
- *Charlie George works on Bruno Albert Avenue*
- *George Ernie works on Charlie Ernie Avenue*

Memory and IQ

David Didau draws a distinction between fluid and crystallized intelligence, arguing that education can and does increase IQ scores by increasing crystallized intelligence, such as vocabulary, math, and verbal reasoning.[cclxxxii] In other words, asking students to memorize facts actually makes them smarter as measured by IQ tests.

Having some experience with the Wechsler Intelligence Scale for Children, I know that vocabulary is one of the subtests, as are similarities, vocabulary, block design, visual puzzles, matrix reasoning, figure weights, digit span, picture span, coding, and symbol search. All of those combine to create the IQ.

Similarities and vocabulary combine for the verbal comprehension score. The similarities test requires students to describe how two words are similar, and vocabulary requires students to define words aloud.[cclxxxiii] If students have never practiced analogizing or have never been exposed to the word and thus do not know it, it will lower their IQ score, regardless of their ability to learn the word. Significant differences exist in the way families from different socio-economic statuses talk to their children[cclxxxiv]—and it matters when our culture assesses those differences in an IQ test.

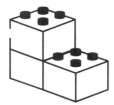

Block design and visual puzzles combine in the visual spatial score. Block design is essentially LEGO-like—students view a design and use blocks to re-create the design.[cclxxxv] Obviously, students who spend lots of time with LEGO products are going to do well with this, while and students whose family can"t afford LEGO products are not going to have as much experience and success—and LEGO products are relatively expensive investments for families, "the Apple of toys."[cclxxxvi] Visual puzzles are similar—--students view a completed puzzle and select pieces that would reconstruct the puzzle.[cclxxxvii] Again, students without significant puzzle experience are not going to do as well—and I have been in many homes where young children did not have access to puzzles.

Matrix reasoning and figure weights combine in the fluid reasoning score. Matrix reasoning requires students to select a missing piece to complete a pattern,[cclxxxviii] which is something that students can learn and practice. Pattern creation and identification is a major part of math instruction.[cclxxxix] The figure weights test is similar—students look at a scale with a missing weight and identify the weight that would keep the scale balanced.[ccxc] Obviously, students can practice using scales in science classes.[ccxci]

Digit span and picture span combine in the working memory score. Picture span requires students to memorize pictures and identify them in order, whereas digit span asks students to listen to strings of numbers read aloud and recall them in the same order, backward order, and ascending order.[ccxcii] But some students are taught mnemonic devices to memorize random sequences.[ccxciii, ccxciv]

Coding and symbol search combine in the processing speed score. Symbol search asks students to scan a group of symbols and mark the target symbol, something at which videogames have been shown to help students improve.[ccxcv] Coding asks students to copy symbols that are paired with numbers.[ccxcvi] Students with poor handwriting skills will suffer in this area.

 Knowing stuff makes a difference in IQ scores.

What to Do

How can teachers help students memorize the vast quantities of information needed to succeed in modern society? As Kirschner and Hendrick note, the two best techniques for teacher implementation are spaced practice: "small, frequent homework assignments that include new and previously treated material, cumulative tests, short review sessions at the beginning of the lesson, spiral curriculum, etc." and the testing effect: "quizzes, practice tests, and review questions."[ccxcvii]

Let's be frank, asking a first-year teacher to create this interwoven set of assignments while designing a high-quality curriculum from scratch is like plopping a high school band student in a professional musician's studio and expecting them to write an orchestral score. Interweaving all these complex threads of student learning is not an easy task.

Online, creating the conditions for memorization is even more difficult because teachers cannot physically dominate the student's personal space and march them through exercises. Instead, teachers must explicitly show students how to memorize knowledge by themselves.

One of the easiest ways to do this is to have students implement a Leitner box. Sebastian Leitner was a German scientist who developed a system for spaced practice of flashcards.[ccxcviii] Classical educators have long used this system.[ccxcix]

Shuffling cards back and forth between the groups in the box helps interleave the cards to provide discrimination practice, allowing students to quickly select the right answer among a small group of choices. Dumping all their different classes in one box varies the practice, which helps students "build a broad schema, an ability to assess changing conditions and adjust responses to fit."[ccc]

 While software does exist that automatically shuffles cards based on Ebbinghaus's forgetting curve and Leitner's algorithm (Tiny Cards, Anki, and Memrise are three of the most popular), not all students can afford the tech. Most students can lay hands on paper, pencils, scissors, and plastic baggies to keep cards sorted.

As students memorize the information, it gradually moves to the back of their recitation schedule, but never entirely disappears. At the end of the year, students have built up a considerable body of knowledge with individualized practice based on their own interleaved, interval-spaced retrieval practice.

To encourage students to keep up practice with their memory work, teachers can reward students with extra credit for submitting audio or video of their practice or recitation. Alternatively, teachers can maintain their own card deck and use it with students during synchronous lessons. If time and money permit, teachers can create class sets using software and track student practice that way.

 Have students create Leitner boxes for memory work.

How to Do It

As a teacher prepares their guided notes for the course module, they can identify the essential vocabulary, procedures (yes, teachers can have students recite the steps for long division, etc.), and concepts. Teachers can post these for students to add to their memory work.

In addition, a good slide deck is a linear outline of the lesson—and so when teachers provide that slide deck to their students, they are providing students with typed notes that students can easily transform into flash cards for retrieval practice.

Typically, students would write the week's memory work on a flash card—the order of the planets in the solar system, Henry VIII's wives, or this week's multiplication facts: third planet from the Sun / Earth, Henry VIII's first wife / Catherine of Aragon, 3 × 7 / 21.

Then, on the first day, students would review the flashcards. The items they missed would go in group one, reviewed daily. The items they answered correctly would go into group two, which is reviewed less often, possibly Monday/Wednesday/Friday. Then on Wednesday, they would review their daily cards (again, cards they know are bumped down to group two) and the group two cards. Known group two cards are bumped down to group three. Unknown group two cards are bumped back to daily. Group three cards are reviewed weekly. Similarly, if group three cards are known, they are bumped down to group four, and if they are unknown, they are bumped back to group two. Group four cards are reviewed once a month. If they are missed, they are bumped back to group three. Group four is never bumped down—reviewing known material once a month makes it stick indefinitely.

If that sounds confusing, here is a sample monthly calendar:

Monday	Tuesday	Wednesday	Thursday	Friday
Group One	Group One	Group One	Group One	Group One
Group Two		Group Two	Group Three	Group Two
Group One	Group One	Group One	Group One	Group One
Group Two		Group Two	Group Three	Group Two
Group One	Group One	Group One	Group One	Group One
Group Two		Group Two	Group Three	Group Two
Group One	Group One	Group One	Group One	Group One
Group Two	Group Four	Group Two	Group Three	Group Two

Hands-On Activities

The kind of retrieval practice that proves most effective is one that reflects what you'll be doing with the knowledge later. It's not just what you know, but how you practice what you know that determines how well the learning serves you later.

–Brown, Roediger, and McDaniel

Although most teachers have been taught that students learn best by doing, there is no factual basis for the learning pyramid with "lecture" at the pointy end and "practice by doing hands-on activities" down near the bottom.[ccci] Similarly, kinesthetic learning styles don't exist.[cccii] If you are one of the 90% of teachers who believe that these things are true,[ccciii] be angry about spending thousands of dollars on a teaching degree that instilled false beliefs.

Discovery learning seems like a good idea. "We remember things better if we discovered them for ourselves" sounds like a reasonable proposition. Did you know that the ancient Sumerians, sometime around 8000 BCE, invented the oldest writing system in the world? Humans took nearly five thousand years, until 3100 BCE, to discover how that system could be used for writing language—and the system still didn't represent sounds. We took another seventeen hundred years, until 1,400 BCE, for Mycenaean Greeks to discover how writing could represent the sounds of language.[ccciv] Teachers don't have thousands of years for our students to discover knowledge for themselves. Every minute in the classroom counts, even more so online.

Although there are curricula whose entire *raison d'être* is problem solving, students do not learn to solve problems by solving problems.[cccv] Students who are successful with those curricula tend to be gifted and already have solid foundation skills in the appropriate domain. In other words, these students are no longer newbies—it is an entire curriculum of extension of procedures. Students successful with these types of curricula have already mastered the procedures. Alternatively, these are students who can master the procedures quickly, without practice (e.g., they're gifted). Either way, students learning with these curricula must have a high tolerance for frustration, because without prior knowledge, they're randomly trying things.[cccvi] This is fine if you have an entire class of knowledgeable, patient, gifted students—more power to you! The rest of us need teaching tactics that work for *all* students.

Hands-on projects are motivating, right? "Kids learn more when they have fun." The argument runs that if teachers were somehow more entertaining, or better performers, our students would be more engaged and learn more.[cccvii] Notice how this set-up shifts responsibility for learning from the student to the teacher. Making teachers responsible for student enthusiasm doesn't increase learning. In fact, researchers have tested the "motivation leads to learning" hypothesis and discovered that it is exactly backwards—learning leads to motivation.[cccviii]

 If you want enthusiastic students, make them successful by teaching them.

Surely, hands-on projects increase students' creativity? Sadly, no. As my college boyfriend succinctly put it when he explained modern art to me, creativity is about breaking the rules by doing something no one else has done before. You cannot break rules if you don't know what the rules are. You can't do something unique if you don't know what has already been done. Allow students to be creative by showing them what has come before so they can build on everyone's experience, not just their own limited understanding.

There are good reasons to assign hands-on assignments. Perhaps teachers want students to be able to work through Euclid's Elements by practicing form drawing. Maybe teachers want students to explore the wonders of the natural world by using a prism to separate light. Sometimes, teachers may need students to commit a task to muscle memory, like how to draw the United States, whisk a béchamel, or titrate a solution.

 Hands-on activities should reinforce prior knowledge, not let students wander aimlessly in "cool" displays.

What to Do

Particularly for younger students, but even at the higher grades, high-quality curricula should include relevant hands-on activities that reinforce the main concept. For more students who are not ready to think about things in a purely abstract way, tangible items like Cuisenaire rods allow them to slowly build useful mental models of key ideas like fractions, decimals, multiplication, and division. A general rule of thumb for teaching is to start learning with concrete manipulatives, move to visual representations, and finally end with abstract representations.[cccix]

However, when teaching online, hands-on activities must be carefully *written to the student.* In addition, unless teachers are willing and able to send home supplies or insist that students purchase supplies, materials for hands-on activities are limited. In addition, about 2% of students are homeless[cccx] and have neither a place to work nor materials.

For this reason, hands-on projects are not ideal for grading. Assign them, expect students to at least watch the video, and assess based on the assumption that students understand the demonstration, but do not expect students to upload anything from the hands-on project.

Even when using synchronous classes, online teachers supervising hands-on activities are the equivalent of a student calling tech support—and nobody likes calling tech support. Our youngest students are particularly bad at creating joint attention online. Most of us do not have sophisticated technology to monitor hands-on activities like studio art, physical education, or sewing, and so these are usually not good content areas for online classes. Given the tech needed, how hard it is to teach students to do the activities, and the high-quality internet access needed, synchronous classes with hands-on activities are a limited option for most classroom teachers.

 Teachers supervising hands-on activities during a synchronous class session is not recommended.

Asynchronous activities are much better choices for online classes. Careful directions for activities ranging from using analemmatic sundials to tell time[cccxi] to mummifying chickens[cccxii] are important in homeschooling curricula. (I skipped the chicken mummification, but we did the sundial.)

Many high-quality curricula for use by individual students have been created with this in mind.

However, as I have experienced with my own children, you can't hand out curriculum "written to the student" and walk away.

 Teacher support is required for answering questions, scheduling, and assessing completed hands-on activities.

How to Do It

- Identify the key concept from the weekly module.
- Use curricula or a reliable outside resource to find a hands-on demonstration of the key concept, or design your own.

> "Written to the student" means that a student is supposed to be able to read and follow the directions without help.

- Ensure that the demonstration uses only inexpensive everyday household items, ask students to obtain the needed items, or provide the items to students.
- Perform the demonstration to make sure it works; record a short (six- to ten minute) video of the demonstration for students who are unable to complete it independently.
- Write directions for the demonstration—to the student.
- Create guided notes for students to complete as they do the project.
- Post the directions, guided notes, and video for the demonstration in the weekly course module.
- Assess through the weekly quiz or other regular evaluation.

Synchronous Class Discussions

Not only do the most effective teachers plan their activities, often minute by minute, but they script their questions in advance.

–Doug Lemov

Keeping in mind that synchronous class discussions are a luxury item when teaching online, there are some best practices for synchronous class design, explored in more detail in another chapter.

Even when teachers have synchronous sessions, due to access limitations and best practices, teachers will have fewer instructional minutes than face-to-face classes. In my experience, most students will do their best to attend a live class session, as it is a key social engagement for them. My Australian students have been known to wake up in the middle of the night to attend a class session, even though a recording is available.

Synchronous class sessions should complement the asynchronous content in the course, not be essential for successful completion of the course. Expect lower attendance rates because it is more difficult for students to attend a synchronous class than it is a face-to-face class.

 Consider synchronous class sessions as part of the spaced repetition of a well-designed course, rather than the central axis of teaching.

How to Prepare:

- Use the guided notes to form an outline of the material to cover in the session.
- Create each slide. One slide should cover one idea, or vocabulary word, and serve as the basis for a flashcard.
- Write extensive notes for each slide. Ideally, these notes can serve as a transcript for students who need one.
- Collect student questions from email and create slides as needed to answer the questions.
- Create slides to cover any upcoming assignments.
- Write a "hook" for the first slide in the notes. Good hooks are often stories or questions.
- Double check that every slide has some kind of check for understanding—polls, chat box questions, audible questions and answers, problems to be completed, etc.
- Where appropriate, ensure that guided practice is included in the slide deck.
- Make sure to include a review slide and include a call for questions at the end of the session.
- Save the slides as a PDF and post them to the weekly course module.

How to Do It:

 Building student community is critical for retaining students in the class. One easy way to do that is to **open the online, synchronous classroom ten to fifteen minutes early** and monitor (but don't participate) in informal student chatting in the online classroom. As Jon Gustafson puts it, this links "should" behaviors (attend class, pay attention) with "want" behaviors that are already rewarding (social interaction).[cccxiii]

Just like in a face-to-face classroom, teachers must **signal the beginning of class**. Teachers can this by turning on the camera, starting the recording, and welcoming all the students to the class, including a shout out to the students who are delayed (students not attending the synchronous course sessions). Last, turn off the camera and take roll, marking it on the roster. This forces students to begin listening to the teacher's voice and allows the teacher to track attendance.

Next, **take administrative questions**—assignment submission issues, upcoming absences, etc. Often, teachers can begin academic instruction by asking for questions from the homework. Students may send the teacher questions anonymously, and the teacher can review them for the entire class. When questions are answered, the teacher should **begin coverage of the academic content**.

 Establish and maintain the same routine for the beginning and end of every synchronous class session.

This routine is **carefully timed with extensive supporting notes**. If possible, write a script, including questions for students to answer via the chat box or poll, jokes, definitions of key terms, outside book suggestions, and exit ticket questions. Incorporate references to other assignments, including selected quotes from the online, written discussion board. In many classes, each slide can be a mini-*I Do/We Do*. Often, *You Do* happens asynchronously, with computer-adaptive technology supporting students as needed.

Here is the class schedule for the synchronous class session of the fourth week of my middle school ancient history class:

- 9:50—I open the class for students to chat among themselves.
- 10:00—I begin the recording, welcoming and taking roll.
- 10:02—I take student questions.
- 10:07—I begin new content with *Written History*.
- 10:10—Sumer and Egypt.
- 10:15—How do we count?
- 10:20—Transaction records.
- 10:25—How do we get from pictures of things to pictures for words to pictures for sounds?
- 10:37—Cuneiform.
- 10:42—Hieratic script.

- 10:45—Loan symbols.
- 10:47—New slide, review of key concepts from lecture, praise for good behavior/effort.
- 10:50—New slide, review of directions for upcoming assignment .

At the end of the class, **end the recording, and then take individual student questions** that are not necessarily about the academic content. The recording is automatically made available to the students. Many students review the recording later, while completing problem sets.

Students strongly dislike any off-topic chatting during a class session. Therefore, teachers should permit only direct questions about the immediate content on the screen during the class. All other questions should be answered before or after class.

 Don't let students distract the synchronous class. Off-topic chatting (either text or voice) is the most disliked part of a synchronous class session.

What Not to Do

Don't ask students to do *anything* during the synchronous class session other than listen and participate. Teachers may want to keep a checklist of participating students and mark it off as they go through the synchronous class session. Teachers can mark one way for a student who answers and mark another when they interact with a student.

Ideally, students should *not* take notes while the synchronous class session is happening, hence the guided notes as an asynchronous assignment. Getting students' attention online is incredibly difficult, and once a teacher has it, they do not want to lose it by having students flip around from screen to screen or writing in their notes. As Adam Boxer argues,[cccxiv] teachers should demand to be the sole focus of student attention. All eyes are to be focused on this screen and only this screen. Every student is expected to answer frequent (every three minutes, on average) questions, disrupting their web surfing.

 Even middle school students can attend to a synchronous class for fifty minutes once or twice a week.

 Do not to split student attention from instruction. Teachers should not expect students to turn on their cameras and interact— this is not a fun social engagement. Ideally, teachers did that before class and sometimes they will do it afterward. I don't use breakout groups because I don't want students to engage in off-topic chatting or waste time with poorly structured group work. They can work by themselves later or in a study group afterward. Don't allow students to interrupt the class for permission to step away—use a nonverbal signal for that, perhaps an "away" message.

In the same way, do not interrupt students when they are solving a problem and selecting the answer in a poll or marking their selection on the whiteboard. Teachers don't need to encourage people to complete the task, because they should expect 100% of students to answer. Don't hum the Jeopardy theme, conduct a conversation, or chat with a student. Do not feel the need to fill up silence. Instead, students are to be focused on thinking about the material. To signal the end of the wait period, simply count down the number of people who have not answered. "Three people have not answered. Two people. Alright, everyone's answered; let's talk about these choices."

For more about structuring content in slides, see the chapter on synchronous sessions later in the book. For more about engaging students see *Teach Like a Champion* by Doug Lemov.

Journals

If you practice elaboration, there's no known limit to how much you can learn. Elaboration is the process of giving new material meaning by expressing it in your own words and connecting it with what you already know.

–Brown, Roediger, and McDaniel

Journals are an underrated feature of many LMSs. As anyone who's kept a diary knows, half the fun is going back and reading what your earlier self wrote. In fact, there are five-year diaries, in which diarists use the same page each day for five years in a row. Facebook's Memories feature is popular for a similar reason.

When using journals for assessment purposes, teachers might consider substituting them for one of the weekly assessments. This signals to students that they should take the assignment seriously. Teachers may wish to use journals for writing assignments in non-composition classes, such as mathematics and science. A good LMS will allow a teacher to use a rubric with a given journal entry, simplifying grading.

Like other weekly assessments, teachers should ensure that the assignment is written and posted two weeks in advance, and that the due date propagates to the central calendar. This allows students to work on the assignment offline, fitting it into their daily schedule. That way, they only need to be online long enough to copy and paste it into the journal text box.

Given the type of assignments I tuck into the journal feature, I generally don't grade these with my formal writing rubric. In fact, I often grade these journals as complete/incomplete, and make students revise it until it is complete. Typically, I'm more concerned with the student getting the work done than I am in a summative assessment.

Sometimes, teachers find that asking students to think about the content is difficult. This difficulty is even more pronounced in an online class, because teachers do not control the student's environment. But, reflecting, or thinking about what happened in the past, connecting it to new materials, and rehearsing what you might do next time is one of the most powerful learning tools.[cccxv] Therefore, I use several types of journal assignments that lean on reflection as a learning tool.

- Ask students to pretend that a friend asked them to help figure out how to do a thing. Students must write their friend a letter that is detailed enough for anyone to pick it up, read it, and figure out how to do the thing. In order to complete this task successfully, students must think about how they did the thing in the past and rehearse how they might do it in the future.
- Ask students to organize what they've learned so far that year, using the table of contents in their textbooks. They can organize it any way they want—but they *cannot* organize it the way it's organized in the table of contents. This is a powerful assignment for thinking about what they've learned and identifying connections between knowledge. Teachers may want to provide students with sample graphic organizers. A low-key way to complete the assignment is to use crayons to highlight a copy of the table of contents, with each color corresponding to a different "box" of content.
- Ask students to make a plan for improving their class skills. Have them list at least three pieces of knowledge, skills, or abilities that they want to improve. Then have students list three concrete actions they will take to improve the items they've listed. Next, students should list three ways that they will self-assess. Finally, have students list a way they can motivate themselves for each item. The final product should have at least twelve items, three for each of the four steps. I provide them with this example:

- *three pieces of knowledge, mathematical skills, or mathematical abilities*
  - *knowledge (times tables)*
  - *skill (factoring trinomials)*
  - *ability (recognizing differences of squares)*
- *three concrete actions*
  - *memorize times tables*
  - *practice factoring trinomials*
  - *memorize four-step checklist for recognizing difference of squares, memorize the first fifteen squares*
- *three ways that you'll know you've improved your skills*
  - *I will be able to recite the times table in less than two minutes.*
  - *I will be able to factor trinomials with 95% accuracy or better.*
  - *I will be able to recite the first fifteen squares and the checklist in less than two minutes; factor differences of squares with 95% accuracy or better.*
- *three ways you can motivate*
  - *Every time I memorize a number on the times table, I'll give myself an M&M.*
  - *Every time I successfully factor ten trinomials, I'll spend five minutes playing Minecraft.*
  - *Every time I recite the checklist and the first fifteen squares in less than two minutes, correctly, I'll give myself one point towards a new album. When I factor ten differences of squares, successfully, I'll give myself five points. When I get twenty-five points, I'll buy a new album.*

The third type of journal can be used on a monthly basis, helping students improve their ability to successfully create a plan for studying. Asking students to use metacognition, or think about their thinking, can be a difficult assignment if they've not practiced it before. Teachers might encounter some pushback, but junior-high-level students and higher can successfully complete this assignment.

These assignments are powerful because they run students up against their own self-perception of their learning. Teachers should remember that online students are working in isolation—with few exceptions, they only have themselves as a measuring stick. Therefore, teaching students how to use measurable, specific assessments for improving their own learning is a valuable skill.

Note that I used objective gauges as examples—students were able to factor trinomials with 95% accuracy, or they were not able to. Students rarely have experience formulating these kinds of standards, so teachers will probably need to assist students in writing these goals. This format might be useful: "Student will be able to _____ (verb: recite, factor, solve, write, etc.) _____ (noun: times tables, helping verbs, battle dates) with _____% accuracy in ____ time."

When providing feedback, don't tell students what they did wrong—instead, tell them how to do it better. For example, rewrite a self-assessment standard for them, and ask them to rewrite the other two the same way when this assignment comes up again next month. Depending on the LMS, the teacher might be able to mark up the journal with a digital red pen.

Weekly Quizzes

> *A single, simple quiz after reading a text or hearing a lecture produces better learning and remembering than rereading the text or reviewing lecture notes.*
>
> –Brown, Roediger, and McDaniel

Along with written discussion questions, quizzes are one of the mainstays of an online course. Recall what Fletcher-Wood said about creating a habit: repetition, context, and rewards. Creating weekly content module quizzes involves all three.

When setting the habit of completing assessments in the course, pick a day and make all the quizzes due that day. My quizzes are always due on Friday, because that permits students a shortened academic day on Friday and allows me to give a quick turnaround for feedback when I grade on Saturdays.

Because I tend to use my quizzes for formative assessment, I always put them at the end of the weekly content module. When teachers assign quizzes, they should make sure the due dates propagate to the LMS calendar. Make sure students can always find the assessment on the same day in the same place—so there is no question about what's due and when.

Reward students for completing the assessment. I tend to make the assessments auto-grading, as much as possible, for a quick sense of reward for completion. There are sophisticated feedback settings built into the LMS—take full advantage.

Getting Started

Begin as you mean to go on. At the end of my orientation, the first synchronous class, I assign a quiz with a Friday due date. While it doesn't cover academic content, it does provide me with critical information about my students that may be difficult for me to obtain from the student information system. Another common option is to quiz students on the class syllabus to ensure that they've read and understood it. Keep in mind that teachers are establishing course expectations with this quiz—mind the question formats, because those will be what student expect later in the course.

In my first quiz, I begin with a variation on Jennifer Gonzalez's Student Inventory.[cccxvi] I ask students' ages, preferred names and pronunciations, their gender pronouns and use preferences, and best emails and phone numbers for contact. Because this is an online class, teachers should ask whether students have taken an online class before and whether students have met the prerequisites. In order to understand how flexible teachers should be with the late policy, teachers need to know if the student has other responsibilities, including whether students are traveling or plan to travel. Then, because online teachers don't have downtimes when students chat about favorite foods, allergies, music, books, movies, TV shows, hobbies, and other skills they're perfecting, ask students about those. Because online classes involve a lot of writing, teachers need to know about student writing experience. Last but not least, ask students what the teacher can do to support them, and add an open space for anything else students wish to share.

One nice thing about using the LMS to do this is that all the answers are auto-populated to a spreadsheet (which teachers should lock with a password, per FERPA guidelines). This way, teachers can quickly and easily read through and extract information for later use.

LMS Quiz Options

 When teachers are ready to create their first content quiz, they should place the quiz within the weekly course module. Each LMS will have an option for different types of assessments, so choose wisely. Teachers will need to title the quiz and provide a description, as well as choose from the different question types. Quizzes can be assigned as graded or just for practice. Teachers can permit multiple attempts or limit the number of attempts, as well as choose to score it using the last attempt or the highest attempt. Timers can be used, and completion can also be forced.

Deadlines are important. Teachers can also make the test available after a certain day, before a certain day, or both. Passwords to attempt the quiz are a common option, as well. Of course, teachers can assign due dates and times, and not permit students to start the quiz after the due date has passed. In addition, teachers can choose whether to include the quiz in the grade book.

When designing the quiz, teachers can decide to show all the questions at once or just one question at a time. If they choose to show one question at a time, teachers can decide that students can be prevented from changing the answer to a question that has already been submitted. Last, teachers can randomize questions for each test attempt.

Some of the more esoteric options include filtering IP addresses (so that students can only take the quiz from certain locations), assigning the quiz to all the students or just some of them, and letting students know that the quiz is now available.

It's worth spending some time exploring the different question types. Often, teachers will need to title each question. Teachers might wish to link it with the textbook: Chapter 5 Section 1, etc. Then teachers will need to enter the actual question—this is where having an integrated question bank from a psychometrician-designed assessment becomes helpful. Often, each answer can be linked with a hint that the teacher writes. Teachers can choose from partial credit options, answer orientation options, random question ordering, and per question feedback (for both correct and incorrect answers). Finally, teachers can include links, files, and images in each question.

This may sound like a lot of work, but each question entered can be added to the course question bank, making it an investment for the future. In an LMS, teachers can categorize each question, label each question with a topic, assign levels of difficulty, and note question key words, using all of these options to search for questions when designing later assessments. In addition, teachers can write notes for themselves about the question.

Adaptive Release

One of the more common options is to require students to earn a certain minimum score on the course module quiz before they can proceed to the next module—adaptive release. Research shows this improves student grades,[cccxvii] but I am not a fan of adaptive release for several reasons.

- The next course module might not be dependent on the current course module, so this setting doesn't necessarily help learning.
- Ideally, enough retrieval practice is included on the quizzes that each week's "mastery" doesn't create a boundary line for minimum sufficiency. Next week will include more practice from this week.
- If something goes wrong with the quiz (and something will go wrong), then using adaptive release has created more work later on, as teachers adjust the settings.
- This setting doesn't allow students flexibility in getting their work done—they need to be able to look ahead and see how much time they're going to need for the next week or the week after. If students have tech week at the theater or a series of away games, or maybe their parent is working a ninety-six-hour shift, students need to be able to schedule their work as it suits them, not the teacher.
- As a parent whose child has taken some of these adaptive release courses, I found it immensely frustrating when the conditions for release were clearly mistaken and my child could not move on in the course.

Feedback

 Feedback comes with many options. Teachers can choose when feedback is available: after completion, one-time only, on a given date, after test availability ends, or after the attempt is graded. Teachers may permit students to see the points per score, as well as all the answers, just the correct answers, or only their submitted answers. In addition, teachers can decide whether they want to show any per-student feedback they may have written. Finally, teachers can choose whether to show students incorrect answers.

Carefully consider the per-question feedback. Explaining why an answer is incorrect assists students with deeper understanding of harder questions. While elaborate feedback doesn't assist with learning for fact practice questions like 3×4, it does help quite a bit when students need to infer from one context to another,[cccxviii] for example, in what sense is multiplying 3×4 like dividing fractions?

Per-question feedback is also an opportunity to refer students with poor study skills to their class material: "See page 65" or "See the Guided Notes for WK 12." Many otherwise excellent students need assistance with structuring their learning efforts to best effect. Assigning frequent, low-stakes quizzes helps them realize what they don't know, and when the teacher directs them to how to find the needed information students learn the habit of looking up what they don't know. Referring to the notes creates a habit of taking notes and using them.

 Always stay positive when offering feedback to students.

Using Quizzes for Retrieval Practice

 If teachers do decide to use the adaptive release mode, combining it with memory work could be a useful adaptation. Teachers could assign a quiz about memory work from the last week, the last month, and the current school year. Then teachers could require students to achieve a certain minimum score ("the optimal success rate for fostering student achievement appears to be about 80 percent"[cccxix]) before they can open that week's module. Ideally, teachers would assign unlimited attempts for zero points—the object here is not to summatively assess students' knowledge, but to require students to do the memory work previously assigned.

 Another option, depending on retrieval practice goals, is a schedule like this, taking advantage of Blake Harvard's Brain/Book/Buddy set-up[cccxx]:

- Synchronous class or recording (Monday).
- Ask students to take the quiz without any notes or their textbook, but don't offer feedback; only percent correct/incorrect (Monday).
- Make a knowledge organizer available (Tuesday).
- Ask students to take the quiz again, using the knowledge organizer. Again, no feedback (Tuesday).
- Assign students a partner and have them discuss the material in a small group (Wednesday).
- Ask the students to take the quiz a final time; this time with feedback (Thursday).

Teachers could choose to assign a grade that is an average of the three scores, not assign a grade at all, assign the series of quizzes for completion credit only, assign this as extra credit, and so on. Note that the elaborated feedback is delayed until the final quiz round. Delaying feedback increases learning.[cccxxi]

Alternatively, consider trying an adaptation of a technique Pooja Agarwal designed for a middle school classroom while conducting research on retrieval practice.[cccxxii]

- Embed short (three- to five- question) low-stakes quizzes about each module's reading and/or recording.
- At the end of the module, assign a cumulative low-stakes quiz (approximately 80% interleaved, varied old material from previous modules, 20% new material from this module).
- Offer a review quiz shortly before each unit exam (twenty-four hours before).

Agarwal's research suggests that this type of quiz structure reduces student anxiety and increases student achievement by a full grade level, on average.[cccxxiii] Empirically speaking, I can verify that this works online, because I do something like this in my mathematics classes, and student achievement is relatively high.

Interleaving means that teachers shuffle the order of the questions—no clustering all the vocabulary together, or all the division problems together.

Varied means that teachers shuffle the questions used from previous modules—a new unlike fraction problem, then a new long division problem, then a new distributive property problem.

 Each quiz should be a little different, in unpredictable ways.

Consider offering untimed, unlimited attempt quizzes as study guides, or offering a PDF of the LMS quiz with correct answers visible so students can download practice working on the types of problems you're actually assigning.

Using Quizzes to Guide Teaching

 One of the benefits of teaching online is the ability to run data analyses on student work. Most LMSs have this feature built in. One way teachers can improve their own teaching is to run and analyze course reports on student progress. Question analysis lets teachers review how well students did on a given question, and rates the question as good, bad, or ugly.

If it's a basic concept and students didn't do well, then the teacher should review the concept in the next synchronous class session, recording, or module. Because I give assessments on Fridays, I run the analysis when I release the upcoming course modules on Saturdays. This way, teachers can find extra outside videos to review concepts students are struggling with, tweak discussion questions so students can spend time thinking about tricky concepts, send an announcement clarifying critical information, and add problems to work with students to the next week's slide deck.

 Don't berate students for poor effort. Instead, scaffold support into the course.

Teachers need to remember that this kind of interleaved, interval-spaced retrieval practice means that students are completing problem sets and quizzes without explicit conceptual organization. While this is fantastic for making it stick,[cccxxiv] it feels harder for students.[cccxxv] Be prepared to compensate by providing more emotional support and warmth.

To help students work their way through this difficulty, Dylan Wiliam suggests explaining the "hypercorrection effect" to students.[cccxxvi] Essentially, the hypercorrection effect means that when students are certain of their answer, ("It is *too* 25!") being corrected means that they are more likely to remember the correct answer. When students are corrected early in the learning process, such as on homework or short, low-stakes quizzes, they're more likely to remember the correct answer in the end.[cccxxvii]

For more about structuring retrieval practice, see *Make It Stick* by Brown, Roediger, and McDaniel.

Chapter Summary

- Written, online **discussion questions**.
  - teach students:
    - where to find the written discussion question
    - when the written discussion answers are due
    - how to find examples of possible written discussion questions
    - what makes a good written discussion answer, using a model
    - how written discussion will be graded, marking up the model and assigning points in the rubric
  - include a mini lesson on communication standards and meaningful participation

- give examples and models
- allow students to choose which questions to answer
- read discussion questions daily and respond to any questions within forty-eight hours

- **Guided notes.**

  - Take your own notes.
  - Use those notes to identify key vocabulary, rules, and concepts.
  - Create an outline of the material with blank spaces for students to fill in with their own notes.

- Include a **sketch or diagram** to label in each weekly module
- Include useful **videos** .
- Create **problem sets**; consider using computer-adaptive learning technology.
- Have students create **Leitner boxes** for memory work.
- **Hands-on activities**.

  - Identify the key concept from the weekly module.
  - Use your curricula or a reliable outside resource to find a hands-on demonstration of the key concept, or design your own.
  - Ensure that the demonstration uses only inexpensive everyday household items, ask students to obtain the needed items, or provide the items to students.
  - Perform the demonstration to make sure it works; record a short (six- to ten-minute) video of the demonstration for students who are unable to complete it independently.
  - Write directions for the demonstration—to the student.
  - Create guided notes for students to complete as they do the project.
  - Post the directions, guided notes, and video for the demonstration in the weekly course module.

- If possible, conduct **synchronous class discussions**.
- Assign weekly **quizzes**, with feedback, and use them for retrieval practice and to guide teaching.

CHAPTER 7
PUTTING IT ALL TOGETHER

In earlier chapters, we have established that teaching online is a complete replacement for face-to-face instruction in a core content area,

> **Create a weekly course module.**

and that it is fundamentally different from teaching a face-to-face class. Ideally, teachers have obtained a high-quality curriculum, with emphases in declarative knowledge, procedural knowledge, and hands-on experiences. The curriculum should include a well-planned scope and sequence of facts and skills covered in a spiral pattern over a school year, as well as professionally designed assessments. Teachers are aware of the need to provide a written, posted schedule weeks in advance, with repetitive types of assignments, using a quality learning management system (LMS) to support teacher-student communication. Now teachers need to create a weekly course module in a way that balances simplicity versus rigor. This chapter leads teachers through that process.

While the understandable first impulse in creating a content module is to recreate a unit from a teacher's face-to-face classroom, this is not a good idea. Teaching online and teaching in a face-to-face classroom share similarities in the same way that riding a bicycle shares similarities with driving a car. When teachers try to recreate their face-to-face classroom online, they're inevitably going to be disappointed and angry. This does not mean that teaching online is necessarily inferior—it's simply different.

One of the major differences between a face-to-face classroom and a well-planned online course is the course module. Whereas teachers are taught to plan units and lessons, experienced online instructors plan by the module. In the course module, the emphasis is not on what the teacher will do, but instead on what the student will do. Course modules should flow in thematic linkages, but they are often not scaffolded like a face-to-face classroom unit. Instead, course modules are more like episodes of a television show, which may have a tightly integrated story arc like Kiefer Sutherland's *24*. Alternatively, the linkages between course modules may be gentle and only slightly dependent on the last episode, like the happy little trees that Bob Ross uses in *The Joy of Painting*.

In my experience, the module is best organized on a weekly basis, as television episodes used to be released. Our world organizes things by weeks, so all but the youngest students have an idea of how long a week is. Students and parents can plan by the week. Weeks do not automatically correspond to lessons or units, so teachers must change the way they approach planning. Remember that every module is like a separate file folder, with its own label and easy-to-read set of instructions. Also, remember that modules contain all the course content.

 Google Classroom topics are not equivalent to modules because the organizational flow is that of a social media feed, rather than a file folder. Finding a particular piece of information on a social media site is hard because they are designed to show new material. Old material needs to be readily available for students. Google Classroom is not an adequate LMS.

Working with the School Calendar

More so than in a regular school calendar, online teachers must organize their content by weeks. Traditionally, instruction doesn't happen when teachers have professional development days or other mandated days without students, but the line between an instructional day and a non-instructional day is blurred when teaching online. Therefore, teachers need to analyze their school calendar for weeks with and without instruction.

It might be helpful to find a traditional calendar that covers a teacher's school calendar and number each week. Teachers should also mark days when students are absent and days the school offices are closed. At this point, teachers will need to make a decision about which days they will expect assignments and which days they will not.

How to Do It

On the following calendar, the first week of school starts on August 10. The first day that the school offices are closed is week 4, September 7 (Labor Day). On that day, teachers should *delay assignments*, but expect students to complete the full module's worth of assignments that week. Bump Monday's assignments to Tuesday, and proceed as normal.

In week 7, students are expected to have an autumn break on Monday and Tuesday—*but do not delay due dates for assignments*. Treat Week 7 as a full module, but do not offer synchronous class sessions on those days. Instead, cover content in the synchronous class sessions more briefly, and offer additional asynchronous videos to compensate.

Why? Because in week 15, students have the rest of the week off. Do not assign *any* work that week, although teachers will have optional, synchronous class sessions that they will use for reviewing difficult material. Students can earn extra credit for attending those sessions.

In exam weeks, teachers will teach no new material and make no assignments other than the final, cumulative exam.

By coordinating days off this way, teachers maintain a weekly module system.

	August 2020						
	Sunday	Monday	Tuesday	Wednesday	Thursday	Friday	Saturday
							1
	2	3	4	5	6	7	8
Orientation	9	10	11	12	13	14	15
Week 1	16	17	18	19	20	21	22
Week 2	23	24	25	26	27	28	29
Week 3	30	31					

	September 2020						
	Sunday	Monday	Tuesday	Wednesday	Thursday	Friday	Saturday
			1	2	3	4	5
Week 4	6	7	8	9	10	11	12
Week 5	13	14	15	16	17	18	19
Week 6	20	21	22	23	24	25	26
Week 7	27	28	29	30			

	October 2020						
	Sunday	Monday	Tuesday	Wednesday	Thursday	Friday	Saturday
					1	2	3
Week 8	4	5	6	7	8	9	10
Week 9	11	12	13	14	15	16	17
Week 10	18	19	20	21	22	23	24
Week 11	25	26	27	28	29	30	31

	November 2020						
	Sunday	Monday	Tuesday	Wednesday	Thursday	Friday	Saturday
Week 12	1	2	3	4	5	6	7
Week 13	8	9	10	11	12	13	14
Week 14	15	16	17	18	19	20	21
Week 15	22	23	24	25	26	27	28
Week 16	29	30					

	December 2020						
	Sunday	Monday	Tuesday	Wednesday	Thursday	Friday	Saturday
			1	2	3	4	5
Week 17	6	7	8	9	10	11	12
Exam week	13	14	15	16	17	18	19
	20	21	22	23	24	25	26
	27	28	29	30	31		

Now that the number of modules in a school year has been established, teachers will need to decide how much content to cover in each module. To some degree, this depends on teacher experience and how a teacher uses the content standards. Most commercial curriculum offers a scope and sequence that teachers can use to correlate with standards. Normally it is best to use curriculum as designed, which may mean mixing up the instructional units, although teachers will often find that they flow together well. When teachers make these decisions, they can use them to write the class description for their syllabus, including desired yearly learning outcomes and goals.

This is an ideal time to schedule long-term projects. For example, I have assigned a six-week biographical essay project, a six- to eight-week science fair project, yearlong timeline projects, etc. This is also a good time to schedule cumulative final exams and repeating assignments (monthly self-assessments, for example).

 Plan now for long-term or repeating assignments, or short one-time-only assignments.

While I don't recommend one-time-only assignments as a habit, I do assign some. In the first week of class, I assign a Student Inventory, which I have tweaked from Jennifer Gonzalez's *Student Inventory*.[cccxxviii] It's much more difficult to get to know students in an online class, and by being deliberate about it, teachers can make a difference in the quality of their interaction. About six weeks in and then in again in February, I assign an anonymous survey based on Jennifer Gonzalez's *How's it Going* form.[cccxxix] Offering students an anonymous way to communicate frustrations and difficulties helps teachers improve the quality of their instruction. Teachers should want to know what students think could be better and how students would improve the class. Ask for suggestions for changes in the pace of the class and the amount of work assigned. Always leave an open-ended comment box—students might surprise teachers with their insight!

Content Standards versus Learning Objectives

Here in the United States, states have content standards and objectives that are to be taught at each grade level. In most cases, those state standards are based on the national standards developed by national organizations, like the National Council for the Social Studies. Sometimes the standards were supported by philanthropic organizations like the Carnegie Corporation of New York (the Next Generation Science Standards). The Common Core standards for math and English were developed similarly. Other subjects also have national standards. For example, there are National Core Arts Standards and World-Readiness Standards for Learning Languages.

Most teachers work in public schools and will therefore use the standards as required by their state. Few teachers are intimately familiar with the standards, especially the progression from grade to grade. Because I'm lucky enough to have spent a good bit of time teaching the same subject at three different grade levels, I've had time to develop a better understanding of the middle school mathematics progression, especially as it's met in the curriculum I use.

But standards and objectives (usually posted on a state website) aren't learning objectives. For example, fundamentally understanding how fractions work, that one-third is more than one-fourth, is something that takes time to develop—mastery doesn't occur in a single lesson. If it did, McDonald's Third Pounder burgers wouldn't have flopped.[cccxxx] Instead, fundamentally understanding fractions is a learning objective that teachers are going to need to touch several times over the course of a year or even several years.

Similarly, writing a biographical essay isn't a standard. It meets "CCSS.ELA-LITERACY.W.7.2 Write informative/explanatory texts to examine a topic and convey ideas, concepts, and information through the selection, organization, and analysis of relevant content."[cccxxxi] The associated sub-standards ask for an introduction, organization, development, transitions, and conclusion, all of which can be met by a biographical essay. But the standards don't actually say anything about a biographical essay, as such.

In short, rather than using standards to create assignments, use assignments to meet standards. Make sure the work will cover the standard, but don't use the standards as the class spine. They're signposts, not the road.

Instead, when designing the content for the course module think in terms of the learning objective—what are the goals for the module? When teachers create the daily problem sets, the learning objective should be foremost. For example, adding like fractions is a learning objective. Alternatively, writing a thesis statement is a learning objective. Each of these is a tiny objective embedded within a larger context of knowledge, skills, and abilities.

This way, when students ask, "What are we doing today?" teachers can confidently answer with a plain English learning objective. "Class, today you are going to learn how to add like fractions."

Using Content Standards with a Textbook

I live in West Virginia, which has adopted the Next Generation Science Standards. There are twenty-one content standards for sixth grade, which leaves eleven weeks open as needed. The first is S.6.LS.1 "Students will construct an explanation that predicts patterns of interactions among organisms across multiple ecosystems."[cccxxxii] That is not obvious; so with a little research, up pops Next Generation Science Standards MS-LS2-2 "Construct an explanation that predicts patterns of interactions among organisms across multiple ecosystems." Some examples are "competitive, predatory, and mutually beneficial."[cccxxxiii]

Because we have wisely purchased a copy of a textbook, in this case *Holt Science & Technology: Life Science*, we can check the index for "predator." Section 3 of Chapter 18 is about "Interactions of Living Things" and includes this sentence: "Ecologists have described four main ways that species and individuals affect each other: competition, predators and prey, symbiotic relationships, and coevolution." Excellent—now we know where we could start our hypothetical school year.

Chapter 18 is the start of Unit 6 in the textbook, which is on ecology. Handily, section 2 of Chapter 18 is titled "Living Things Need Energy" and reviews the role of photosynthesis (S.6.LS.3), as well as food chains and webs (S.6.LS.4). Luckily, it even comes with a handy bit of math practice to meet S.6.LS.5 "Students will analyze and interpret data to provide evidence for the effects of resource availability on organisms and populations of organisms in an ecosystem."[cccxxxiv] Section 3, "Types of Interactions," provides material for S.6.LS.6.

The only two standards not covered in Chapter 18 are S.6.LS.2 "Students will evaluate competing design solutions for maintaining biodiversity and ecosystem services" and S.6.LS.7 "Students will construct an argument supported by empirical evidence that changes to physical or biological components of an ecosystem affect populations."[cccxxxv] Further research shows that the skills practice lab in Chapter 19 can easily meet S.6.LS.2 and can be done inexpensively, offline. The language arts activity in Chapter 19 can meet the last standard—but will require some scaffolding.

Altogether, the four chapters of unit 6 in the textbook cover nearly one-third of the required content standards. Given the required scaffolding to review photosynthesis and animal behavior (arguably worth reviewing the two relevant chapters), that is six total chapters. One-third of the thirty-two instructional weeks is about ten, so a teacher has four more weeks they could add, covering a chapter a week. Using a week to review scientific methods (Chapter 1) would be productive, as would another week on evolution (Chapters 7 and 8, relevant to ecosystem effects on biodiversity). This saves the last week for review and working on the final details of the major writing assignment and the lab report. Conveniently, those assignments will help meet several of the general reading and writing standards.

This process should be repeated until a tentative plan, including types of assignments, is written for each weekly content module in the school year.

Using Content Standards without a Textbook

Perhaps a teacher is, unluckily, in one of the many states that does not have a paper textbook. Given the copyright constraints for online classes, and the widespread lack of broadband for students, one can make a reasonable argument that hunting down used copies of an older edition is a worthwhile use of a teacher's time. For example, the 2007 edition of the textbook mentioned previously is currently $3.50 a copy on the used book market. Many sellers will cut a deal when selling a classroom set.

Spending $112 on a set of thirty textbooks will save a teacher a lot of time. On average, teachers spend seven hours a week hunting for materials online, over 250 hours during the course of a school year.[cccxxxvi] On average, public school teachers in the United States earn $60,483 per year,[cccxxxvii] and they are usually contracted for a forty-hour workweek.[cccxxxviii] That divides out to about twenty-nine dollars per hour. While we all know that many teachers work far longer than their contracted workweek, it's worth pointing out that buying an inexpensive used class set of textbooks pays for itself by freeing up teacher labor *in the first week*. Savvy administrators who are moving toward online K-12 classes will ensure their students have paper textbooks, even if the textbooks are used.

However, if for whatever reason a teacher cannot lay hands on a textbook, they should spend time now researching sources for good texts that can be used offline. Open educational resources are popular free resource libraries, although the lack of expertise in instructional design means that these materials are often of poorer quality than professionally designed curricula. The history of the movement also means that most materials are more suitable for higher education than K-12. In addition, Creative Commons licenses often used with open educational resources material frequently do not permit posting on websites—teachers should read the licensing restrictions carefully. Private schools are often subject to significantly more copyright restrictions than public schools. In the case of the science standards used earlier, a teacher might use a CK-12 Flexbook for a downloadable, optical character recognition–capable, printable PDF that can be posted to the LMS.

While it is tempting to simply search through materials from third-party (for-profit or not-for-profit) lesson-sharing websites and download those, teachers should be wary of these resources. While teachers may sometimes run across a good supplement for an individual unit, using these sources as the spine of a course has several issues. First, copyright issues mean that the laws are different for online courses, as are the use restrictions. Materials that are fine to copy and distribute in a face-to-face classroom often cannot be legally posted on websites. Second, most of these materials have little to no differentiation for students with print issues, students who are English language learners or English as an additional language learners, or students with other special educational needs. Often, these materials are of poor quality and do not build into a coherent, high-quality curriculum. Finally, given the online teaching environment, many of these materials are simply unsuitable for teaching online.

 The expansive fair use policy that applies to in-classroom use of copyrighted material does not automatically translate to online classes.

As a practical equity issue, it is important that by far **the majority of material teachers make available to students through the LMS should be quickly**

downloadable (or not required), so that students can work offline. My general rule of thumb is to assign what can be downloaded on a trip through a fast-food drive-through, using the restaurant's Wi-Fi. This means text files are a good resource, as are optical character recognition–capable PDFs and small image files. Test downloading the file on your phone from the LMS, and if takes longer than two minutes, back up and try it with a different file type, like a text file.

Whatever the resource, teachers should locate materials that they can use to support their class for each weekly content module in the school year, along with a tentative plan for assignments.

Creating a Schedule

When teachers finish weekly planning, they should be able to add a section to the syllabus that looks like the following chart. Parents and students need to know what the class is covering, and when, so that they can arrange their schedules to make sure that students have extra time for more difficult topics or assignments. Keep in mind that these are not set in stone—especially in the first year, teachers will probably need to adjust these somewhat.

Note that these chart headers will convert easily into the title for each of the weekly course modules. For example: *Week 1: August 17 – 23 Scientific Method*

Here is a tentative schedule for the first part of our hypothetical science class:

Week	Chapter	Assignment	Topic
0	--	Introduction	Orientation
1	1	DQs HW/Quiz	Scientific Method
2	7	DQs HW/Quiz	Evolution
3	8	DQs HW/Quiz	History of Life
4	13	DQs HW/Quiz	Plant Processes
5	14	DQs HW/Quiz	Animals and Behavior writing: topic selection

Week	Chapter	Assignment	Topic
6	18	DQs HW/Quiz	Interactions of Living Things writing: note taking
7	19	DQs HW/Quiz	Natural Cycles writing: thesis statement begin lab: nitrogen cycle
8	20	DQs HW/Quiz	Ecosystems writing: introduction/conclusion continue lab: nitrogen cycle
9	21	DQs HW/Quiz	Environmental Challenges writing: rough draft due continue lab: nitrogen cycle
10	--	DQs Test	Review writing: final draft due lab: lab report due, with growth chart

Assignments and Weights

Part of weekly planning is deciding what types of assignments are useful for a given course and how much they're going to be worth. Clearly, each teacher's situation will be slightly different. Some teachers may have required assignments and assignment types, and others may have complete freedom. No matter the situation, teachers need to be able to explain to students what will be required of them, how it will be evaluated, and what is good enough. One way to do that is to provide both a written description of each assignment and a description of the grading breakdown for the course. By having this ready in advance, there are fewer questions about what students will be doing in the class.

Remember that teachers should not make attending the live video sessions the main part of their course. Classroom teachers are arguably the star of the face-to-face classroom stage, but in the online classroom teachers play a supporting role. Even when teachers are onstage, online students are distracted, sipping beverages and flipping through their programs.[cccxxxix] For this reason, every piece of necessary information reviewed in live class sessions should be available in writing in the course module, and students should be taught how to find the information.

Don't require extensive writing. Particularly, don't give lengthy writing assignments as a substitute for face-to-face checks for understanding. I once took an undergraduate online course that required more than five thousand words per week, more than many professional authors can write. Yes, I wrote a scathing course review. Add up all the writing assigned for each content module (yes, this includes discussion questions and any required pieces of text during synchronous lecture), and make a limit. My limit ranges from five hundred to one thousand words for school-aged students.

Don't require students (or parents) to upload all the work that has been assigned. Busy working parents have limited time (especially parents living in poverty). In addition, uploading assignments can be tricky. Teachers must explicitly train students in how to upload work. Further, if parents are taking their children to a fast-food restaurant for the free Wi-Fi, the bandwidth is usually limited, which means that uploading large files like videos or high-quality photos is difficult or impossible.

Finally, teachers have limited time. Each time teachers assign work to be uploaded, teachers need to have the common courtesy to offer feedback, which takes time. Offer students the option of uploading a scan of every assignment, but don't require it.

Here is a sample from our hypothetical class:

Written Assignments:

- *Journal:* Students will write about their learning experience on a regular basis. 5% of final grade
- *Weekly Discussion Questions:* Discussion questions will be drawn from the text. Each student must write a meaningful reply to a question by midnight, EST, Monday, and meaningfully respond to two other students' responses by midnight, EST, on Wednesday. See the Assignment policies for more information about meaningful participation. 15% of final grade

Quizzes and Tests:

- *Weekly Quizzes:* Students will complete problems drawn from the text as well as non-text material. 20% of final grade
- *Tests:* Students will complete problems drawn from the text as well as non-text material. 20% of final grade
- *Comprehensive Exams:* There will be two comprehensive exams. 10% of final grade.

Other Assignments/Requirements:

- *Homework:* Students will complete a variety of tasks and exercises. 20% of final grade, total
- *Timeline:* Students will maintain a historical timeline of major scientific discoveries. 10% of final grade

Grading breakdown:

Course Work	Percentage
Homework	20
Weekly quizzes	20
Tests	20
Discussion questions	15
Journal	5
Timeline	10
Comprehensive final exams—2	10
Total	100

Internet Access and Websites

Among the oldest and wealthiest students in 2017, about 80% used the internet at home, according to the National Center for Education Statistics.[cccxl] In the same study, for the youngest, poorest students, fully half did not use the internet at home. According to the Pew Research Center, about 37% of households are smartphone-only users.[cccxli]

If we make a generous assumption that since 2017 internet use among students has gone up to the standard of the wealthiest students, 80% of all students would have internet access at home. A total of 37% of those students would have internet only on their smartphone. That would mean 29% of all students would have smartphone-only internet access. At best, about half ($80 - 29 = 51$) would have broadband internet access.

Not all internet access is created equal. The Federal Communications Commission recommends that students have between five and twenty-five Mbps of internet access each, but the typical broadband speed of mobile phones is only ten Mbps. If one student is on their LMS, and the other student is in a synchronous session, twelve to twenty-five Mbps is recommended.[cccxlii] For our hypothetical one-third of students, even if parents can use their phone as a wireless hotspot, two students can't both attend a synchronous session at the same time or both watch assigned YouTube videos at the same time. Therefore, teachers need to limit the amount of internet-intensive activities they assign in a weekly content module.

Even in our hypothetical half of households with a wide pipe of broadband internet access, the type of website assigned matters. For example, many educational websites use older technology, like Flash animation.[cccxliii] Adobe support for Flash ends in 2020, and many households do not have devices that permit Flash content to work. Furthermore, even in the wealthiest, most tech-savvy households, there are a limited number of devices.

Outside Apps and Websites

While everything the students need should be contained within the LMS, if a teacher does decide that an outside website or app is essential to the course, such as computer-adaptive software, then that expectation should be made clear up front. Parents will have to figure out how to access the website and make sure their child knows how to do it independently. (If students can't do it independently, it shouldn't be used.) Recall that teachers must explicitly demonstrate in a recorded video how to access the website or app, and show students exactly what they're to be doing once they're in.

This emphasis on keeping learning simple also applies to gamification. While initially students may want to jump through the hoops for the novelty factor, they often get bored quickly with poor quality games and then most unsupervised students wander off to YouTube. As Clark and Mayer write in *e-Learning and the Science of Instruction*, "there is not research support for wholesale conversion of traditional training formats to game-based formats." Establish a habit of completing problem sets because it is the best way to learn, not because it is fun. Taking satisfaction in a job well done is a valuable life skill.

Keep in mind that that most online supplements, apps, and extensions are not recommended for several reasons.

1. Digital extras are usually *meant for face-to-face classrooms*, so they are rarely useful for the all-online classroom. Their inputs and outputs are often designed to be displayed on digital whiteboards, used with class devices like clickers, and so on.
2. Just like in a face-to-face classroom, teachers must *consider the trade-offs*. Teachers will have to learn how to use the website or app, and because teachers only have so much time, teachers will have to take

that time away from the time devoted to assessment, feedback, and reaching out to students. So, when adding in "extras," the question is, "Is it really worth it?" Often, teachers are better off refining *teacher talk*[cccxliv] (extra important online[cccxlv]), improving concept presentation, making connections with students, and so on.

3. *Overwhelming students* with the number of locations and gadgets and apps is easy to do. Teachers will spend significant time teaching students where to locate materials in the online classroom. Adding multiple websites? Students (and parents) would be overwhelmed.[cccxlvi] Often, they'll simply skip the assignment.

4. Why would teachers use something that *doesn't directly improve student learning*? Very rarely do shiny new websites or apps have any evidence to support learning. If it's not directly useful in improving student learning, then it has no place in the classroom. Fun apps aren't fun when students (or parents) are in frustrated tears.

5. Many websites and apps are not fully accessible to students who use screen readers like JAWS or even the built-in accessibility options. Recall that according to both the US Department of Education and the US Department of Justice,[cccxlvii] *it is illegal to use public funds to purchase technology that supplies inaccessible content*, both at the collegiate and K-12 level.[cccxlviii]

6. Very few websites or apps offer any information or activities that aren't contained in a high-quality textbook and an LMS. In some ways, *teaching online is about paring down teaching to the bare bones needed to convey information.* As Dr. Willingham says, students remember what they think about.[cccxlix] Make it the content and not the context. Why spend money on flashy websites when teachers could invest that money in textbooks, instead?

Be prepared to justify the use of the outside website to parents or administrators who are unhappy with the decision. Write a FAQ list about the resource, explaining your reasoning and explaining how the resource is beneficial to students and families.

 Teaching online is about paring down teaching to the bare bones needed to convey information.

Creating a Weekly Calendar for Students

As discussed earlier, this type of course design is an elaborately structured, self-reinforcing creation designed to improve student learning. For students, meeting all the expectations can feel overwhelming, particularly for students with special education needs. When parents see this type of course, they can also feel overwhelmed as they begin to plan for their child's device access, internet access, and a quiet space for their child to work.

When students and parents feel like they've jumped into the deep end of the pool, offer them a life preserver in the form of a daily and weekly calendar along with a list of familiar assignments to be completed, including time expectations. Especially for students with attention deficit/hyperactivity disorder, who often have difficulty with executive functioning, making plans, and goals,[ccl] a systematic plan with repetitive daily, weekly, and monthly goals helps create success.[ccli] As many as one in five students suffer from anxiety, especially given recent world events.[cclii] "Predictability is very important for anxious children,"[ccliii] and creating a predictable routine helps them be successful.

Another benefit is that by completing a repetitive, limited set of assignments on the same day every week, students focus on the content, not the context. For students who are new to learning online, figuring out how to do a task may take up more of their attention than the content of the task itself. But students learn better when they're thinking about content, not how to use software.[cccliv]

This set-up benefits teachers, because once they are familiar with the handful of assignments they're creating, they can quickly create a new set by copying and pasting the format from last week's class. Remember, different content areas lend themselves to different tasks—problem sets in math, map work in geography, etc. In addition, tasks should be carefully chosen for specific learning goals.

Learning is improved when teachers think clearly and carefully about goals and expectations for students. When teachers are creating weekly modules and calendars in advance, a scope and sequence is helpful. Usually, teachers should have the topic of each weekly module planned months before school starts, along with a rough plan of what assignments they will use and when they will make them due.

How to Do It

Over the years, I've refined my content module calendar to include both a weekly list and a daily calendar. Visual schedules are common in special education, but they benefit everyone, which is why your phone comes with a calendar app. Note that all of these assignments are *also* in the LMS calendar, so students can see what is due for all their classes, day by day. This way, it is easy for a student to find what they've been assigned to do. In my experience, some parents print these out and stick them on the refrigerator, while others export the LMS calendar to their personal digital calendars and use that for scheduling.

 Keep the style of the module calendar the same every week.

What follows is a sample calendar. Note that Week 2 is underlined, meaning that it is a link to open the "folder" for that week. Inside is the folder is where all the directions and files for each activity are located. Teachers will have to demonstrate finding the modules and how to open each module. To make it easier, set the modules as the first things student see when they click on the class link after using their Single Sign On.

While the times might seem excessive, it averages out to seventy-two minutes per weekday, including video conference sessions. By the time teachers combine instructional face-to-face class time and homework, seventy-two minutes per day for a middle school core content class is a reasonable expectation.

Also notice that most of the work is done offline, with the exception of the discussion question, the online lab, and the video conference sessions. The diagram, reading excerpt, and contents of the guided notes are all discussed in the video conference session, so students can self-check their work. The online lab has feedback within the simulation.

 Ensure video conference sessions are recorded and that students can download the recordings and watch offline.

Another feature of this calendar is the clarity between different types of assignments. Within the folder it's clearer, but only the discussion questions, summary, and the weekly quiz are turned in that week. The weekly quiz is auto-graded, while the teacher uses a rubric to grade the discussion questions. The summary is for completion credit. The timeline is an ongoing assignment that is turned in at the end of every term. This saves teacher time and student frustration, because the students do not have to upload many papers in an average content module. The quiz assesses facts from the sedimentary rock diagram, the *Origin of the Species* excerpt, and the textbook reading, as well as the results of the online lab, so students must complete those in order to score well.

 The title of the weekly module is a good place to write the learning objectives for the week.

<u>Week 2: Understanding how Evolution Works</u>

1) At the end of Week 2, students will have:

- Attended the video conference session
- Answered the Discussion Question (ten minutes)
- Responded to two other students (fifteen minutes)
- Completed the Sedimentary Rock diagram (fifteen minutes)
- Read and summarized the *Origin of the Species* excerpt (twenty minutes)
- Completed the *Galapagos Islands* lab (twenty minutes per day/sixty minutes)
- Read Chapter 7 and completed the Guided Notes (twenty minutes per day/sixty minutes)
- Added *adaptation, evolution, natural selection* to your Leitner box (five minutes)
- Added dates to your timeline (ten minutes)
- Completed the quiz in the LMS (thirty minutes)

2) Your calendar for Week 2 is below.

Monday	Tuesday	Wednesday	Thursday	Friday
Day 1	**Day 2**	**Day 3**	**Day 4**	**Day 5**
Aug 26	**Aug 27**	**Aug 28**	**Aug 29**	**Aug 30**
DQ Due (ten minutes)	Lecture 1 pm	**Two DQ Responses Due (fifteen minutes)**	Lecture 1 pm	**Quiz (thirty minutes)**
Read Chapter 7, Section 1 and completed the Guided Notes (twenty minutes)	Read Chapter 7, Section 2 and complete the Guided Notes (twenty minutes)	Read Chapter 7, Section 3 and complete the Guided Notes (twenty minutes)	Read and summarize the *Origin of the Species* excerpt (twenty minutes)	
Add adaptation, evolution, natural selection to your Leitner box (five minutes)	Complete Part A of the *Galapagos Islands* lab (twenty minutes)	Complete Part B of the *Galapagos Islands* lab (twenty minutes)	Complete Part C of the *Galapagos Islands* lab (twenty minutes) Add dates to your timeline (ten minutes)	
Complete the Sedimentary Rock diagram (twenty minutes) fifty-five minutes	Review Memory Work (five minutes) Complete the Sedimentary Rock diagram (fifteen minutes) sixty minutes + class session	Review Memory Work (five minutes) sixty minutes	Review Memory Work (five minutes) fifty-five minutes + class session	

Inside the Course Module

In each course module, the assignments should make sense to students. Everything should be clearly labeled, with a minimum of diversion. Even links to outside resources should be tucked away. Every link outside the course is an opportunity for students to surf away from learning. In the following list, students would have to click on the "useful videos" link to open up another page with the names of the outside videos.

As Daisy Christodoulou notes in *Teachers vs. Tech*, distraction is one of the main pitfalls of online learning, and offering students an abundance of hypermedia, or "a mixture of images, text, and hyperlinks" leads to less learning, rather than more.[ccclv] Teachers don't need to decorate the content module with pretty clip art and photos and whiz-bang videos. Carefully curated videos are helpful, but teachers should minimize visual clutter. Teachers don't win a prize for the best-decorated online classroom—and in fact Kripa Sundar notes in the research that she conducted with Olusola Adesope that these "seductive details" impair students' learning.[ccclvi] Make the inside of the course module plain.

Each item in an LMS module should be a link to an in-LMS page, a document, or outside resource set. Everything that students need should be all in one place. Remember to use file types that work on multiple devices—phones, tablets, and desktop computers with varying operating systems. Text files and optical character recognition–capable PDFs are preferred. If the assignment is in a document, instructions written to the student should explain how to complete it and, if needed, how to submit it. If possible, consider auto-releasing encouraging notes when students complete assignments. Inside a module, students should work their way from top to bottom, finishing the week with an assessment on Friday.

- Live Session Link and Recordings (LMS link)
- Week 2 Discussion Questions (LMS link)
- Week 2 Diagram (PDF)
- Week 2 Demonstration (online lab simulation)
- Week 2 Guided Notes (PDF)
- Week 2 Slides (PDF)
- Week 2 Quiz (LMS link)
- Week 2 Optional Videos (LMS link)
  - Outside Video 1 (YouTube)
  - Outside Video 2 (YouTube)
  - Outside Video 3 (YouTube)
  - Outside Video 4 (YouTube)

- Outside Video 5 (YouTube)
- Outside Video 6 (YouTube)

Weekly Checklist for Teachers

Once teachers have a content coverage plan and an idea of the types of assignments they're planning to use, they need to plan how they are going to spend their limited preparation time. In the spirit of Atul Gawande's *The Checklist Manifesto*, a weekly checklist, adapted to an individual teacher's personal situation, might be useful. Here is a sample checklist for a single class:

☐ create and title a blank content module with WK #, date, and subject

- ☐ create and post a PDF or Word doc of the guided notes in the content module
- ☐ create and post a slide deck in the content module
- ☐ research and write a teacher script for slide deck
- ☐ create and post written discussion questions in the content module
- ☐ find and post links to outside supplemental videos in the content module
- ☐ create and post a PDF or Word doc of the sketch/diagram in the content module
- ☐ double-check that the sketch/diagram is covered in the textbook and/or slide deck
- ☐ create and post a PDF or Word doc hands-on assignment in the content module
- ☐ double-check that the expected result of the hands-on assignment is covered in the slide deck
- ☐ create and post auto-graded daily problem sets in the content module
- ☐ create and post a weekly assessment in the content module
- ☐ create and post any non-graded assignments, like readings
- ☐ create and post a weekly calendar filled in with assignments by day on the outside of the content module
- ☐ create and post a list of content module assignments on the outside of the content module

  - ☐ *attend lecture date/time*
  - ☐ *answer discussion questions*
  - ☐ *respond to two other students*
  - ☐ *add vocabulary _____, _____, _____ to your memory work*

    ☐ *read the textbook chapter ____, section _____ and take notes*
      using the notes sheet
    ☐ *read pgs. ___ from your other book*
    ☐ *label this week's sketch*
    ☐ *complete problem sets*
    ☐ *complete guided notes*
    ☐ *complete hands-on assignment*
    ☐ *complete the quiz*

☐ use the LMS student view to ensure that all assignments are visible inside the content module, in the order in which teachers want students to complete them
☐ use the LMS student view to double-check that the assignments are posted in the correct order in the grade view
☐ double-check that all assignments have posted to the central LMS calendar
☐ grade this week's work

    ☐ use a rubric to grade this week's written discussion questions
    ☐ review the "just for fun" discussion boards to ensure proper behavior
    ☐ grade this week's problem sets
    ☐ use data analysis from problem sets to adjust next week's slide deck as needed
    ☐ grade this week's assessment

☐ clear the inbox

    ☐ email parents and students about missing assignments or any failing grades from last week
    ☐ email parents and students about any behavior issues
    ☐ email parents and students about any academic issues or large upcoming assignments
    ☐ respond to any parent/student emails

☐ post weekly announcement with policy reminders, upcoming breaks, etc.

Ongoing Projects

Not all work online can or should be completed within a single weekly content module. However, the work should be segmented so that a single part can be completed within a content module. Be very clear about student expectations, and finish the plan before beginning the project, so work can be scheduled in advance each week. Note that these projects must be added to the teacher's weekly checklist and the students' weekly checklist.

Essay Writing Example

For the writing assignment defined earlier, our hypothetical science students are going to research and write about famous interactions between populations and the environment, such as hypoxic "dead zones" in the Gulf of Mexico, the Great Pacific Garbage Gyre, and the Isle Royale wolf research. This would help them meet a required standard.

> MS-LS2-4 *"Construct an argument supported by empirical evidence that changes to physical or biological components of an ecosystem affect populations. [Clarification Statement: Emphasis is on recognizing patterns in data and making warranted inferences about changes in populations, and on evaluating empirical evidence supporting arguments about changes to ecosystems.]* "[ccclvii]

This standard also links to *"Construct an oral and written argument supported by empirical evidence and scientific reasoning to support or refute an explanation or a model for a phenomenon or a solution to a problem."*[ccclviii]

However, most of our hypothetical students are on the younger side (ages eleven and twelve), and it is possible that this is the first time they've written a formal academic essay. Therefore, they are going to need significant scaffolding. With that need in mind, here is a sample six-week program of instruction that students are to complete in addition to the "regular" weekly content module assignments.

Week 1:

- Two weeks before students are to begin the work, research and select four to six famous interactions. Locate three to five sources per famous interaction. These resources need to be suitable for middle school students who have difficulty researching.
- In the slide deck for two weeks from then, add a mini lesson about finding sources, citations, and evaluating websites, as well as the list of famous interactions.
- As part of the weekly assessment for week 3, add a multiple-choice question with the names of the famous interactions so teachers know which one each student chooses. Add a short-answer essay question for students to list three sources for their famous interaction.

Week 2:

- The next weekend, add a mini lesson about taking notes to the slide deck for week 4, as well as slides with fully and partially worked examples of the specific note-taking students will complete.
- Each student is to complete specific notes for three separate types of body paragraphs. Each body paragraph note set is set in a worksheet that students can download and print from PDF format or fill out as a document. In turn, students must scan and upload the PDF, or complete the document and upload it. Add a drop box in the week 4 content folder for students to use when uploading.

Week 3:

- Teach the lesson prepared in week 1 about finding sources, and offer the famous interactions that were pre-selected, so students can choose their topic.
- That weekend, assess students' sources, and if needed, give feedback with better sources for each of the famous interactions.
- Also that weekend, create a set of slides about thesis statements, with exemplars and a partially worked model.
- In the assessment two weeks from that date, add a short-answer essay question where students are to write their thesis statement.

Week 4:

- Teach the lesson about taking notes, modeling how to use text to take the precise notes needed for the essay with the three specified body paragraphs.
- Assess students' notes and citations from their uploaded PDFs or annotated Word documents, and give formative feedback when needed.
- For the week 6 slide deck, add slides for a mini lesson about writing introductions and conclusions, including specific sentence types and the order in which sentences were to be written.
- For part of the week 6 assessment, add two parts to the worksheet for students to complete and upload with their introductions and conclusions. Then add a drop box for students to upload their completed worksheet.

Week 5:

- Teach the lesson about thesis statements that prepared in week 3.

- This weekend, assess students' thesis statement, and if needed, schedule one-to-one synchronous meetings or phone calls to work through writing a thesis statement that conforms to the expected model.
- In the slide deck creating for two weeks from then, add slides for a mini lesson about sentence types, word choices, style choices, transitions, and the grading rubric, as well as a brief introduction to works cited pages.
- Last, create a drop box for students to upload their rough drafts in week 7, attaching the essay-grading rubric, and making it visible to students.

Week 6:

- Teach the mini lesson about writing introductions and conclusions, giving exemplars and modeling the use of summarization of body paragraphs.
- Students turn in their introductions and conclusions. Assess each set, marking them up as needed.
- In the slide deck, add a slide to review the rubric with students in week 8.
- Finally, create a drop box for students to upload their final drafts in week 8.

Week 7:

- Teach the mini lesson about informative, lively essays with vivid language and colorful details.
- Assess their rough drafts using the rubric.
- Create a drop box for students to turn in their final draft revisions.

Week 8:

- Review the rubric as a class, noting point values and taking questions.
- Students turn in their final draft. Assess it.

Week 9:

- Grade any final draft revisions. (Permissible only for students who made less than an A on the final draft, as per course policy.)

Again, don't use many outside websites or apps. When creating assignments, remember that for many students internet access is a time-constrained, limited resource. In this essay process, no outside websites are required. Students can and do use websites for sources, but they are not required to do so.

Don't use big files. Note that in the multi-week essay assignment, students only have to download two small files and upload four times. Even in relatively well-off households, students are often competing with siblings and parents who are working from home for access to bandwidth and the best devices. Keeping file uploads and downloads to a minimum helps students and parents.

Don't assign complex extended assignments that require adult assistance. Each week, the work should be written to the student. When worksheets are clear and simple, students can complete them mostly independently. When needed, students can reference the models and exemplars on the slide decks. While essay writing isn't usually work that can be auto-graded, each week's uploaded work is the least amount needed for assessing learning. For example, the week with the thesis statement only had students write one sentence, something students can usually do by themselves.

Working with Younger Students

One of the key parts of teaching younger children is "joint attention," or when both the teacher and the student are engaged with the same item, sight, or idea.[ccclix] Joint attention is crucial for pre-K and the early years and helps immensely at all ages. The problem is, of course, that young children often see the world like William James put it in his *Principles of Psychology*, "as one great blooming, buzzing confusion."[ccclx] In other words, items off the screen in their homes easily distract them.

Therefore, teachers cannot expect the average five- or six-year-old to sit through a lengthy videoconference and attend to the teacher in the same way a nine- or ten-year-old would. Many people have had the experience of talking to a young child on the phone with the sinking sensation that while the child may talk at you, they are definitely not listening. "Honey, put your mommy back on the phone, please!" In addition, because online classes are so print-intensive and young children are not yet fluent readers, the asynchronous modality is not productive for the youngest learners.

For a successful online learning experience, another human must be with our youngest learners, redirecting the child's attention to the screen, supporting the teacher. Because 82% of children have siblings,[ccclxi] 68% of children live with their married parents,[ccclxii] and 64% of married couples with children have two working parents,[ccclxiii] this is often an unreasonable expectation. This is even less feasible for the next most common household arrangement (23% of children),[ccclxiv] children with a single, working mother (23% of children and 75% of single mothers).[ccclxv]

Many young students will enjoy a synchronous session with adult support. They may even develop an attachment to a teacher that they have never met face-to-face. For example, my six-year-old is currently enjoying her foreign language tutorial with a favored instructor who lives in Massachusetts. But twenty minutes at a time, three days a week is not enough to create lasting learning, even though it's a standard instructional period for a young child. In order for my child to learn the new vocabulary, I must reinforce her new language skills with daily practice—I must be a co-teacher.

While having a parent as a co-teacher seems like less work for the online teacher, remember that most parents are not education professionals and parents are busy with their own jobs. Parents need clear instructions for short (five- to ten-minute) daily tasks. Do not expect them to do any of the heavy lifting in terms of course planning, instructional goals, or content selection. At best, an appropriate expectation is a daily checklist of two or three items per subject with scripted lessons. In some ways, this type of instruction is actually more work because teachers have to take parents' needs into consideration as well as the students' needs.

A similar problem exists with web- or app-based tasks. While young children have seemingly endless patience for unboxing videos and Minecraft, those are much less difficult tasks than learning to read or beginning mathematics. The typical reward system used in a K-2 classroom does not translate to an online class. In addition, parents do not have infinite patience or internet access, making logging into multiple apps and websites a limited resource for teachers.

Online Assignments for Younger Students

Many web-based assignments are a virtual scavenger hunt. For example, "Find the purple square." Are students learning about the content? Or are they learning to hunt and click and poke at areas of the screen (i.e., the context)? For young children, this requires motor coordination on small screens (like mom's phone) that they might not have. At best, these kinds of assignments are inequitable for children with fine motor issues. At worst, they are frustrating, no matter that they look good on a teacher's home computer with a nineteen-inch screen.

While manipulatives are often plentiful and useful in the early learning classroom, teachers cannot assume that parents have or are willing to buy anything outside of the bare necessities of daily life. When teachers assign activities like making gears from candy, unless the teacher sent home the required materials and a set of instructions written to the student, the odds are good that the activity is not going to happen. In addition, much like Pinterest fails, what looks good on the screen may be an utter failure in practice. Unless a teacher has actually sat down and performed the activity with a child of the appropriate age, they should not assign it.

Similarly, if students aren't old enough to independently answer the questions in writing, teachers should not assign written answers—or online questions and answers that the parents must read to students and type in for them. Parents have enough on their plate without extensively scribing for their children and then figuring out how to use their device to scan and upload work they've helped their young child complete. In addition, limited internet access means that it is not appropriate for teachers to require extensive proof of work in terms of worksheets.

Be careful about what is assigned to be turned in. If teachers are going to require that parents of young children go through the effort of uploading work, then teachers owe individual, upbeat feedback for each student as a matter of common courtesy. Otherwise, teachers have assigned busywork.

Sometimes it's difficult to figure out whether students can complete the task independently. Err on the side of caution and don't assign it. Or pick up the phone and call the student to talk to them about it. Make short videos with questions and have parents make five-second videos of students answering questions, which parents can then text the teacher. Any of those three options are easier for parents than scanning and uploading worksheets for which parents had to supervise completion.

Working with Parents of Younger Students

Instead of bending over backwards to create assignments that the youngest learners can do independently, give clear written directions to the parent. If this sounds odd, there is a whole genre of curricula written to the parent instead of the student. These are called scripted curricula and they are consistent bestsellers. For example, as I write this *Teach Your Child to Read in 100 Easy Lessons*, published in 1986, is the 219th most popular book sold on Amazon.

These curricula exist for almost every content area, including math, reading, grammar, science, Spanish, composition, art, and history. Using these kinds of curricula and acknowledging and respecting the parent's role as co-teacher can lead to high-quality learning. In a recent article for NPR, Anya Kamenetz mentioned that a program designed to work with low-income families as co-teachers made significant reading gains for three-fourths of students in just five weeks.[ccclxvi]

When working with parents of young students, teachers often run up against their own expectations of what families should look like and how they should treat their children. This extends beyond class issues to matters of race and culture. Teachers should educate themselves about their students and take some time to reflect about the ways their own experiences and expectations compare and contrast with those of their students. Equity in education is a complicated issue, and for more information, teachers might want to read books such as *Culturally Responsive Teaching and The Brain* by Zaretta Hammond or *Other People's Children* by Lisa Delpit.

Chapter Summary

- Use a weekly course module.
- Divide the school calendar into instructional weeks.
- Schedule long-term or repeating assignments.
- Use learning objectives, not content standards.
- Use a textbook or open educational resources to cover content standards.
- Create a weekly pacing schedule, with assignments.
- Create assignment descriptions and grading breakdowns.
- Use as little Internet access as possible.
- Use few outside apps and websites, if any.
- Create a weekly calendar and checklist for students.
- Place assignments chronologically inside the course module.
- Create a weekly checklist for teachers.
- Plan long-term projects in advance.
- Make offline assignments for younger students.
- Work with parents as co-teachers.

CHAPTER 8

BACK TO SCHOOL

While starting a new school year with students that teachers have never met face-to-face seems intimidating, teachers can create a working relationship with online students. First impressions matter, so preparation is important. Just as the content module should not be centered around the synchronous class session, welcoming students to class isn't structured around meeting them in those synchronous class sessions.

> Reach out to students and create a relationship by sharing yourself, making students aware of content, and clarifying expectations.

One way to begin a successful school year for an online class is to look at it from the perspective of a student and their parent. When students meet the mandatory attendance laws, almost inevitably the process ends with the student walking into the school building where the teacher awaits them. This is not true online. There is no clear demarcation with parent drop-offs, buses, or subways delivering students to the classroom.

Gathering Data

Online teachers must be prepared to do outreach to get their students to show up. Ideally, teachers will have access to the student information system, or SIS, that will let them find the names and contact information for all the students enrolled in classes. With any luck, teachers will have access to email addresses, but teachers should be prepared to make phone calls. Often data updates rapidly as last-minute students show up (or leave) right before school starts, but the student information system is a good place to start.

About two weeks before the first day of school, organize this information with the student's first name, last name, student identification number, parent or guardian name, student email address, guardian email address, and phone number. Spreadsheets are useful here, but not required. Make a note for students with a working email addresses, phones, and postal addresses. If needed, note which parents require translations into other languages or forms of communication (such as Braille). Figure out how to get information into the correct language or format. Perhaps the school district employs an interpreter.

My advice is to collect all the information for all the students in a given class in one place. I'm teaching three sections of algebra I next year, but all those students will be lumped together in a single spreadsheet. In the learning management system (LMS), all the students across all three sections will participate together in the online discussion board, and so on. This way, I maintain one grade book per class, as opposed to three grade books for three sections.

School administration should assign synchronous class meeting days and times, to ensure that teachers don't overlap with each other. One recommendation is to keep the same times as the face-to-face class for synchronous sessions. However, synchronous online classes should meet less frequently than face-to-face classes due to the difficulty in getting students online and the addition of offline assignments. Instead, use the "off" days as work time for students.

Posting the First Assignments

Before students have access to the online classroom, post the first two weeks of assignments. Link to the live session from *within* every module. This is important, because teachers want students to make a habit of going to the online classroom. If the school doesn't have an online orientation week, create one in the classroom as a content module to be completed before the first week of class.

Now is a good time to set a theme for the course in the LMS. Most LMSs allow teachers to customize the colors of the classes and apply background images. Use built-in, high-contrast themes because they're more likely to be handicapped accessible. Students taking multiple classes often appreciate this subtle way teachers can help them differentiate between classes. Do not "customize" the theme, because any kind of customization is likely to violate accessibility rules.

In that week, set the first discussion questions as introductory questions with directions. For example, below is my standard orientation discussion question. This kind of question helps welcome students and their families and helps provide acceptance of varied student backgrounds and successes. Teachers should demonstrate positive framing in their responses and ensure that they respond to every student in the first week. Typically, students post on Monday, and I dedicate two or three hours on Tuesday evening to responding to students.

> Each week, I will post at least one, and usually more than one, Discussion Question. Choose only one question to answer. Do not use the internet to look up the answer.

> For your two response posts, while you must respond to another student, you don't have to respond only in the question you chose—and you may use the internet, if needed. If you have questions, contact me!

This first week, read my introductory biography below, and then post your own. Respond to two other students' bios.

> *I am your instructor! I am excited to teach this as an online course. I have been teaching online since 1999, when I taught videoconferenced classes. While I worked toward my teaching certifications, I was employed first as an online instructor of community college courses and then as a public school teacher. Along the way, I've done technical writing, web design, public relations, data analysis, and a whole host of "other duties as assigned."*

> *In my spare time, I enjoy reading, photography, cooking, and sewing. I live in wild, wonderful West Virginia with my husband, our two children, and my mother. Our menagerie currently consists of a leopard gecko, a veiled chameleon, a betta fish, a big old dog, four chickens, and assorted cats.*

Getting to Know Students

Assign a quiz in the orientation module. Typically, I use a variation on Jennifer Gonzalez's *Student Inventory.*[ccclxvii] Because information is often out of date or unavailable in student records, ask for students' ages, preferred names, and their pronunciations. Many students have nicknames or middle names that they prefer, and even though teachers may not be addressing students in a face-to-face class session, getting their preferred name right signals that they matter.

Likewise, ask for gender pronouns and use preferences. While this is useful for transgender and nonbinary students, there are also students whose first languages don't clearly distinguish gender through pronouns. My social studies teaching methods professor shared a story with my class about a school that failed to ask the gender of a child whose parents didn't speak much English. The student's teachers spent weeks trying to figure out the child's gender. Because online teachers don't line students up and walk them to the bathroom, and students often have gender-neutral names like Morgan, Jamie, or Alex, it's best just to ask.

Many people have more than one email address and phone number. Students often have multiple email addresses that parents don't list on contact forms, and while it's not necessary that teachers have all of a student's email addresses, asking students for the best email address and phone number for contacting them is useful. Often, students don't use their names when registering email addresses, and rarely do they sign their names to emails. At the beginning of the school year, I regularly reply with, "I'd love to answer your question, but who is this?" In my experience, parents want online teachers to take responsibility for instruction, but occasionally teachers will need to contact parents quickly, and the phone is the best way to do that. Asking for a parent's phone number is a reasonable request.

Student experience matters in taking and teaching online classes. Teachers should ask whether a student has taken an online class before, and if so, what their experience has been. Students who have successfully completed a regular content area class entirely online will need less assistance than a student who has only taken an online class in the spring of 2020.

If teachers have a class that has prerequisites, ask whether students have met them. Often, online course registration is structured much like ordering delivery online, and important details are missed. Every now and then, teachers will find that a student had no idea there were prerequisites. Alternatively, a student may need to be bumped up a level and before class starts is the best time to handle it. Ask about what else a student is studying—their course loads may be surprising.

While face-to-face teachers are often guaranteed a student's presence in the classroom due to truancy laws, online teachers have no such promise. Taking an online class requires a level of organization that is difficult to maintain when students travel or have other outside commitments like jobs. Ask if students move from house to house, are employed, or are planning to travel or be offline during the school year. This way, teachers can reasonably offer deadline flexibility to some students, and teachers will know when to post work further in advance. For example, I often post work a month in advance at the winter holidays because so many families travel then or observe religious obligations that require students to be offline.

In many face-to-face classrooms, details about students come up during class discussions. Because there are fewer direct instructional minutes in online classes, even with synchronous class sessions, these details are often simply not mentioned. Make it a point to ask students about their favorite foods, allergies, music, books, movies, television shows, hobbies, and other skills they're perfecting. Students appreciate that their teacher wants to know about them, and this lays the groundwork for hooking student interest later on. By working to learn about each student as an individual, and using what they've learned to help design their instruction, teachers promote equity in the classroom.

Because online classes involve a lot of writing, teachers need to know about student writing experience. I ask students to select a on continuum from "I don't write" to "I wrote a novel last summer." A surprising number of students choose the novel option. When teachers have some idea of students' current writing skills, they can better design scaffolding for the writing expectations in the class.

In a competently run school, teachers are informed of Individualized Educational Plan or 504 plan requirements for every applicable student before class starts. However, this does not always happen. In addition, not all students are able to obtain an Individualized Educational Plan or 504 plan, but these students still have learning exceptionalities, health conditions, or mental health concerns that will affect their ability to do well in a class. Therefore, students should be asked what they want their teachers to know about their physical or mental health.

Finally, ask students what the teacher can do to support them. Every year, my heart hurts when students plead for my patience, beg me not to give up on them, and blithely confess to their status as poor students. Rarely, students will put in a concrete request, like having notes or written directions. Knowing how students perceive themselves goes a long way toward creating a welcoming learning environment.

Quiz Options

Another common first quiz is to test students on the class syllabus, to ensure that they have read and understood it. Teachers might also consider creating a short, low-stakes quiz about the welcome-back email content as the first assignment.

Keep in mind that teachers are establishing course expectations with this quiz—mind the question formats, because those will be what students expect later in the course.

One nice thing about using the LMS to do this is that all the answers are auto-populated to a spreadsheet (which teachers should lock with a password, per Family Educational Rights and Privacy Act guidelines). This way, teachers can quickly and easily read through, and extract information for later use. If teachers are hesitant about using the LMS, they can set up a Google Form that auto-populates to a Google Sheet.

Reaching Out

A week before the orientation module starts, send out a general welcome email to parents and students. Keep in mind that this is the important first impression, so spend time on the message. While teachers might be tempted to make it pretty, with pastel backgrounds and flowery script, resist the temptation. Remember, the odds are good that parents are reading it on a cheap phone with a generic email app, and all the hard design work will be for naught—or worse, make the email difficult to read.

Instead, go high-contrast black and white, with a default font. Use text only, and make sure it's well-formatted. Send a test email to another email account and check the email on a desktop computer, a tablet email app, and a phone app. Font too small for easy reading? Fix that. Weird formatting issues? Fix that.

The first email should include:

- ☐ A greeting, personalized by parent and student name if possible.
- ☐ A line or two welcoming them to the course.
- ☐ A note about the first synchronous session with the date and time, with a link to the LMS.
- ☐ A note about the minimum device and internet access students will need, along with a list of any particular course materials.
- ☐ If teachers are creating a quiz about the email as the first assignment, note it in the email.
- ☐ A paragraph about the teacher with a line about their credentials. Other possible pieces of background information include hobbies, location, a little bit about family, and pets. Be wary of crossing the line between a one-paragraph short biography and inappropriate overtures of friendship. Here is an example:

  I have been teaching online since 1999, including college algebra from 2006 to 2013. I enjoy teaching so much that I went back to school to earn a second master's degree in secondary education. Now, I am certified to teach social studies, general science, and math in grades five through adult, and students with visual impairments from birth to adulthood. In my spare time, I enjoy reading, photography, cooking, and sewing. I live in wild, wonderful West Virginia with my husband, our two children, and my mother. Our menagerie currently consists of a leopard gecko, a beta fish, a veiled chameleon, a big old dog, two mice, chickens, and assorted cats.

- ☐ A bit about course expectations, with strengths and weaknesses of the online course and how students can compensate, including a request for any information about special education needs:

The best way I can teach you is to learn about you, because the more I know about you, the better I can help you learn. This is more difficult online, because I can't see your face. So please complete the New Student Survey by Friday, August 17. If you have a special education need, let me know so that I may accommodate you.

Because this class is online, almost all I can see is your written words. As a result, your written words are very important. One way to guarantee your success in this, or any other class, is to work on your writing skills. While it's tempting to write angry words, I expect each student to behave with good manners. In addition, the more effective your written words are, the better your assignment grades will be! My goal is for you to succeed, so if you have questions or concerns, please let me know.

Keep in mind that this is your class. You and the rest of your class will learn the material from through reading, discussion, problem solving, and lecture. However, that does not mean I will not answer questions. Questions are good! They mean that you are reading and thinking about the material, which is the best way to learn anything.

To recap, the way to do your best in this class is to:

- ◆ work on your writing
- ◆ participate
- ◆ follow the rules
- ◆ ask questions

Do these four things and this class be will great!

☐ The teacher's name, title, the school name, the teacher's email, a phone number, and the teacher's office hours.

Teacher Hardware and Software

Preparation is required to run a good synchronous session. Teachers need to have the right devices to make the session work. Ideally, teachers will have a desktop or laptop computer, a headset with a microphone, speakers, a comfortably sized computer monitor, and a high-quality internet connection.

Hardwired connections are the best quality, so teachers should be prepared to upgrade their connections if necessary. I have fifty-five Mbps download and five Mbps upload, and I rarely have complaints about the quality of my streaming audio and video. In addition, many teachers will not be working at home alone, and their children or spouses will probably also need to use the internet while they are working. Teaching online requires more bandwidth than streaming videos, even on multiple devices. Students can get away with inferior internet connections because they'll be uploading less data than the instructor.

Laptops can be hooked up to larger computer monitors if necessary. Teachers will be loading their slide deck, the chat box, and a whiteboard all on the same screen, so they need the space. Widescreen monitors are optimal in this situation. While some people prefer document cameras, I recommend a pen tablet for most teachers. Pen tablets allow teachers to draw directly on the screen, reducing the number of outgoing video streams and therefore decreasing bandwidth requirements for teachers and students.

Because teachers are going to be spending a large portion of their days typing, an ergonomic keyboard helps prevent repetitive strain injuries like tendinitis. Alt codes, or characters that don't have specific keys, like © or ≠, are often helpful in chat boxes, but require a specific number pad that many laptops do not have but are usually available on ergonomic keyboards. In my experience, track pads are inferior to mice for precisely locating the cursor on the screen, so teachers may want to invest in a high-quality gaming mouse as well.

Sometimes, teachers will need to scan documents or images. In the olden days, a dedicated flatbed scanner was preferable, but newer apps have excellent free scan-to-PDF functions for use with smart phones. Teacher will want to investigate their options and select one before panicking at 1:30 am. Similarly, teachers will need to print documents or images, and so teachers should figure out whether they want to rely on printers at school, use a local a copy shop, or buy their own printer. Personally, I purchased an inexpensive, reliable black-and-white laser printer that takes generic drums and toner, saving me hundreds of dollars in ink each year.

Once teachers have invested in all this hardware, they will want to make sure it doesn't get fried with power surges and outages. If teachers have the money, an uninterruptible power supply (UPS) is a worthwhile investment. Many UPSs filter voltage spikes and brownouts, providing "clean" electricity to prolong the life of expensive hardware. In addition, because a UPS provides battery backup when the power goes out, teachers can close out the synchronous class session instead of just disappearing from class.

When teachers have access to an LMS, very little specialized software is required because everything they need is contained within the LMS and backed up in the cloud. However, teachers will want to familiarize themselves with an easy way to take screenshots. Screenshots are often useful as proof of student misbehavior during synchronous class sessions. Screenshots are also valuable when teachers want to quickly preserve student work on virtual whiteboards, because many whiteboards don't save from session to session. If the LMS does not include a whiteboard, then teachers will want to select one for use during synchronous class sessions.

Teachers should always have a Plan B and a Plan C for device or internet failure. For example, I primarily use a custom desktop rig that my husband built for me, but I also have access to a laptop should our power go out and I need to borrow a friend's Wi-Fi to teach class. My Plan C is to use the LMS app on my smartphone over cellular data, which I have done more than once.

First Synchronous Session

Several days before the first synchronous session, teachers should prepare a slide deck. In the slide deck should be an introductory slide, with the school logo, the date, the teacher's name, and a note that the session will begin soon. This will go up first, before anyone else arrives. The date and topic should always be on the first slide because when students review recordings, they will use the label to locate the session, even if they can't quite remember when the material was covered.

Because this is the first session, teachers cannot guarantee that students know how to use their devices or the LMS, so the first few slides should be a systematic wordless workshop showing students how to set the software so students can access their microphone, speakers, and chat box. Keep in mind that most computers will have multiple inputs and outputs, so teachers might need to show students how to select the microphone and speaker they're going to use. If students are accessing the synchronous session through the web, students might have accidentally muted the browser tab, so if students are having difficulty hearing the teacher make sure to have them check that setting.

Keep in mind that teachers are not tech support. School administration should have provided students with detailed instructions on how to log into the LMS, reset their passwords if necessary, find their class, find their class page, and locate the synchronous session. Districts and schools are responsible for setting device requirements, not teachers. In addition, the school administration should have given students explicit instructions on how to check their audio and video settings. Equally, if students wish to switch in or out of a class, that should not be a teacher responsibility. School administration should provide that support.

Teachers are not tech support. The LMS provider should offer help (help desk tickets) as should the school information technology department.

Once teachers have shown everyone how to set up their software so students can hear, see, and speak, teachers will want to use another wordless workshop to teach students how to use the chat box. This is an excellent time to take roll by having them put their name in the chat box. Depending on the default settings in the LMS, teachers may wish to have students turn off audiovisual notifications that interfere with concentration during class.

At this point, students tend to feel more confident in their ability to attend the session. This is when I show a slide with a photograph of myself, my family, my teaching license, and some carefully selected social media screenshots. This helps make me more human and provides some authentic touchstones for creating connection in the online classroom.

 Never friend students on social media.

One useful classroom practice, online or offline, is teaching students how and when to raise their hand, so this is the focus of the next slide. One of my favorite rules in a face-to-face classroom is "Raise Your Hand and Wait to Be Called On." I do not tolerate idle chatter and students talking over each other. Online, the LMS tracks the order in which students raised their virtual hands, so teachers can have students "line up" to take turns at onscreen activities. This is particularly helpful when tracking participation in a course. My younger students frequently "run around" and get back in line to do "board work" on a slide.

Technique 34 in *Teach Like a Champion* is "Seat Signals." While students spacing out of class are less distracting online, that does not mean that a student who interrupts a carefully prepared question and answer session with repeated requests to step away from their computer is any less troublesome. Therefore, developing easy-to-use, clear-cut signals for students who need to step away from the class is essential. Fortunately, most LMSs come with a way for participants to set an "away" status. Establishing classroom norms from the start means that this is the point in the orientation when students are taught not to interrupt the class with a request to step away, but to set their status as away and go.

This is also a good time to teach students to use the wordless feedback buttons built into the system that are typically located in the same area as the status buttons, and we practice using the "confused," "faster," and "slower" settings as displayed on the slide. Because teachers cannot see students' faces throughout the lesson, having students use these settings is helpful in adjusting the lesson on the fly.

One of students' favorite parts of synchronous sessions is getting to draw on the board, whether they are nine or sixteen. Therefore, teachers should take time to teach students to use the editing tools. Just like a dry-erase board, a whiteboard is a virtual blank space. All LMS videoconferencing software has digital markers in a handful of colors. Depending on the particular software, teachers and students may be able place and resize shapes, move objects, add text, and erase all or a portion of the whiteboard. Some have the ability to save drawings (content annotation) for later reference. Others might display several whiteboards at once, so a teacher can monitor several students' work at the same time.

One way to build community in an online class is to ask students to locate themselves on a map. Make sure that it is *not* a detailed map—teachers don't want students to feel uncomfortable about their personal safety by giving away too much information. Instead, use a blank world map and ask students to mark their approximate location. This builds camaraderie from the get-go, and lets students feel seen.

Now it's time to get down to business. Take a screenshot of what students see when they first click into class and show them how to find their weekly content modules. Tell students what kinds of assignments will be required and how they'll be evaluated in the class. Open the content module in the next slide and show them what the inside of the module looks like. Point them to the "help" links, including how to submit a trouble ticket and how to find directions for accessing recordings.

Help students stay organized. Make a slide with an overview of the weekly course schedule, with the set days per week that an assignment is due, and review what kinds of assignments are due on which days. Keep students interactive—ask them to use the course tools to show understanding. I often use a "thumbs up to move on" requirement, letting them know I can see who gave up a thumbs up and who did not.

Don't forget to review course policies, including attendance. Generally, there are separate synchronous and asynchronous attendance policies. Sometimes teachers will require asynchronous students to submit some kind of exit ticket to verify that they have watched class recordings. I don't think it's fair to require extra work of students who are already at a disadvantage, so I don't use that policy. Instead, I require the same graded work for all students, and I don't give points for attendance. Many online schools have policies about mixing synchronous and asynchronous sessions.

> Enrolled students are expected to attend class on a regular basis. If the student does not attend class, or is late for class, the responsibility for missed material and work falls upon the student. Attendance will be taken at the beginning of each lecture.

Other course policies include responsibility for readings:

> Students are responsible for all the material in the textbook, whether or not specific material is discussed during class.

Electronic devices:

> Students are welcome to have other electronic devices that support their educational endeavors. All background noises should be silenced as a courtesy to other students. If students must leave the class for any reason, they should simply note themselves as being "Away."

Learning differences:

> If students have a documented learning disability, a serious hearing or vision problem, or any other special need that might affect their performance and participation in class, please inform me during the first week of class so that I might make appropriate accommodations. Lecture slides and transcripts are available upon request.

Learning environment:

> I expect to maintain a positive learning environment based upon open communication, mutual respect, and non-discrimination. I will not discriminate based on race, gender, age, disability, veteran status, religious tradition, sexual orientation, color, or national origin. Any suggestions as to how to further a positive and open environment will be appreciated and given thoughtful consideration.

Late policy:

> Assignments are due by 12 am Eastern Standard Time (–5:00 UTC) on the date listed in the syllabus. Late work will receive a letter grade reduction for every day that it is late, up to five days. After five days, late work will not be accepted. Essay assignments are to be submitted via BlackBoard in either .pdf, .doc, or .docx format.

Assignment formatting:

> *Math Formatting:* The object of the course is not technology. Therefore, while the use of LaTeX, MathType, Geogebra, and other software tools is encouraged, it is not required. A LaTeX editor is built into the LMS for student use. At certain points, students may be expected to demonstrate use of a straightedge and compass, unless a student's documented exceptionality prevents such assignments. If students choose to hand-sketch and handwrite assignments that do not require handwork (i.e., can be done with LaTeX, etc.), easily legible handwriting is required. In addition, all assignments, whether created with software or drawn by hand, must be uploaded to the LMS in digital format. Therefore, emailed or texted assignments will not be accepted.

> *Style for Written Assignments:* Formatting is to be twelve-point Times New Roman, double-spaced, with 1" margins. Use a single space between sentences, always use the Oxford comma, avoid the use of passive voice, and do not use the first person or address the audience directly. Students are to refer to the APA Style Manual. If students wish to purchase a hard copy, use ISBN-13: 978-1433805615 or ISBN-10: 1433805618.

Assignment style, revision, and partial credit:

> *Partial Credit/Showing Your Work:* Requirements vary by problem type. Students are not required to show their work for homework and weekly quiz problems—however, if they do not show their work, and get the problem wrong, they cannot get partial credit. Partial credit is only given for homework and weekly quiz problems when all work is shown. Test problems drawn from the book require that students show work in order to receive any credit.

> *Written Assignment Prior Review:* Students may submit an outline for feedback one week in advance of the deadline. Papers will be returned with written feedback at least twenty-four hours prior to the submission deadline. This option is not available for the final exam.

> *Written Assignment Revision:* Within one week after receiving graded papers, students may revise papers for an improved grade, not to exceed one letter grade above the original grade. This option is not available for the final exam.

Although this may seem excessive, the only reason to make a policy is that there has been a need for the policy in the past. At some point, every one of these policies has been used when working with students. There is no need to linger on these policies, because these are all copied from the syllabus. This is a review to ensure that students remember the key points. After every other slide or so, ask students to show a thumbs up to move on. This is creating a habit of attending to the lecture.

 Don't just read slides. Instead, restate the main points in your own words.

When I had my first child, I was an older parent who'd never spent much time around younger children. I had never done any babysitting, and I had never had any close extended family, friends, or neighbors with young children. Instead, I took classes on infant care when I was pregnant and read many books on childcare and discipline. One of the books, *Positive Discipline*, made an excellent point—tell children what you want them to do. "Don't touch that" isn't nearly as useful as "Hold this, please." Even teenagers don't have a fully myelinated prefrontal cortex to provide adult levels of inhibitory control.[ccclxviii] Instead of telling them to stop, always direct and, if needed, redirect.

Therefore, teachers should establish behavioral expectations right from the start. This is especially important online, because people are often more unkind online than they are face-to-face. In combination with students' poor self-control, this can be a recipe for disaster. Instead, clearly outline the standards for communication in the class, and remind students that nothing is ever "gone" online—screenshots and servers are always recording.

Here is my standard policy:

> Your communication skills are on display in this class. A positive attitude and tone are keys to success. Read your messages before you send them—especially if you disagree. We can't see your expression or hear your voice. The written word is much harsher than the spoken one. Always respond with tact and eliminate any sarcasm.

> No personal attacks, forms of harassment, discrimination, or threatening messages will be tolerated. I take electronic communication seriously—so should you. Never send a message you composed while you were angry or upset. Wait until you cool down. By now you should know that all messages are retained either on the server or on a backup. Just because you deleted it on your device doesn't mean it's gone.

> We do not discuss (or vent about) other instructors, other classes, students, etc. Always keep your posts "clean" and respectful. If it isn't something you would tell your parent, don't post it.

In order to hammer the point home, teachers should follow this up with a list of what students should do. Frequently teachers may wish to review a list of examples of meaningful participation for the online, written discussion questions, copied and pasted from the syllabus. Students often have questions here, so be prepared to stop and discuss, especially as regards to how a teacher will evaluate their writing.

Sharing a related experience

Commenting on others' experiences

Asking others questions about their ideas and/or experiences

Offering a different perspective about an idea that is being discussed

Describing an interesting idea from the week's reading and explaining what you learned

Asking the group a question about something in the course

Disagreeing (respectfully)

Describing a problem and asking for help

Describing how you've used something you've learned in the course

Sharing a relevant resource

Describing relevant research and sharing information on how to find it

Noting, briefly, the content and/or purpose of a useful website and providing a link (it is a violation of copyright law to copy the actual page)

Many students have terrible study habits, so teachers may want to follow this up with another quick prescriptive set of behavioral expectations. Students are often surprised when teachers mention taking breaks, eating, drinking, and sleeping. Pointing out that losing sleep lowers IQ[ccclxix] often helps students make sleep a priority.

Have a schedule and stick to it.

Keep everything you need to study in one place .

Study in a quiet and comfortable place.

Study when you are rested and alert.

Don''t study while you are hungry or upset.

Take a ten-minute break and stretch every fifty minutes or so.

Keep organized notes you can read.

Use your table of contents.

Take notes mainly on what you don't understand.

Use retrieval practice.

When teachers have synchronous class sessions, teachers should establish expected etiquette for participating in the chat room. Many younger students only have experience with unmonitored videogame chat sessions, which are notorious for profanity, bullying, and other inappropriate content.[ccclxx] Making it clear that those kinds of behaviors are not tolerated helps establish a culture of respect and safety in the online classroom. Online teachers have the additional burden of helping students learn to keep themselves safe by not asking for or disclosing personal information.

When addressing someone in the chat, use their name.

Don't take over the conversation.

Be polite. You can't see facial expressions or hear tones of voice.

State your question.

Give me a chance to answer you.

Don't spam or flood the room with repeated questions, statements, emojis, or links.

Avoid typing in all caps. It is hard on the eyes to read and rude. It is the internet equivalent of shouting.

Don't ask for a person's age/gender/location. It is rude and unnecessary. If you want to know something about a person, be patient.

As part of my periodic student surveys, I ask students an open-ended question about what they dislike most about taking online classes and almost every year, students respond with off-topic chatting. Use that bit of information to let students know that even when their peers aren't saying anything, they're sitting there and being annoyed at the person derailing the synchronous class conversation. For example, during a class session with a student who is distracting the class, all I need to do is ask, "Students, what do y'all hate most about online classes?" In almost every case, the student stops their poor behavior.

With a particularly obstinate student, teachers might need to mute a student or remove them from the synchronous session. In that case, follow up with an email to the parent (BCCd to your supervisor) letting the parent know what happened and why the teacher chose to mute or remove the student. Additionally, teachers should offer suggestions for the next synchronous class session, such as, "Next week, if John has a question or comment, he should type it in the chat box and wait for me to respond. If I don't answer it then, he can bring it up at the end of class."

 Students dislike off-topic chatting. Don't let it happen.

One way to help students evaluate whether a given statement is rude or inappropriate is to go down the list and give examples of common poor behavior, having the class point out the appropriate behavior. "Class, should I ask a question, and then ask another one without waiting for an answer? What should I do instead? Class, should I type like this? How should I have typed that? Class, should I say, 'Hey you'? How should I say that question?" For students with poor social skills, reinforcing anticipated behavior with good and bad examples helps clarify expectations.

Online classes are scary for many students (and the parents who are inevitably watching in the background). Reviewing how the course is going to work and how students are going to be evaluated helps ease their fears. The syllabus should contain the grading breakdown for the course, and while ideally  parents and students have reviewed the syllabus, don't take their perusal for granted. Instead, review the grading breakdown for the course.

Part of the grading breakdown almost certainly includes online, written discussion questions, so teachers should have a slide with a model of a good online, written class discussion. Point out exactly what makes the model good and use the earlier examples from meaningful participation to show students how them can write their own high-quality discussion questions. Draw a correlation between the model and the rubric so students understand precisely how to get a good grade. Many students will have questions, so be prepared to take time to explain. Point out how the late work policy applies to the written discussion questions, and show students where to find the late work policy.

 Tell students when they can expect assignments to be graded, and keep your word.

If there is time, include a slide about why we should study what we're studying in the class. While other teachers may have a different philosophy of education,

179

I believe that Lord Morley's aphorism about truth is an excellent goal of education.

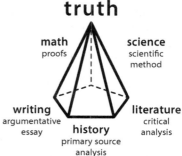

> *An educated man is one who knows when a thing is proved and when it is not. An uneducated man does not know.*
>
> –quoted in A Defence of Classical Education

Explaining to students that the goal of a given strand of education is for them to be able to understand whether some truth has been proven provides students with an underlying reason for studying, especially when teachers can quickly lay out the skills progression for a given field. For example, "You need to learn to write complete sentences so you can use them in a paragraph. After you learn how to write paragraphs, you can begin to write essays. After you learn to write an essay, you can learn to write an argumentative essay. Then you can persuade people that you know the truth. Today, we're going to learn to identify the four basic sentence types."

When teachers wrap up the first online session, provide students with a way to contact their teacher in case of dire emergency. In my experience, students always want to know what constitutes an emergency, so I tell them the truth—students have texted me about hurricanes, forest fires, wide-spread flooding, hospitalizations, and so on. I tell students about messages like, "Mrs. Ostaff, my mom is driving down the interstate and there's a forest fire in our rearview mirror." Letting students know that they can and should share important information helps establish trust.

Finally, this is a good time for teachers to link to the student survey. Sending students directly to the next task is a good practice. This is also when teachers can establish a routine of five to ten minutes after class where students can ask questions semi-privately, with the recording off. By providing a Q&A session at the beginning and end of class, students are less likely to interrupt during class with off-topic questions.

 A day or two before the chosen date and time, run a test session in the LMS with a trusted friend or co-worker. Make sure all systems are a go and the presentation is clear.

Orientation Week Checklist

☐ Post the syllabus. Make sure it includes

- School name
- Class title
- School year
- Teacher name
- Date and time for synchronous class sessions
- Teacher email address
- Office hours location and policy
- Class website
- Required textbooks, any lab equipment, manipulatives, website memberships, etc.
- Class description
- Assignment descriptions
- Grade breakdown
- Class assignment schedule
- Weekly calendar with the pacing guide
- Assignment policies
- Teacher contact and availability policy
- Attendance policy
- Work archiving policy
- Electronic devices policy
- Disability policy
- Religious observances policy
- Non-discrimination policy
- Cheating policy

☐ Post the teacher's contact information in an easy-to-find location in the class in the LMS. Include their email, perhaps a phone number, and the office hours policy. I use this:

Office hours are scheduled by appointment in fifteen-minute increments. I am also available outside of office hours, by prior request and mutual agreement.

☐ Post the email response policy. This is mine:

Please email me with any questions or concerns you have regarding the course. I will respond to any email within twenty-hour hours during weekdays (but this is not guaranteed for emails submitted over the weekend). Instructor availability is limited on weekends.

☐ Create an *About Me* link and fill it with a professional photo and a short autobiography.

☐ Post the first two weeks of course modules, including the orientation module. Don't forget to create an introductory discussion.

☐ Post a welcome announcement, often a copy of the welcome email.

☐ Set up the grade book. Don't forget to use the student view of the class in the LMS to ensure the visible grades make sense and are in sequential order.

☐ Double check that the central calendar includes the assignment dates from the class. If needed, add deadlines for readings and other non-graded activities.

☐ Lock videoconference classrooms. Just like teachers know better than to allow students free range in their face-to-face classrooms, never permit students to hang out unsupervised in the synchronous class. Always "lock" the classroom so that it's only available when the teacher is prepared to monitor the session. No one wants to deal with students misbehaving online in a space for which the teacher or school is responsible.

☐ Ideally, teachers will set up repeating synchronous sessions in the LMS with obvious labels. For example, "Monday/Wednesday 1 pm Pre-Algebra." Don't forget to allow recording downloads so asynchronous students can watch the session and all students can review concepts as necessary. A good LMS will ensure the recording of the chat is anonymized to prevent a Family Educational Rights and Privacy Act violation. Do not allow unsupervised private chats during synchronous class sessions.

☐ Create a discussion board for off-topic chatting in the class. By posting a location, with behavior rules, teachers can direct students there when they want to make friends or share non-class-related information. This helps promote a positive classroom atmosphere for student relationships, while ensuring rules and expectations for behavior are clear and direct, preventing potential disruption in other places in the online classroom.

Chapter Summary

- Gather student data.
- Create an orientation week.
- Post the first two weeks of assignments.
- Create a quiz that allows teachers to get to know students.

- Send a "welcome" email.
- Ensure that you, as the teacher, have needed hardware, software, and internet access.
- Prepare for the first synchronous session, with a slide deck that includes:
  - how to use the software
  - setting synchronous student behavior rules
  - showing students where and how to find assignments
  - review class policies about:
    - readings
    - device use
    - learning differences
    - learning environment
    - late policy
    - assignment formatting
    - assignment style, revision, and partial credit
    - class communication
    - meaningful participation
    - study habits
    - chat etiquette
  - grading breakdown
  - rubrics
  - rationale for studying this content
  - teacher contact information
- Complete an Orientation Week Checklist.

CHAPTER 9

BUILDING AN ONLINE CLASSROOM MANAGEMENT SYSTEM

New teachers often end up spending exorbitant amounts of time tracking down work and students, but teachers can create a system with clear boundaries and expectations for student academic behavior.

> **Set clear boundaries and expectations for students.**

When teachers use a method that makes doing the work the path of least resistance for students, students do the work, reducing both time spent and frustration for teachers and students. Providing both incentives and consequences as part of a well-balanced class behavioral management system helps student learning. Keeping close track of student work helps teachers nudge students into getting assignments done. Frequent, positive communication helps build good working relationships with students.

In order to make this happen, teachers need to have computer skills. Required skills include turning computers on and off, finding and starting applications, typing and using a spellchecker, being comfortable resizing and dragging windows around, saving and organizing files and file folders, finding lost files, uploading and downloading files, printing to PDF, and creating slide decks.

Email in Online Classes

In particular, online teachers need to be comfortable using email programs, attaching files, saving and downloading files, and some more advanced features. Because communication is so important, teachers should use a flagging and filing system for their email. For example, teachers could flag requests for help so when they have time to sit down to help students, they can find the requests. Teachers could file emails they will need later, so if a student emails with a note like, "I'm going to miss class Mar. 22-27," teachers can track the email down when reviewing their attendance sheet at the end of the year. Teachers could also create VIP contacts (i.e., supervisors) that are automatically moved to the top of their email inbox.

Tell students to email with the smallest questions and then respond to those emails. Even if a teacher doesn't know the answer to the question, respond back with a "I'm looking into that, and I'll get back to you!" That way, students know that you've received their emails and are looking into the question. Always write in a positive, upbeat manner—this communication sets the tone for the relationship with the student.

Teachers should check their email frequently. If they let it go too long, the unread list will quickly become overwhelming. I check my email at breakfast, just before classes, lunch, just after classes, and before bed, at a minimum. Be prepared to spend at least an hour every day writing and thoughtfully responding.

Because an online teacher gets so many emails, do not permit students to clutter a teacher's inbox with assignments. Instead, insist students submit assignments via the LMS or a dedicated email address. Sorting assignments from everything else is a Herculean task for which online teachers do not have time.

Part of the online teacher's job is sending follow-up emails. When I had my first professional office job, my supervisor insisted I document all contact, and I thought it was a foolish waste of time. Mea culpa. An email that includes "Here is a copy of the email I sent Dec. 13th re: this assignment" has frequently proven useful in dealing with upset students, parents, and supervisors. When a teacher has a telephone or non-recorded synchronous session with a parent, they should take a couple of minutes to send an email reviewing what was covered during the conversation, and list any actions to be taken in the future. Recording synchronous session with parents is not a bad idea.

Another useful skill is learning how to rename an email contact (a surprisingly high number of families maintain a family email address with the contact name "Mom"). For example, it's often helpful to nickname an email contact with the student name (in this case, Isabel) and the parent name (in this case, Elijah), like so: "Elijah 'Isabel' Smith." When this type of nickname is used, composing an email about a particular student doesn't require a teacher to memorize all the parent names.

Often, teachers will want to address a whole class virtually, in which case they may want to create an email list. An email list means that a teacher can type in the name of the list, for example, "Algebra I" and all the included email addresses automatically fill in. Use this wisely however—the BCC field is the most appropriate place to write this, because email addresses are often seen as private and because teachers do not want to set up an accidental, never-ending "reply-all" situation.

Time Management for Teachers

Teachers should offer multiple points of contact. Discussion boards, email, text-chats during lecture, office hours, and 1:1 tutoring sessions should all be available to students. However, insist that phone calls or synchronous meetings outside of class or office hours happen only by emailed appointment agreed upon in advance by both parties. This policy can be included in the syllabus. One way to set the appointment is to send three times that are good for the teacher: one in the morning, one in the afternoon, and one in the evening, across three different days. Allow the student or parent to choose one of the days and times. Do not let parents dictate how a teacher spends their time.

Alternatively, teachers can use a free online scheduler (sometimes included in an LMS) and allow students to self-schedule in fifteen-minute increments during specified times. Although this procedure often increases student willingness to make appointments,[ccclxxi] teachers need to be aware that they'll need to keep those hours always free, just in case a student does make an appointment. Don't set the availability as wide open, because teachers need to have down time too.

If teachers have input into scheduling synchronous class sessions, consider bumping synchronous class sessions back to two or three times a week for core content areas. The other days, teachers can slot office hours into those times. Just as a teacher would assign a problem set during class and give one or two students their attention while everyone else works, teachers can use office hours for scheduling one-to-one or small group meetings with some students while the other students work independently.

In order to protect themselves from burnout, teachers should set times that they will never be available and let students and parents know in advance. For example, I am not available on Fridays after 6 pm, and for twenty-four hours on Sunday. Boundaries are important for a teacher's mental health. In addition, establishing firm boundaries limits opportunities for parents or students to demand inappropriate levels of contact from a teacher. Just because a teacher is working from home does not mean that they need to be available all the time. Teachers provide a public service, but they are not servants.

A teacher's time is limited. Instead of trying to be everything to everyone, encourage students to work together without a teacher's direct supervision. Often, students can answer each other's question without taking up their teacher's time. In situations where social distancing is in effect, setting up these study groups can be critical for a student's sense of belonging. Discussion boards for a given assignment are useful, but in middle school students can create flashcard decks together, share notes in joint documents, and create study sets. Older students frequently set up their own unofficial chat and text groups for studying together.

Leverage for Getting Students to Turn in Work

Building a functional system begins with good policies. From the beginning, students should have clear behavioral expectations about assignments, participation, and communication. These policies should be inserted into the class syllabus, reviewed in the orientation session, and posted in the LMS. Competent school administrators will have reinforced expectations with policies reviewed during class registration, written in student and parent handbooks, and posted on the school website.

It is hard to overstate the difficulty of getting students to turn in work in an online class. For most students, nearly anything else is more interesting than doing online schoolwork at home. In normal times, streaming videos, sunny afternoons, and games are all compelling distractions. Add in family distress, pandemics, and natural disasters, and an online class becomes the least important task in a student's life.

Student health and safety always come first, but in the end students will be healthier and safer with more education. As Hummer and Hernandez write in *The Effect of Educational Attainment on Adult Mortality in the U.S.*, "remaining life expectancy at age 25—an important overall indicator of adult population health—is about a decade shorter for people who do not have a high school degree compared with those who have completed college."[ccclxxii] Teachers need to do their best to compel students to do the work so that students can earn those high school degrees and, if they choose to do so, attend college.

A draconian late policy helps teachers enforce consequences for failure to complete work. Teachers should not use this policy to enforce cruel expectations on students, but instead use it as leverage when students fail to meet a reasonable standard. Remember, teachers have posted assignments at least two weeks in advance, so students and parents can plan to get the work done and turned in. Because assignments are repetitive and written to the student, students don't need to have their hand held when completing the work—they already know how to do it. Short supporting videos explaining tricky concepts are available in the content module. During the synchronous class, teachers have explained exactly how students are to complete the task, with sequential steps, worked examples, and models.

> Assignments are due by 12 am Eastern Standard Time (–5:00 UTC) on the date listed in the syllabus. Late work will receive a letter grade reduction for every day that it is late, up to five days. After five days, late work will not be accepted. Essay assignments are to be submitted

via the learning management system in either .pdf, .doc, .docx, or .rtf format.

Students have the teacher's contact information. Barring an emergency, there is no reason an average student cannot get work in by the deadline or contact the teacher and let them know why the work will be late or missing. Teachers should use their best judgment to be flexible and waive the policy as they need.

Because students have such extensive support, a teacher rarely needs to take this policy to the mat. However, when students write an email with hat in hand asking to turn in late work, this policy means that the teacher has the power to deny full credit to students who have failed to turn in work on time without a good excuse. This policy also means that when a parent emails a teacher at the end of the semester, asking the teacher to accept a month or two of late work, the teacher can respond with, "I'm not comfortable accepting that much late work, as per the syllabus."

It's Not About You

An experienced teacher knows students' failure to comply with class expectations isn't personal. Students' issues are not the teacher's issues, and the missing work isn't necessarily indicative of anything about a particular teacher. Teachers can do everything right and an individual student might not succeed in meeting expectations.

Neither does missing work make a student a bad person. Something happened and the student's plan for getting the work done failed, but the odds are good there was a plan. As John Lennon once sang, "Life is what happens to you while you're busy making other plans."[ccclxxiii] There is no need to do anything but enforce the policy and move on.

Teachers are role models, and part of what they model is emotional self-regulation. Given the inherent power imbalance between a teacher and students, a teacher imposing their bad mood or anger in the classroom does not help learning. When a teacher is calm and focused, the students are more likely to be calm and focused. Emotional compartmentalization is a key skill for teachers.

Always be positive. No matter how angry a teacher might be when a student fails to complete assignments or acts out in a synchronous session or a nasty email, a teacher should not react with anger. Instead, the teacher should maintain calm control, of both themselves and the situation. Assume that students didn't mean to write the email snarkily, that their repeated interruptions during lecture mean they're enthusiastic, and so on.

By always reframing the situation in a positive light, refusing to engage in a power struggle, and establishing expectations for future behavior, teachers help students succeed. Teachers should never write an email while they are angry or upset. If the email needs an immediate response, but a teacher is finding it difficult to write from a calm, upbeat perspective, they should be able to ask their supervisor for assistance.

The Carrot—Make It Easy for Students to Do the Work

One important caveat is that teachers should never assign work during a synchronous session. This may be strange to teachers who are accustomed to checking for understanding in a face-to-face classroom and creating assignments based on that feedback. But in an online, synchronous session, teachers do not have the same kind of nonverbal communication and cannot easily tell how well students understand the content or the assignment. Most students will pay attention, but many will not be able to recall and use the information.[ccclxxiv] Parents will write angry emails about their student's lack of comprehension or knowledge of the assignment.

 Teachers should never assign work during a synchronous session.

Make it easy for students to know what is due and when it is due. Always post work on the front of each content module. This calendar, filled with repetitive assignment types, is helpful for all students but critical for students with special education needs. Another benefit is that by completing a repetitive, limited set of assignments on the same day every week, students focus on the content, not the context.

Make it easy for students to do the work by giving them assignments with known times and performance standards. New assignments are more difficult because students are figuring out how to use the software, rather than thinking about the content. As an added benefit, this reduces teacher workload because teachers don't have to instruct students on how to do the assignment, just the content. This way, there are no panicky emails from confused students that require an immediate answer before breakfast.

Make it easy for students to figure out what is due each day with standardized assignments and calendars. These also make life easier for teachers because teachers can copy and paste the content module from last week, updating it with this week's content. Although different content areas lend themselves to different tasks—problem sets in math, map work in geography, etc.—teachers should ensure that students meet the learning objectives for the week through the assigned tasks.

Make it easy for students to make their own plans to get the work done. The content module calendar should include both a weekly list and a daily calendar. Students can copy and paste these tasks to their own calendar app, or even print them out and stick them on the refrigerator. Teachers should ensure all assignments are *also* in the LMS calendar, making it easier for students to track assignments for all their classes at once. Often, this makes it easier for parents because they can export the LMS calendar feed to their own calendar apps and track that way.

 Keep the style of the module calendar the same every week.

Make it easy for students with limited internet access by not requiring students to turn everything into the LMS. This is not to say that teachers should assign busy work. Each assignment should serve a specific, essential step on the stairway to mastery. But not all work needs to be uploaded and graded by the teacher. Much work can be auto-graded or self-checked. Will everything always be done? No, of course not. That's okay—teachers should design the weekly assessment to be impossible to make a good grade on unless students have done the work. It only takes a week or two for students to figure that out.

- It's much faster to flip through paper than it is to load a document, write on the document with a virtual pen, save the document, and deliver it to the student. What a teacher can do in fifteen seconds with a red pen will take them at least a minute online. Multiply each minute by 140 and what took a teacher thirty minutes during a planning period now takes 140 minutes of staring at a screen. Therefore, teachers should be selective about the work they decide to mark up. Offer students the option of uploading the work, but don't overwork students—or yourself.
- Even if only some of the questions are matching, multiple choice, fill in the blank, or ordering questions that can be graded by the LMS, choosing that option will save teachers' time when reviewing the short-answer essay questions.

Make it easy for students with print issues to access the content. Ensure that the textbook is available in audio for students with reading difficulty. If students have a diagnosed print access issue, BookShare offers free audio versions of most textbooks, trade books, and fiction books for qualifying US students, and a low-cost membership for others with qualifying conditions. Inside the weekly content module, teachers should link to videos that cover all the key concepts in the reading. This is a great place to offer links to websites and videos that provide extensions on the topic for gifted students.

Make it easy for students with dysgraphia and executive functioning issues to access the concept maps and notes. Usually the answers to the sketch (often difficult for students with dysgraphia) are available in the textbook. Teachers should review the sketch and the answers to the skeleton notes during lecture. Remember, the teacher has based the slide deck on the skeleton notes, so reviewing the notes doesn't need to be overt. However, teachers should explicitly call out the video that covers this week's hands-on activity, because not every student will be able to do a project every week due to lack of materials or access to workspace.

Make it easy for students with other kinds of learning issues.

- Because so many students who prefer online classes have anxiety issues, teachers might consider not requiring written or oral participation during synchronous class sessions. In my classes, students are still required to participate in polls and sometimes marking on the board, but I don't require out loud expression. Although this seems counterintuitive to many extroverts, speaking aloud doesn't increase student learning. In fact, many face-to-face classroom teachers struggle to keep students from talking. Often, the silent students are some of my best students, scoring 95% and above in the class.
- Requiring handwritten participation unfairly penalizes students with dysgraphia or other fine motor issues. Similarly, requiring handwritten verbal work in an online class is nonsensical for students in middle school and up. Mathematics work requirements vary by teaching philosophy and individualized educational plan.
- Teachers might consider not using timed assessments. I'm more interested in whether students know the material than how fast they can recall it, or how fast they can write, and it's not as if the bell is going to ring for the next class. This helps students with anxiety issues and dyscalculia, too.
- Along those lines, teachers should provide copies of slides in advance. These slides should include copies of concepts/problems worked during class and reviews of past problems. The lectures should be recorded for posterity and anonymized to protect student privacy.

The Stick—Make It Difficult for Students Who Don't Do the Work

The flip side of making it easy to do the work is to make it difficult to not to the work. Teachers shouldn't shame students or be inflexible, but they should establish clear policies that ensure that when a student would rather play videogames than do the weekly assessment, the burden of the effort should be on the student. Yes, I really did receive an email from a high school student who said they chose to stay up all night with the new *Call of Duty* rather than turn in their weekly quiz. I was amused, but I didn't give them a pass on getting it done.

Therefore, without a valid excuse from the student or parent, teachers should not contort themselves with providing missed work to students. Teachers don't need to bend over backwards because all the work is already in the content module. Students don't need anything else from the teacher. The teacher does not owe coddling to students who didn't get the work in on time and didn't have family emergencies or similar issues. Extra assistance is not fair to the students who did the work and got it in on time. This is enshrined in my attendance policy:

> Enrolled students are expected to attend class on a regular basis. If the student does not attend class, or is late for class, the responsibility for missed material and work falls upon the student. Attendance will be taken at the beginning of each synchronous session. A student who misses more than 25% of any course will not receive a grade or certificate of completion.

Although some teachers may feel uncomfortable with this stance, remember that students are aware of these policies from the first day of the class, because teachers reviewed the policies during the orientation session. Because teachers recorded the orientation, all students had an opportunity to watch it. Teachers should record every synchronous class so students can easily go back and watch what they missed. Course modules mean that all work is readily available to students all the time. In addition, these policies are clearly listed in the syllabus, written in announcements, and noted within the course module in the directions for the assignments.

Note that students should not be excused from turning in late work without consultation with the parent and possibly an administrator. The expectation is always that students will complete the work, even if it is late. Teachers should assign a zero for every late assignment, whether or not teachers have discussed an alternative due date with a student. Even when a student and the teacher agree that the student can turn in something late, students should receive a zero until the work is turned in.

Place a zero in the grade book, but leave the assignment open for completion and update the grade book when the work is completed—within a reasonable period. In my classes, students who don't get late work in by the grading day but who do contact me with a reasonable explanation receive a standard one-week extension.

Executive functioning issues are common for students with attention deficit/ hyperactive disorder, dyslexia, and other issues. "The dog ate my homework" isn't just in face-to-face classes. In addition, software isn't perfect. An LMS does intermittently lose assignments through timed-out settings or other errors. While leniency for the rare problem is appropriately merciful, lost work is still the student's responsibility. Teachers can't grade what they don't have. If students lose their work and therefore don't turn it in, teachers should have an applicable policy.

> Students are responsible for keeping their own copies of their work, including work posted to the LMS. Teachers do not have access to student passwords. If students store work in password-protected area like a cloud folder, students should have multiple copies of their username and password so they can look it up if they forget the information. Before posting an assignment to learning management system:
>
> 1. File hardcopy work in a safe place.
> 2. Store electronic copies in a dedicated folder. Label each file with the student name, class, assignment, and date: "John Smith-Latin-1-Essay 3-Autumn 2020." Label each folder with the class name: "Johns Pre-Algebra HW."

If the student is not turning in the work because they didn't do it, teachers can use some nudges. By establishing protocols for students who want exceptions to the rules, teachers can document the exceptions and patterns of behavior. Good protocols put most of the responsibility on the student to take action, rather than the teacher. This documentation is particularly helpful when parents protest a child's grade—they've received a notice about every missing assignment and therefore cannot claim ignorance of the situation. Documentation is also of use when teachers reach out to administration about students who are not participating in the class.

- *Every late assignment gets a weekly form email home* to the parent or guardian, whether an alternative due date has been discussed or not. Even if a student and a teacher agree that the student can turn in something late, they and their parent will get that email. That ensures that everyone is one the same page. Better too much communication than too little. Three assignments that week? Three emails.
- *Every request for late work permission must come to the teacher via email.* If a student says in a synchronous class session, "Oh, I'm going to Disney World next week, and I'm not going to be here," the teacher

should respond with, "Have fun on your trip! Thanks for letting me know in advance. Drop me an email and remind me, please, so I will know to take your late work." When the teacher receives that email, they should always confirm by CCing the parent with an upbeat, "Great, thanks for letting me know!" With this procedure, the student, parents, and teachers are clear on what is happening, when, and why.

- *Every time a student turns in work that's more than two weeks late, they must write the teacher an email and let the teacher know that they turned in a specific assignment and want credit.* Two weeks is a good cut-off. Within that period, a teacher will probably want to go back, check for late work in the assignment drop box, and silently add it to the grade. After that time? Not without an explicit request via email, which a teacher may—or may not—grant based on past behavior patterns, prior written requests, and so on.

The Follow Through—What to Do When Students Don't Do the Work

Most parents are appreciative when a teacher sends them a form email about a missing assignment. Typically, they'll have the student turn in the assignment immediately. Therefore, when a student who is normally good about getting their work in drops the ball, the email ensures the work slides into the LMS. Often the student doesn't respond but the work mysteriously shows up.

If a student has a repeated pattern of slightly late work (for example, turning it on Fridays instead of Thursdays), a teacher should use their best judgment. A teacher might let it slide, as the easiest thing to do is just to grade the work. If it's habitual, there is often a good reason for it. Maybe the parent in charge of overseeing the student's schoolwork has a long shift on Thursdays. Maybe the student has to watch their siblings on Thursdays. As long as the work gets in by my grading deadline on Saturday, I have better things to do than fuss about a twenty-four-hour difference. Tracking down the reason a student's work is routinely twenty-four hours late will require extra work with delicate handling that might not be worth the effort.

On the other hand, a normally diligent student might faithfully attend synchronous class sessions but suddenly stop turning in work for a couple of weeks. That is a sign to reach out to the parent. Especially in the ten- to fifteen-year-old age group, students can become overwhelmed by a concept and then be intimidated by asking for help. Then students perceive catching up in the class as a Sisyphean task.

Teachers should nip that cycle in the bud immediately, picking up the phone and calling the parent. "Good afternoon, I wonder if you have a moment. Sara is a great student, and she's showing up to the lectures, but I'm missing a good bit of work for her. Can I help?" Often, parents are either not aware of the issue or have forgotten to tell the teacher about a family crisis. Teachers can direct parents to resources for their student, like setting up one-to-one office hours to discuss tricky concepts, sharing tutoring information, or providing links to helpful videos and websites.

Every now and then, a student will disappear from a class. The LMS will show that they stopped logging in and have not turned in homework or attended a synchronous class session. This is when school administration needs to step in, contacting the parent and determining the issue. Sometimes there is a family crisis and the family needs a week or two of breathing room. Teachers can choose to waive these assignments for students, or with the school administration's consent, turn the class into a pass/fail or audit-style class. Often, the parent found a new education option for their child and forgot to withdraw the student from the class, in which case the administration handles the paperwork.

Working with Parents Who Push Back

Unfortunately, there is a perception of online classes as being easier than face-to-face classes. This accusation is often not without merit, and so every now and then parents push back on the amount of work in a rigorous online class. There are several appropriate responses, depending on the situation. A competent administration will welcome a BCC on emails with upset parents, so they are not surprised if a parent puts a call into the school.

Distracted Students

Teachers should begin by reviewing previous interactions with the student. If the student seems to be capable based on completed work, the teacher might say something like, "That sounds really frustrating. Unfortunately, your student is the only one having difficulty with this series of assignments. Is there something I can clarify? How long are they spending on the assignment?"

Some students tell their parents they're working on homework, but are in fact making videos or streaming videos unrelated to class assignments. Most LMSs track the time that a student spends in a given area, on each assignment, and for each question. A carefully selected screenshot of this data provides support for a compelling argument that perhaps the student needs to have their browser locked down or certain sites blocked until after the work is done.

Struggling Students

Some students struggle. When teachers check for understanding during the synchronous class session, some students are consistently wrong. Ideally, the teacher will have already pointed the student to extra resources. However, some parents push back because they feel that the work is too hard, and they want the teacher to lighten their child's load.

Helping every student succeed does not always mean lightening the load. Acknowledge the parent's frustration and offer support. Teachers might write something like, "I noticed that Tommy is working really hard in this class. Maybe there is a concept he's just not getting. Let's set a meeting time/date for us to go over these concepts and see what he's confused about. Here are three days and times when I'm available. Do any of these days work for you?"

In many courses of study, concepts scaffold on one another, and a student might have stumbled their way through a passing grade without a good understanding of a critical topic. That poor understanding is now blocking their current success. A teacher needs to sit down with the student, pick out the thread that has been hastily and poorly stitched, and work with the student to sew a firm foundation of understanding that helps them succeed. Often this will mean setting up regular weekly meetings, either individually or in small groups. This does not always mean exempting students from the work.

Students with Tech Issues

When a student is perfectly capable, and the work that is turned in is of high quality, tech issues might be to blame. Teachers can identify this by noting students who often show up a minute or two late to synchronous sessions because they're having trouble logging in. These students might leave a synchronous session without notice because their connection is poor. Alternatively, these students might howl with complaint because they wrote something, but it disappeared from the LMS and they don't understand why.

Their parents become immensely frustrated and push back on the assignments not because their child can't do them, but because the parent finds the hardware and software exasperating. A competent administration will have anticipated this issue and provided a section of the school website with explicit directions for how to turn in assignments, log into synchronous class sessions, and so on. Teachers should have explored this section of the website.

Parents who have difficulty with tech rarely know about this assistance, so teachers should point these parents and their students to the help. Teachers should gently volunteer the resources by writing something like: "Yes, that does seem difficult. You might find this video of how to upload a Word doc to be helpful." or "Here's a series of screenshots to lead you through the assignment uploading process."

Families in Distress

When parents push back because their families are stressed, school administration and teachers can work together to accommodate the families. One way that can happen is to require fewer assignments, but keep the standard for the work high. Teachers might permit parents to opt their child out of the online, written discussion questions or opt out of the synchronous class sessions.

Another alternative might be a change in the way the course is graded. Allowing students to take a class with a pass/fail grade can reduce stress for families. Something rarely used but often appreciated is allowing students to audit a course. When students audit a course, they complete all the assignments and attend all the synchronous class sessions, but administration keeps their name on a private list. At the end of the year, the student receives a certificate of attendance, rather than a grade. This way, if students need to miss assignments or class sessions, they can do so with less stress. Parents appreciate this because their student stays with the class and gains as much education as possible.

Monitoring Student Work

All of this depends on conscientious monitoring of student work. Fortunately, most LMS grade books are filled with useful features to help teachers in this task. One of the most useful features is the "Last Access" setting. Students aren't going to do the work if they're not going to log in regularly and find the work. Keep a weather eye on this data, and if a student hasn't logged in recently, reach out.

Don't spend hours chasing down missing work. Teachers should let students know what day of the week they grade the work for a class (I grade work every Saturday). To help ensure that all work is collected, teachers should add reviewing the grade book for late work to their weekly checklist. When teachers use an LMS, it will often flag all late work in the online grade book.

Remember that just because a student turned in late work doesn't mean that teacher must automatically attend to the assignment. Students can wait until the next grading day. Poor preparation on their part doesn't constitute an emergency on the teacher's part.

Using the LMS to Track Student Progress

In an LMS students see their grades by due date, and teachers see grades by assignment. An LMS will track when an assignment was turned in and automatically mark it late. After teachers grade the assignment, or the grade is posted automatically by the LMS, the grades usually are released to the students. Often, when students see that zero for a missing assignment, they go back and complete the work. Then, the LMS grade book marks it as needing to be graded, usually with some kind of sticker to draw a teacher's attention.

When teachers select outside websites or apps, they should ensure that student progress monitoring is clear, including tracking dates and times for work completion. Marking work as late is a basic function that should be included in any regularly used outside website or app. In addition, these external websites and apps should have an export data tool that allows teachers to download scores or other progress, usually in .csv format for importing into spreadsheet software.

Sometimes the LMS allows teachers to upload scores into the LMS directly from the .csv file. Once that data is integrated into the LMS, many LMSs allow teachers to sort the grade book by scores on an assignment and email students directly from the grade book, saving a lot of time.

Using a Spreadsheet with an LMS to Track Student Progress

Because teachers have gathered student data from the student information system before school started, they probably have a spreadsheet ready for adding student progress from outside websites or apps. This spreadsheet should have each student's identification number, name, class section, student email, guardian email, and assignment scores. In addition, the spreadsheet is an excellent place to track student attendance if teachers choose not to track it within the LMS. If it's cloud-based (Dropbox, Google Drive, etc.), teachers can pull the information up on their phones and send quick notes or voice messages even when they're away from their work computer.

Teachers can download the scores from the external website, sort them by student identification number, copy and paste them into their spreadsheet, and then hand-enter them by hand into the LMS. Although this seems tedious, the process is significantly faster than having students upload work, digitally mark the work, save the work, and then send the work back to students.

Using Only a Spreadsheet to Track Student Progress

Even if teachers do not have access to an LMS, and they are taking student work via email or Google Drive, a spreadsheet is a perfectly adequate student progress tracking method. Teachers can see at a glance who has been showing up to lecture through coded attendance. Note who showed up, who is always asynchronous, who was tardy, and who never showed up. Teachers can also easily see an individual student's grades, as well as calculate class averages on a given assignment.

Contacting Parents about Student Progress

In any case, teachers should update scores at least once a week, entering zeroes for missing work as necessary. If teachers have created a spreadsheet, they can then sort it by column, smallest to largest. Then teachers can copy email addresses for all the students who have not turned in work (and their parents), and paste the email addresses in the BCC field of their email software. Using the CC (carbon copy, sending an email to more than one person at a time while making it clear that the other person is getting a copy) and the BCC (blind carbon copy, sending a secret copy to another person) features are helpful. Remember not to CC students or parents for this particular email, as that would be a violation of Family Educational Rights and Privacy Act.

Once teachers have created that week's email list, they can copy and paste a form email for the missing work. Teachers might write something like the following sample, identifying the problem, the solution, ways in which support is offered to the student, alternatives for distraction or being online, and multiple ways to contact the teacher for support.

Stereotype threat is the lowered score that results when students are reminded that they belong to a group stereotyped as being bad at academics, like being a girl or being Black.[ccclxxv] Although an online teacher can't control a student's environment, the Aspen Institute writes that teachers can diminish the impact of stereotype threat by affirming that "the student is seen as competent and valued and by a focus on tasks as the basis for ongoing improvement, rather than as judgments of ability."[ccclxxvi] Notice the positive framing in the following email. There is no guilt tripping, no anger, no assumption of bad behavior or lack of ability, no calling out individual students. Instead, there is the expectation that students can and will complete the task.

Dear Parent,

Your student's quiz, due yesterday, has not yet been turned it in. If we have discussed alternative due dates, then those apply. I encourage you to remind your student to go ahead and turn this in.

In class, I go through all concepts in lecture and offer students time to ask questions. The classes are recorded for students to review. I also provide copies of the class slides and knowledge organizers for further reference.

Outside of class, I am willing to meet with students, to work through specific problems and concepts with one student at a time. The school also offers a tutoring service.

Extra practice is available through _____. Areas in which the student can use extra practice are found _____.

When a student is doing homework in _____, customized support is available, allowing students to see examples of problems and videos of teachers explaining problems, for nearly all homework problems.

Also, when working in _____, if students want personalized assistance from me on a particular problem, I am only a click away via the Contact Instructor button. I return most emailed questions on the same day.

When it comes to the revision of work in class, students can attempt each homework problem three times, allowing for mastery through practice. Also, students may print the homework assignments and work offline using their textbooks. Then students only need to be online long enough to type in the answers. This avoids the distraction of the internet.

Every problem students complete is checked, but I will also look over scratch work if uploaded to the LMS drop box. If students do this, I can then help them identify areas of need. I will also assign partial credit.

I hope this helps!

A variation on this email works well for students who have earned low grades on that week's assignments. My rule is to send an email when a student scores below a 70% on any assignment. Parents and students should never be surprised by a report card or progress report. Remember, most parents are too busy to log in and check their student's grades on a regular basis. They're expecting the teacher to handle their student's progress.

Having regular contact also means that parents will learn to wait before emailing the teacher, trusting that they'll be informed if their student did badly on a quiz. This reduces the number of emails in the teacher's inbox, and thus reduces the teacher's workload. The student knows that the teacher will be in contact with their parent, so the teacher doesn't need to lean into guilting the student to do better, because the parents will do that in the teacher's place.

Don't forget to email parents with occasional praise as well. A group email for a class that breaks the curve, a shout-out to a parent when their child goes beyond the standard on an assignment, asking permission to share a student's work on the school's social media feeds—these all help parents invest in their child's education while rewarding students for hard work.

Within the class or via email, respond to every student at least once a week. Give students specific, meaningful praise for doing well. This does not imply that one should praise a student for doing the bare minimum in meeting expectations. Instead, a teacher should notice when a student works hard or performs above expectations. If a teacher has many students, they might consider making themselves a roster and checking it off to ensure that every student is "seen" every week.

Random emails like "Best in class on last week's quiz!" can mean a great deal to a lonely student. Take the opportunity to shout out to a student during a synchronous class session with "Great answer, Maria! How did you know?" Using quiet praise for the quietest students on assignment feedback can be significant. For example, a teacher could ask, "Ever thought about being an engineer?"

Using Announcements in an LMS to Reinforce Policies

In a good LMS, teachers can reinforce individual policies and behaviors with pre-planned weekly announcements that are automatically posted in a class on a given date and automatically emailed to students and parents on that date. For example, the first announcement should always be the "welcome" email. Following this up with an explanation that the teacher will be lenient about deadlines as students learn to use the LMS reduces the number of panicky emails to which a teacher awakes.

Often, the next useful announcement will be links to directions on how to use the LMS, followed by an explanation of rubrics and how to find them. If teachers choose to use an outside website, they should write an announcement with systematic explanations for how to use it. In the first couple of weeks of class, technical issues abound, so an announcement with a series of steps and links for resolving common technical issues is helpful. Frequently, students have difficulty attending live sessions or panic about how to turn their assignment if the LMS is down, so the next week's announcement might be about the class policy for these issues.

Two or three weeks into class, students begin to notice that their discussion question work isn't making the grade, so now is a good time to review the examples for meaningful participation. As students get more comfortable, they become less formal, so it's appropriate to write the expectations for class communication as an announcement.

An announcement about study skills is useful as students begin to become concerned about their overall grade, usually six weeks or so into the semester. Likewise, the next announcement could be reviewing the grading breakdown and how to calculate one's own grade. When students become concerned, they should reach out for assistance, so make an announcement telling them how to do it and review the policies for contacting the teacher. If the school offers an autumn break or other regular days off, always write an announcement the week before, so students are aware of the schedule change.

Remind students how to turn in their work, reviewing policies for partial credit and file formatting. About a month in advance, remind students about deadlines (date and time) for turning in work and specify any differences for final exams. If attendance is marked in the classes (and it should be), write an announcement reviewing the attendance policy. The next week, review the class policy for when synchronous class students watch recordings instead of attending.

Make an announcement about the end of each grading term, with specific dates, and let students know when term or semester final grades will be available. Don't forget to let students know that the teacher will be unavailable over holiday breaks. My students know that as a rule, I am unavailable after 6 pm EST on Friday, and all day on Sunday. In addition, when school is closed, I rarely check my work email. Establishing clear availability boundaries helps teachers' mental health, staving off burnout.

As the winter holidays come around, take the time to reiterate the non-discrimination policy. A couple of weeks before final exams, review the class policy for content not covered in synchronous sessions, the academic honesty policy, and the plagiarism policy. Hopefully, teachers can copy and paste these from the school policy.

As the pressure of final exams begins to rise, make an announcement about learning exceptionalities and access issues, so that students can request accommodations in advance. Similarly, make an announcement about device use during synchronous sessions and the exam. Parents receive these emails as well, and when teachers request that students limit outside resources for exams, parents are often good about compliance. This includes calculator use, if applicable.

After students return from the mid-year break, teachers might wish to remind students about how to archive their work offline, out of the LMS. Now is a good time to make an announcement about the late work policy.

Often, new students show up at the mid-year, so teachers should write an announcement as a "welcome" to new students, with a list of previously covered topics and links to corresponding records, links to any recordings that teachers feel students must absolutely watch to catch up, directions on how to access the recordings, and any other relevant information. By sending this out to the class as a whole, current students are made aware that new students are joining them, something that is not always obvious in an online class. Without exception, my current students have been kind and welcoming to new students.

As students grind through the short, gray days of winter, a general malaise tends to fall over classrooms, online and offline. Now is a good time to write an encouraging announcement, giving praise for effort and manners. Acknowledge that this time of year can be difficult and inspire students to "just keep swimming." Review good study practices, and if possible, insert a cheerful picture.

In my experience, a lot of work tends to be done in this stretch of the school year, so announcements with specific resources about the content are often welcomed. Teachers can write announcements about teacher-created materials in the course module, for example.

Prepare for spring break and the end-of-year schedule well in advance by anticipating student and parent questions with an announcement that lists the dates for spring break, any other days off, the last days of school, and the final exam schedule, if applicable. Refer to late policies and exceptions.

Students often have stress about making it through the last quarter of class, so write an announcement that discusses resources for assistance, including asking questions during synchronous sessions, office hours availability, hints and examples for content within the LMS, reminders for students to email the teacher, any study resources, how to improve their scores, and how to obtain partial credit.

 Announcing deadlines, reviewing policies, and writing about other classroom administration issues helps reduce teacher workload by reducing the number of emails from students.

Chapter Summary

- Become an email power user.
- Offer multiple points of contact, but set boundaries about availability.
- Know that students are distracted, so set boundaries about late work.
- Don't take it personally. Always stay calm.
- Publish to-do lists, daily calendars, and repetitive assignments well in advance.
- Don't make heavy use of the internet; offer alternatives to print for students who need it.
- Don't let students off the hook for late work.
- Promptly inform the responsible individuals when students have missing work, poor-quality work, or great work.
- Create an expectation that students should ask permission to turn in work late.
- Meticulously track student work and respond as appropriate.
- Be flexible with families under stress, but keep standards high.
- Use the announcements feature in an LMS to remind students of expectations, policies, and deadlines.

CHAPTER 10

WORKING WITH PARENTS (OR THEIR DESIGNEES)

Although many face-to-face teachers justifiably pride themselves on handling all issues within the boundaries of their classroom, there is no physical classroom when teaching online. Instead, teachers must adjust to working with students who are supervised by their parents, guardians, older siblings, neighbors, grandparents, aunts, uncles, cousins, babysitters, child center care workers, etc. A teacher's job is to teach, and the job of these responsible individuals is to ensure health and safety. The tension between these two goals can be a difficult adjustment in an online class. In this chapter, I attempt to discuss some common issues around working with parents and offer some solutions.

Older students, usually age twelve and up, are often not directly supervised. For example, I've had students who took a bus downtown and used the free Wi-Fi at the mall to attend class. Other students popped in between rehearsals or participated after professional sports practice. Ensuring that their work is done means striking a delicate balance between the teacher, the student, and an adult who may not be closely supervising the student. Often, students may be supervised by a third party. In that case, teachers might consider CCing that person as well as the parent or guardian.

In my experience, many teachers are dubious, at best, about working with parents. In a 2018 EdChoice survey, only 36% of teachers said they trusted parents.[ccclxxvii] That attitude is self-defeating when teaching online because teachers will interact with the student's in-person supervisor far more than in a face-to-face setting. Teachers must place trust in these individuals while they do their schoolwork. There is no other functional option.

For example, a common issue is when a student fails to turn in work. In that case, a teacher might write an email like the following and send it to the student, the parent or guardian, and the person who is actually supervising the student. That third party could be a teacher's aide, a private tutor, or the older sibling.

> Dear Parent,
>
> Your student's quiz, due yesterday, has not yet been turned it in. If we have discussed alternative due dates, then those apply. I encourage you to remind your student to go ahead and turn this in.

In class, I go through all concepts in lecture and offer students time to ask questions. The classes are recorded for students to review. I also provide copies of the class slides, and knowledge organizers for further reference.

Outside of class, I am willing to meet with students, to work through specific problems and concepts with one student at a time. The school also offers a tutoring service.

Extra practice is available through _____. Areas in which the student can use extra practice are found _____.

When a student is doing homework in _____, customized support is available, allowing students to see examples of problems and videos of teachers explaining problems, for nearly all homework problems.

Also, when working in _____, if students want personalized assistance from me on a particular problem, I am only a click away via the Contact Instructor button. I return most emailed questions on the same day.

When it comes to the revision of work in class, students can attempt each homework problem three times, allowing for mastery through practice. Also, students may print the homework assignments and work offline using their textbooks. Then, students only need to be online long enough to type in the answers. This avoids the distraction of the internet.

Every problem students complete is checked, but I will also look over scratch work if uploaded to the LMS drop box. If students do this, I can then help them identify areas of need. I will also assign partial credit.

I hope this helps!

In addition, teachers should assume the best of these responsible individuals, whether they are older siblings, grandparents, or the parents themselves. They may not always agree with teachers, and they may not follow through with a teacher's request, but most of these people will give teachers the courtesy of listening to the request. In return, teachers should use their power wisely by reserving contact for priority issues and treating them with respect and kindness.

Create a Good Working Relationship

Online teachers need to create a good working relationship with the people who supervise students. This begins in the planning stages, when teachers create a pacing schedule for the course and display it in the syllabus. This allows the student's supervisor to better plan their schedules. When sending the initial welcome email, remember to explain how and when you'll contact parents. My default is to email them, so that's how I initially contact them.

Dear Parents and Students,

Welcome to World Geography! Our first meeting will be Friday, August 14, at 11 am Eastern Daylight Time in the Classroom & Recordings link on the left-hand side of the class.

Keep in mind that students will need to be able to stream video to participate in the class, using a computer or tablet. Our LMS is _____. In this class, students will need Goode's World Atlas, 23rd edition. Please contact me if your student will not have a copy before class begins.

A little bit about me: I have been teaching online since 1999, including college algebra from 2006 to 2013. I enjoy teaching so much that I went back to school to earn a second master's degree in secondary education. Now, I am certified to teach social studies, general science, and math in grades five through adult, and students with visual impairments from birth to adulthood. In my spare time, I enjoy reading, photography, cooking, and sewing. I live in wild, wonderful West Virginia with my husband, our two children, and my mother. Our menagerie currently consists of a leopard gecko, a betta fish, a veiled chameleon, a big old dog, two mice, chickens, and assorted cats.

The best way I can teach you is to learn about you, because the more I know about you, the better I can help you learn. This is more difficult online, because I can't see your face. So please complete the New Student Survey by Friday, August 14. If you have a special education need, let me know so that I may accommodate you.

Because this class is online, almost all I can see is your written words. As a result, your written words are very important. One way to guarantee your success in this, or any other class, is to work on your writing skills. While it's tempting to write angry words, I expect each student to behave with good manners. In addition, the more effective your written words are, the better your assignment grades will be! My goal is for you to succeed, so if you have questions or concerns, please let me know.

Keep in mind that this is your class. You and the rest of your class will learn the material from through reading, discussion, problem solving, and lecture. However, that does not mean I will not answer questions. Questions are good! They mean that you are reading and thinking about the material, which is the best way to learn anything.

To recap, the way to do your best in this class is to:

- work on your writing
- participate
- follow the rules
- ask questions

Do these four things and this class be will great!

Mrs. Courtney Ostaff, Instructor

School Name

School Email, School Phone

Office Hours Available by Appointment

When teachers choose the limited, repetitive assignments they're going to use in their classes, they need to select items that secondary students can complete as independently as possible, reducing the burden on the supervisor. Frequently, parents will reach out to advocate for their child, who may or may not have an individualized educational plan or 504 plan. My standard email response often looks like this:

Good evening,

It's great to hear from you! I'm always happy to have good communication with parents! I'll keep an eye out for that 504 plan—and in the meantime, I'm happy to work with you on an individualized plan to make _____ successful in the course.

One of the joys of online classes is the ability to be flexible, and I'm always happy to accommodate families. Thanks for giving me a heads up!

If there is anything I can do, please let me know!

Parents might worry about specific learning disabilities, such as dyslexia. Notice that I'm taking the parent's concerns seriously. In addition, I'm requiring peers to adjust their behavior as well. Also note that the email asks the parent to reach out with any later issues.

> Good afternoon,
>
> Thanks for the heads up! I'll remind everyone that this is not a writing class, and we're not judging people on the basis of their writing. :) The Discussion Questions are meant to be small assignments, not stressful, and I offer a video option nearly every week. I know that dyslexia often has associated issues that make math difficult, so if any of those pop up (tears with homework, for example), let me know, and we can adjust accordingly.
>
> I'm always open to feedback, so please feel free to reach out often!

According to a recent study discussed in EdWeek, about 61% of teachers are white women with college degrees; according to the *Washington Post*, fewer than half of public school students are white.[ccclxxviii] Pew reports that in the United States in 2019, 93% of college graduates had broadband access at home.[ccclxxix] Teachers often assume that students have practically unlimited internet access, but that same Pew study reported that only 66% of Black adults and 61% of Hispanic adults had broadband at home. Responsible individuals have often dug deep to make sure the student is available, has a device, and has internet access. Creating a good functioning relationship with responsible individuals means having respect for the effort they put in to help students work online.

Sometimes, parents will reach out and ask for exemptions from internet-intensive activities. A teacher should use their best judgment when replying. In this hypothetical case, a parent is having difficulty with arranging for their child to attend the initial orientation session and is worried about their child doing well in the class.

> Good evening,
>
> Thanks for checking in. The orientation will be recorded. It's optional to attend, but I strongly recommend that he watch it (and if you have time, you're more than welcome to watch it with him.) I review the class rules and expectations, as well as the year's schedule, so that we hit the ground running on the 19th.

Likewise, the student survey is optional. It's just a way for me to get to know my students better, as I have less nonverbal information than I would in a classroom setting. All of the information is kept confidential. Students change courses through the first week of class, so I typically don't actually settle down to read the responses until after the first week, so it's not problematic if he does it later.

Saxon Alg. I is a strong program—it is the only commercially available direct instruction program available in the United States, and it uses modern cognitive science applications like interleaved, interval-spaced retrieval practice. I have every expectation that he'll do well.

I hope that helps!

Avoid the curse of expertise by simplifying what is expected of responsible individuals. Use an LMS to create a single, central portal for all classes students are taking, with a central calendar so that all students and responsible individuals in the school can easily see what is due and when for all classes at once. Don't use outside websites and videos unless they're essential to the course. Make life easier for the students and their responsible individuals by ensuring the central portal has an app or is otherwise optimized for mobile access. Don't ask them to navigate a half-dozen websites with separate passwords and calendars—that expectation is disrespectful of their time and effort.

Most people have a daily routine. Teachers can leverage that routine to help students get schoolwork done by creating an assignment calendar. Always post the calendar on the front of each content module. Assignments with known times and performance standards help students incorporate the work into their daily routine. The content module calendar should include both a weekly list and a daily calendar, because schedules vary. For some, it's easier to check off a list, while others appreciate the day-by-day planning. Of course, this should all be pushed out to the single, central LMS calendar, so that students and responsible adults can plan for more than one class at a time.

For example, one of the more common emails at the beginning of the semester is about traveling. Many families plan to travel in August, or at the winter holidays. My standard email often looks like this:

Good afternoon,

It's lovely to hear from you! One of the joys of online classes is flexibility, and I'm happy to work with parents to adapt the schedule as much as possible.

The first hands-on activity is a fun one, and I hope that y'all get a chance to run through it. Just in case family circumstances do not permit it, I always post a video of the demonstration in the "Useful Video" section of that week's Assignments folder, usually accessible via YouTube.

Here is a materials list for the first month:

- Week 1 items
- Week 2 items
- Week 3 items
- Week 4 items
- Week 5 items

I hope that helps!

If a teacher absolutely must use an outside website or app, be prepared to justify that decision to responsible individuals or administrators who are unhappy with the decision. Teachers should be prepared by writing a Frequently Asked Questions about the resource, explaining their reasoning and explaining how the resource is beneficial to students and families.

Don't imagine that the responsible individuals will explain anything to secondary students. That's the teacher's job. Instead, create work written to the student. Students should be able to understand the knowledge, skills, or abilities independently, without assistance from the responsible adult. Asking the responsible individuals to teach a concept to the student is an unreasonable expectation.

For younger students, respect the time of the responsible individual by providing them with scripted curriculum that strips down the task to the bare minimum. A good rule of thumb is no more than fifteen total minutes of seatwork per year of age through third grade. For example, an eight-year-old should be doing no more than two hours a day of focused, seated academics.

Don't ask the responsible individual to spend any time or effort coming up with how to teach—only a third of responsible individuals routinely check their K-8 child's homework.[ccclxxx] Instead, provide the responsible individuals with the exact words to say and the responses for which they're looking—a script. In my experience, most responsible individuals will use scripted lessons. There is a reason why Saxon math and *Teach Your Child to Read in 100 Easy Lessons* have been bestsellers for decades.

Responsible individuals should have a *Parent Observer* account in the LMS. These are limited accounts that allow responsible individuals to see a list of assignments and the student's submissions, scores, course progression, teacher contact, and so on.

Recall that online teachers do not control the student's home environment. I've had students attend synchronous classes from their empty shower, because the bathroom was the only room in the motor home that had a locking door for privacy. Make life easier for the responsible individuals by not insisting that students show up on camera—frequently there are screaming babies, loud music, and other distractions that the student and the responsible individuals cannot control. Sometimes students attend from hospital beds. Asking these students to be on camera is a violation of their HIPAA privacy rights. Instead of making demands that the responsible individuals cannot meet, be grateful that students showed up by any means.

Synchronous class sessions should teach students how to do the task, but teachers should never assign work during the synchronous session to be completed later. Instead, that work should have been posted weeks ago so responsible individuals can make plans for the student to have access to devices and internet access with which to complete work. If a teacher assigns work during a live session and makes it due soon, the responsible individual has now been subjected to just-in-time scheduling, one of the most despised modern labor practices.[ccclxxxi] Throwing chaos into a family's evening plans does not help create a good working relationship with the responsible individual.

Assume that the responsible adult is watching all videos and synchronous class sessions. It's not uncommon for my synchronous classes to be casted to the living room television, where the whole family to watches and learns. Friends, family, and neighbors often sit in on synchronous classes. There is no classroom door and relative privacy—teachers may direct their words to the student, but the whole community is watching. Don't be upset about this. Instead, welcome Cousin Ava to the synchronous class every week. The more, the merrier!

Make Reasonable Requests

Welcome the responsible individual to the class at the beginning of the school year and ask for their updated contact information in the teacher's New Student Survey. Frequently, the school's student information system is out of date or only has contact information for legal guardians. Online teachers need contact information for the responsible individual, not just the legal guardian.

Most responsible individuals read their email. They're under no obligation to reply to teachers, but 81% of US adults own a smartphone and therefore have easy access to their email.[ccclxxxii] Remember that the quality of internet access is highly variable for responsible individuals. Use text-only emails. Avoid pretty fonts or unnecessary pictures or attachments because the odds are good that a lot of smartphone email apps won't read them correctly. Use the subject heading wisely. My standard subject header is *School Name - Class Name – Week # - Assignment Name.*

Likewise, most responsible individuals will hand students a piece of paper. According to a market research survey in 2007, 84% of households owned a printer.[ccclxxxiii] That's a somewhat higher percentage than other research suggests, but it's safe to say that many responsible adults are capable of printing out documents for students. However, printing is an expensive request and should not be a required task. Teachers in public schools might consider surveying responsible individuals about their willingness to print work and mailing copies for those who cannot print.

According to Common Sense Media, the average eight- to twelve-year-old spends almost five hours a day watching a screen outside of schoolwork, and teenagers average almost seven and a half hours.[ccclxxxiv] Therefore, it is a realistic request to ask a responsible individual to set their child in front of a short video. Because some students

> Do not assume that responsible individuals are tracking the student's progress. Email, call, or text about missing assignments, poor grades, etc.

do not have internet access at home, teachers shouldn't require all students to watch many videos but strongly encouraging students to watch the video is practical.

Nearly all parents (97%, according to the National Center for Education Statistics) support literacy activities, and in fact, most parents (81%) read to their children.[ccclxxxv] Textbooks are a great resource that responsible individuals will almost certainly help teachers use. Ensuring that book reading actually happens will vary, and teachers must consistently apply consequences for undone work, but asking the responsible individual to make the initial push is a reasonable expectation.

Likewise, 95% of responsible individuals will check to ensure that an elementary (K-8) student's work is done, although that drops to 65% of responsible individuals for grades nine to twelve.[ccclxxxvi] Therefore, most responsible individuals understand that children have work to do, although again, follow through varies. Don't expect the responsible individual to figure out how to turn it in online, though. If teachers instruct students how to do it, students as young as ten can upload work themselves.

Parent Communication Strategies

Things that are the same online include report cards—yes, I do them. But they are not printed pieces of paper. Instead, they're another column in the grade book in the LMS. Teachers can write the current grade in the textbooks, along with a summary of student strength and weaknesses in that quarter, as well as expectations for the upcoming term. Teachers should send a note to parents letting them know when the report cards or progress reports are ready to view.

Along those lines, most online teachers do not send pieces of work home, because the work is already online for parents to view as needed in parent observer accounts. Alternatively, parents can log in with their student's username and password. In my experience, parents rarely do this, assuming that teachers will let them know if something needs their attention. In turn, teachers should try to honor this trust by reaching out via email within seven days if a student's work is an issue. Remember, teachers can reach out with praise too.

Phone calls are used both offline and online. Because online teachers work much more closely with parents or their designees, online teachers tend to call more frequently about issues that can't be handled via email. Occasionally, teachers may choose to conference with a parent in the synchronous classroom. However, the school at which I work does not have parent-teacher conferences. Instead, we meet on an as-needed basis with parents. My general rule is to offer times spread across three days at different times—one in the morning, one in the afternoon, and one in the evening. Most of the time, one of those options will work for a meeting. Afterwards, write up what was said and email the summary to all the participants. Often, these notes come in handy when communication issues arise.

Because good online teachers maintain frequent contact with parents, and because teachers will have clarity of assignments within content modules, newsletters home to parents are redundant. Parents have a copy of the syllabus to let them know what the class is doing and when it happens. If teachers feel something is urgent and they need to share it with all parents, they can send an email from the LMS.

Maintaining and projecting warmth via email is an intentional mode that online teachers need to practice to perfect. If this seems intimidating, Understood has an excellent handout on writing emails to parents titled, "Anatomy of an Effective Email to Parents and Caregivers." It's available on their website in the Partnering with Families section.

Because our student population is international—I have students from Alaska to Abu Dhabi to Australia—we do not have a parent-teacher organization or local school improvement council. Similarly, we don't make home visits, publish items in local newspapers, or have grandparent days. But online teachers can ask parents for permission to showcase their child's excellent work on the school's social media sites. In addition, teachers should assume that the whole household is watching synchronous class sessions, because they often are. Siblings, cousins, and grandparents often sit in on classes.

Chapter Summary

- Create a good working relationship by being respectful of time and effort.
- Make reasonable requests by limiting expectations.

CHAPTER 11

CONDUCTING A SYNCHRONOUS CLASS

When planning a synchronous instructional session, teachers should carefully design a scripted lesson with a set opening routine, an activation of prior knowledge that leads naturally to an explanation, a model, a demonstration with checks for understanding, guided practice, and a closing routine followed by independent practice supported by content module assignments. In this chapter, I review how this works in practice, step by step.

> Teachers should carefully design a scripted lesson with a set opening routine, an activation of prior knowledge that leads naturally to an explanation, a model, a demonstration with checks for understanding, guided practice, and a closing routine followed by independent practice in content module assignments.

First, don't hide the content, or feel that you need to make learning fun like the way parents sometimes hide spinach in spaghetti sauce. Bring enthusiasm to the lesson, instead. Research supports this: instructor-directed online learning has a greater effect on student learning (+0.39) than collaborative instruction (+0.25) or independent work (+0.05).[ccclxxxvii]

The Big 3 learning management system (LMS) providers provide breakout rooms for small group work within a class—but teachers might look into separating a larger class into smaller sections, and setting up synchronous class schedule for each section instead. If teachers do want to switch it up and use breakout groups, each group member should have a clearly defined, rehearsed role. The teacher must have a way to confirm that the group members performed the work, possibly through a summary activity.

Teacher Affect Matters

One critical part of good synchronous sessions is that my personal affect is *the same every day*. I am always cheerful, upbeat, and positive. I've taught classes when I was up all night with a sick child, the same day my child had surgery, and when my husband called to tell me that he'd lost his job. These are not my students' problems. Part of being a professional is the ability to compartmentalize emotions,

KEEP CALM AND TEACH ON

packing them away to present a warm, supportive aspect to students. Even when I can't quite manage—when I have the flu or bronchitis—I'll be upfront with students and apologize that I can't give them my best that day.

The other side of this coin is that because students are children, they can be emotional or have stress that seems less troubling to adults. Take them seriously, and stay composed. By keeping calm, the teacher provides students with a safe harbor from their anxiety or frustration. Teachers become trustworthy people, becoming those to whom students can safely confess, "Mrs. Ostaff, I don't understand this." This is vitally important for good teaching, because teachers need to know when students don't understand. Be worthy of that confession by offering reassurance and a plan to fix it. "It's okay. You'll get there. Now, here's how we're going to do this."

Never take student criticism personally. Especially online, students tend to be harsher than they would face to face, even more so than adults. Don't let yourself snap at students. Instead, establish a routine to get the class back on track when a student disrupts it with rudeness.

In my classes, I establish the routine at orientation when I share the results of the previous year's *"How's It Going?"* survey. Every year, the survey results indicate the most-hated part of an online class is off-topic chatting. Despite this, students rarely say anything when it happens. By sharing this information, I can quickly shut down students who derail the discussion. All I have to do is ask, "Students, what is the most disliked part of an online class?" The suspicion that peers are sitting there silently seething is enough to get all but the most adversarial student back on track. Those students can be muted or booted by the teacher, and the teacher should follow up with them later.

How to Prepare

- Use the guided notes to form an outline of the material to cover in the session.
- Create each slide. One slide should cover one idea, or vocabulary word, and serve as the basis for a flashcard. *Canva* and *The Noun Project* are good resources for visual aids.
- Write extensive notes for each slide. These notes can serve as a transcript for students.
- Collect student questions from email and create slides as needed to answer the questions.
- Create slides to cover any upcoming assignments.
- Write a "hook" for the first slide in the notes. Good hooks are often stories or questions.

- Double check that every slide has some kind of check for understanding—polls, chat box questions, audible questions and answers, problems to be completed, etc.
- Where appropriate, ensure that guided practice is included in the slide deck.
- Make sure to include a review slide and include a call for questions at the end of the session.
- Save the slides as a PDF and post them to the weekly course module.

Some teachers are good enough to wing it with deep content knowledge and charisma, but the rest of us to work hard to create a good lesson, especially online. I typically spend three to five hours per week, per class, preparing slides for one or two fifty-minute synchronous sessions. Each procedural emphasis lesson takes about twenty-five minutes in a synchronous session. Fortunately, good teaching is good teaching, online or offline. The same principles apply when creating a lesson to deliver in a face-to-face class or in a synchronous session, with a few twists.

By the time a teacher is ready to prepare a synchronous lesson, they will have already selected a curriculum, determined the applicable standards, figured out the three to five learning objectives for the weekly content module, and designed the assignments for the content module. At this point, the teacher should be quite familiar with the concepts for the lesson, including the specific independent practice and all the variations of the problem expected in the independent practice.

 The slide deck is the last part of the content module to be prepared.

When creating a slide deck, make sure it is carefully timed with extensive supporting notes. This is an excellent time to include references to other assignments, including selected quotes from the online, written discussion board. Teachers want to make sure that students know teachers are paying attention to their work.

Here is the class schedule for the synchronous class session of the fourth week of my middle school ancient history class. I wrote these times in my notes for each slide, so that I could check myself as I went along. Staying on track when teaching online can be tricky, because teachers should demand students participate at least once every three minutes and change slides every five to ten minutes.

- 9:50: I open the class for students to chat among themselves.
- 10:00: I begin the recording, welcoming students and taking roll.
- 10:02: I take student questions.

- 10:07: I begin new content with *Written History*.
- 10:10: Sumer and Egypt.
- 10:15: How do we count?
- 10:20: Transaction records.
- 10:25: How do we get from pictures of things to pictures for words to pictures for sounds?
- 10:37: Cuneiform.
- 10:42: Hieratic script.
- 10:45: Loan symbols.
- 10:47: New slide, review of key concepts from lecture, praise for good behavior/effort.
- 10:50: New slide, review of directions for upcoming assignment .

Set an Opening Routine

Good online teaching provides opportunities for students to bond as a class. One easy way to do this online is to show up to class ten to fifteen minutes early to allow students to chat before a synchronous class starts. Always keep a weather eye on the chat to head off any problems before they develop, but don't interfere unless it's necessary. This is a good time to check email in another window, prepare any last-minute announcements, or quickly review the content for the synchronous session.

Now is the time to load the slide deck. The first slide should always have the class title, teacher name, the scheduled class (WK ___, Day 1), and the subject of the day's synchronous session. It doesn't hurt to put the school's logo. The recordings might be passed around, and teachers want to be clear what's happening on the video.

If teachers want students to take showing up to class on time seriously, teachers must take it seriously. My classes always begin on the top of the hour, so at the fifty-nine-minute mark, I un-mute myself and turn on my webcam and the recording. I smile and wave, and then turn off my video to save bandwidth. In my morning classes, I often sing "good morning" *Singing in the Rain* style instead of waving. To wake them up in the afternoon, I have fun imitating Robin Williams in *Good Morning, Vietnam*. "Good afternoon, Algebra I!"

Then I follow up my greeting by taking attendance. This might seem odd when most LMSs offer an automated attendance checker, but in my experience, the automated attendance checking is not very reliable. In addition, this gives students thirty seconds or so to get themselves together and forces them to attend to my voice from the beginning of the session. By the second or third class, they know better than to trickle in after the recording has started. Teachers can't expect all the students to always show up, given the difficulty of getting online, and that's okay. A total of 80% to 90% attendance is a good goal.

Synchronous class sessions do not need students to turn on their cameras—and for privacy concerns and bandwidth concerns, I do not require it. Remember, synchronous sessions do not always equal videoconferencing. Telephones exist, and students can dial into online synchronous sessions. This is a frequent hack for my students with poor connections: they log into the synchronous session, mute themselves, watch the live video, and listen via telephone.

When teachers create an emphasis on attendance, students know that their presence is expected. I deliberately list all the students who are not present—no one is overlooked—and wish them well. Usually students let me know ahead of time, so I might say something like, "Everybody wish John good luck at his hockey game!" Asynchronous students get a shout-out as well, because they are vital members of the class community.

Because I teach two sections of most classes—the first section meets on Monday/Wednesday and the second section meets on Tuesday/Thursday—I repeat Monday's lessons on Tuesday and Wednesday's lessons on Thursday. At the Well-Trained Mind Academy, students are assigned to a section, or they are "delayed," meaning that they participate in the class but don't attend the synchronous sessions. As part of my goal to make life easier for families, I do not care which section students attend. If students want to attend on Monday and Thursday, or Tuesday and Wednesday, that schedule is fine by me. Similarly, if my delayed Australian students want to wake up in the middle of the night and attend a synchronous session, they are welcome. Life is too short to be cranky about students swapping back and forth.

Finally, I wrap up the introductory ritual with an acknowledgment of the late students, sleepy students, traveling students, and delayed students who are watching the recording. This helps remind students that they can go back and watch the recording as they need. Students who missed class are implicitly expected to watch the recording and see their greeting.

Note that this routine is relentlessly upbeat and positive. No one is shamed for missing class. The default assumption is that students would be there if they could have managed it. If my attendance sheet shows that a student is regularly missing class, I might circle the date to remind myself to drop a note to the parent after class.

Next, I take questions. Up until this point, students have been mostly quiet, perhaps greeting each other in the text chat while I take roll. By the second month of class, most students know to save questions for this moment, and have typed them out so that they can just hit enter and post them in the text chat. Typically, these questions are either administrative or content related. Administrative questions might be about difficulties uploading an assignment or confusion about the directions for an upcoming assignment. Content questions are great, because they segue into the next part of the class.

Usually I will spend five to ten minutes reviewing questions that students had about the assignment from the previous day or week. Because the LMS offers question analysis, I frequently review the most-missed questions on Friday's assessment. Students are encouraged to email me directly, send me an anonymous question from the computer-adaptive software, or take screenshots that they can upload in the synchronous class session. Even if students answered the question correctly but are still confused about the concept, I'm happy to explain it. I encourage this by labeling the questions as gifts. "Did anyone bring me any presents today?!"

Never discourage students from asking questions. One way I push students is to tell them an old saw I heard about a car sales clerk. While probably apocryphal, the idea that only one customer buys a car for every twenty that walks away translates into the notion that if one person in a twenty-student class has a question, the other nineteen probably also have that question. I make it clear that by asking an on-topic question, a student is helping others and being a good classmate. This is strong incentive for most students.

Set an introductory routine by:

- showing up early
- loading the prepared slide deck
- starting the recording
- greeting students
- taking roll
- noting missing students
- taking administrative questions
- reviewing questions

Conducting the Lesson

Experienced teachers know that they will often need to review background knowledge before introducing a new learning objective, and this is my favorite way to begin a lesson. Review can take several different forms, all leading into the new topic of the day's lesson.

- A teacher could freehand sketch a concept map of previous lessons on a blank slide, prompting students for the appropriate key words as the diagram is completed. "What are the two classes of bony fish?" At the end, an obvious blank spot could prompt, "See this? This is what we're going to discuss today." Explicitly mapping how knowledge is related is valuable, especially for younger students.
- A teacher could start with a brief story with supporting images on a slide. Even my high school students enjoy a story time about something they already know that leads naturally into the day's topic. For example, I often begin discussion of the Cartesian plane (coordinate system) with a brief biographical sketch of René Descartes, beginning with his life as a precocious, sickly college student, his original career as a mercenary, and then his decision to opt for a life of the mind, writing *La Géométrie* and creating the idea of analytical geometry: "which is why this is called a Cartesian plane!"
- A teacher could begin with a posted problem—"Remember this?"— and take a whole-class poll on multiple-choice answers shown underneath the problem. The problem should be easier, because students should have mastered it earlier. In addition, the problem should be essential to the day's topic—it's not so much retrieval practice as it is prior knowledge. Ideally, each wrong answer will be just slightly wrong. Teachers can move down the list of answers and require students to identify why the wrong answers are incorrect. This style of opener has the advantage of settling down an unruly class to focus on the content. In addition, when teachers have quite a bit to cover and limited time to do it in, the straightforward approach saves time. "Now, we're going to take this and add a little twist."

When students are on-topic and have had their background knowledge refreshed, the teacher is in a good place to trot out the learning objective on a separate slide. "Today, we are going to *verb noun*." The verb should be explicit, specific, and measurable. For example:

- "Today, we are going to *add fractions*."
- "Today, we are going to *list and describe the stages of meiosis*."
- "Today, we are going to *compose a thesis sentence*."
- "Today, we are going to *identify and describe steps in the development of written language*."
- "Today, we are going to *read a story and use supporting evidence to identify a theme*."

Notice how often the nouns lend themselves to key vocabulary for adding to the memory work. Because students will ask, teachers need to have a clear definition for each of the verbs. What does compose mean? How does one identify something? The specificity lends itself to clear expectations. Either the fraction was added correctly or it was not. Either all the stages of meiosis were listed or they were not. Each objective should be measurable. According to Barak Rosenshine, "the optimal success rate for fostering student achievement appears to be about 80 percent."[ccclxxxviii] A student should be able to successfully read a short story and identify a theme at least eight out of ten times.

Now that students are all clear on the topic of the day, teachers can begin with the presentation of new material. Different class goals lend themselves to different ways of presenting new materials. Having clarity on the type of class affects how teachers approach most lesson presentations. In Chapter 2, I listed three common class types.

survey course—skims over major content areas; requires intense vocabulary study

- western history from 1500 to present; fifth-grade biology

Survey courses require that teachers identify major themes in the area under study so students have a framework with which to understand the learning objective. For example, in middle school biology courses, often a quarter of the school year is given over to human body systems. Within that theme, teachers can trace components of the knowledge (traditionally, eleven major organ systems), and then subdivide each of those into their constituent parts. The integumentary system can be further divided into the skin, hair, nails, and sometimes glands.

The problem sets therefore consist of identifying each level of the division and being able to describe how those parts are related. For instance, the skin contains blood vessels, which are traditionally part of the circulatory system.

This type of course requires significant investment in vocabulary study. Ideally, teachers will have created a set of guided notes from the textbook or booklet. Students will then have completed the notes and defined the terms using their text. During the synchronous lesson, teachers review the terms and discuss them with students. Freehand sketching a concept map at the beginning of the lesson and calling on students to fill the diagram helps make sure that students can understand the words out of the framework of their text and gives them practice in using the words. In addition, the key vocabulary should be discussed in the optional videos and in the written discussion board. Quizzes should include retrieval practice for key vocabulary, using interleaved, interval-spaced practice.

In a survey course, a teacher might begin by reviewing the theme in a concept map, noting the missing pieces, and then listing and defining each new piece. Online, each defined term should have its own slide, with a short, clear definition in a high-contrast color scheme, preferably with a visual example. Teachers should not *just* read the slides, but they should read the slides for students with visual impairments, dyslexia, and other special education needs.

When teaching these lessons, teachers should be prepared with extensive research about the terms and concepts, centering ideas within a wide, scripted set of background knowledge. Another way to think of this is practicing zooming deep into a body of knowledge and then zooming out of the body of the knowledge to the larger picture. This is where lesson flexibility comes into play.

If students have more knowledge than expected, teachers can go deeper because they've researched the topic. If students have less knowledge than expected, teachers can spend more time breaking the concept down by inserting blank slides, freehand drawing connections between topics, and redefining difficult terms. In order to do this well, teachers must have prepared more notes than they'll need for each slide.

Teachers often model how they organize the concepts, and check for understanding by providing students with blank organizers, asking students where each piece fits, and then requiring students to justify their decision. Teachers can freehand these on a blank slide or put the diagram they'd asked students to label in their skeleton notes on a slide. Now is a good time to review guided notes, as well.

Asking several students to create mnemonics on a blank slide can help reveal any misunderstandings in student understanding. A common mnemonic for the order of the planets is "My Very Educated Mother Just Served Us Noodles" (Mercury, Venus, Earth, Mars, Jupiter, Saturn, Uranus, Neptune). But if a student created a mnemonic with a different order, a teacher would know the student doesn't fully have the organization required and needs help with their memory work.

methods course—mastery of facts, concepts, and procedures; requires rigorous practice

> ◵ algebra I; elements of art and composition; expository writing

Methods courses have a heavy emphasis on procedures and concepts. Students traditionally demonstrate mastery by using procedures to solve problem sets. My algebra I students learn seven procedures for solving quadratic equations and must be able to complete all seven, as well as be able to explicitly describe when each procedure is the most appropriate (have conceptual understanding). Students spend a great deal of time practicing procedures and, ideally, honing discrimination between appropriate uses of procedures through interleaved, interval-spaced, varied problem sets.

Before demonstrating the procedure, do not forget to clearly define the concept underlying each procedure in words. Define terms from the ground up and have the definitions already written on the slide. Teachers might be amazed how often students say, "I never knew that!" when they start with the basic, underlying terms.

It's a running joke in my math classes that many people think they prefer math class to reading class because there are fewer vocabulary words, and yet here they are, scrabbling to learn all the vocabulary that I explicitly list and define in each lesson. Good definitions help students internalize the procedures into a schema of understanding. For example, my algebra I students learn three methods to solve systems of equations with two variables, and the definition for each includes "solve a system of equation with two variables by . . ."

When presenting information for a methods course, teachers should be prepared with worked examples, particularly for complex problems. Often, I present worked examples of underlying skills and then show students how the underlying skill builds to the current skill. However, if the problem is lengthy or complex, I find that it is often better not to scare students by showing them a board full of complex text, but instead to insert a blank slide and narrate as I work a problem. To help compensate for less than stellar writing, the next slide will have the same problem neatly typed up for students to review later.

For example, in the "I Do" stage, I walk algebra students through adding 1/2 and 3/4 on a blank slide, gradually replacing each numeral with a variable, but keeping the procedure the same. Students can trace the similarities and differences as the examples are shown. Each problem is a different slide. At the end, I type up all five problems on the same slide so students can compare the procedures. (MathType is my preferred software for typing in MS PowerPoint.)

Key to this style of presentation is teacher talk, or thinking aloud as I make choices to solve problems on the whiteboard. I script this in advance and reuse the script throughout the year. My goal is to have students internalize the script so that when they go to work independently, they hear my voice in their head prompting the next step. If this sounds odd, rest assured that I can still hear my ballet teacher from thirty years ago prompting me to "Make a diamond in your back." Many of us might still remember hearing a coach shout, "Keep your eye on the ball!" We want that same level of internal support when students perform procedures in methods classes. Common teacher talk questions include the following:

- What should I do first?
- Next? And then?
- How do I know what kind of problem this is?
- How did we get . . .?
- Why did I do that?
- Because _____ I did . . .?
- What would happen if I didn't . . .?
- How do you know?
- What's missing from this?
- Almost! What should we have done instead?
- How do we always finish these types of problems?

Checking for understanding can occur in the "We Do" stage when I pretend to forget a step and have a student tell me what to do next. "We Do" is also useful for having two, three, or more students solve prepared problems on a single slide, so students can see that multiple paths lead to correct answers. In my opinion, the best lessons are when several students work together to solve a single problem, such as assigning each student a coordinate point and having them graph it on a slide prepared with a Cartesian plane, so the class works together to graph a single line. This type of problem has a built-in check for understanding, because if a student's point is not on the line, the student doesn't understand the concept.

As students gain familiarity with the procedures, include non-examples. In my experience, this works best when teachers tuck them on an ordinary slide. Don't distinguish them in any way. Then, when students are puzzled as to why the procedure doesn't work, the teacher can point out the way that this problem doesn't conform to the procedure. This way, students are more likely to remember the difference. Have students refer back to the definition of the underlying concept to distinguish why this problem didn't work.

Another way to include non-examples is to let students tell teachers the wrong way to solve a problem, and then when it doesn't work, locate the error and circle the mistake or misunderstanding. Do not call out the student who made the error. Instead, point out that all students need to be aware of this common error. By the end of the lesson, students should be able to list when the procedure doesn't apply and common errors of which they should be aware. Ideally, at the end of the lesson the teacher would have these prepared on a slide that students may want to take a screenshot of for future reference.

Teachers should include enough examples so that students gain fluency before the end of the lesson. When possible, I like to emphasize that there are many ways to solve a problem and that what I'm teaching them is the quickest route. I routinely allow a volunteer to solve a problem on a slide, or part of a problem, and then have the whole class examine the correctly worked problem. "How many of you would have done this? Mmhmm. Can you do it this way? Mmhmm. But how can we do this faster?" This is not about embarrassing students, but about showing students ways to make their life easier. I'm externalizing the most efficient route to solving the problem.

Finally, faded, worked examples are excellent. In this case, teachers have partially solved problems on the board and let students work their way through increasingly large chunks of the problem type. Often, this may take a half-dozen slides to go from fully worked problems to blank slides with only the initial problem. Then teachers should have another three or four slides prepared with only the initial problem, so students can practice together before they separate out for independent practice in the course module assignments.

Always have more problems prepared than students will need, just in case. All students should answer every problem at the end of the "We Do" portion even if that means that the teacher prepares several slides of multiple-choice questions for use with the polling feature in the LMS. Alternatives include having students write their answer on the prepared slide in set slots or drawing lines for matching problems. Teachers can require all students prepare typed answers in the chat box, but not hit enter until the teacher gives the cue, to prevent copying. Remember, teachers should aim for 80% of the class to earn an 80% on these problems. That's four out of five questions answered correctly.

Remediation course—must begin at first principles and work forward; designed to fill gaps

- preparation for pre-algebra; conceptual physics

Remedial courses often have fewer, precise goals and begin at first principles. Students in a remedial reading course might find themselves reviewing phonics from the first letter sounds. Often, students are in remedial courses because they have gaps in their underlying background knowledge. Their courses should be designed to fill the gaps. These courses will have less complicated themes but still require an outlay of student time on assignments.

These classes are often difficult to teach because teachers must have a deep underlying knowledge of the structure of the content area in order to identify common underlying gaps in knowledge. Then teachers must be able to clearly and directly trace the development of a given piece of knowledge, skill, or ability across several grade levels in order to lead students through the material without skipping any necessary steps.

In other words, teachers must prepare the content as if for a survey course but teach using the tools and techniques of a procedural course. However, the teaching has to be different from the average classroom, because if the average tools and techniques worked for these students, they wouldn't be in the class. In addition, teachers must establish good working relationships with students who are typically unhappy and unsuccessful with traditional academics. This is a difficult undertaking.

Although teachers should never assume that students are not gifted, students with working memory issues are seldom well served by traditional classrooms. Working memory is the part of the brain where people temporarily store information and work with it, a bit like RAM for a computer. Scientists' best estimate is that working memory is limited to between four and nine items at a time, for about thirty seconds at a time.[ccclxxxix] Typically, gifted students have a larger working memory capacity,[cccxc] whereas students with attention and memory problems tend to have poorer working memory capacity.[cccxci]

Because students with working memory issues frequently show up in remedial classes, teachers should attend to their needs. One thing these students need is consistent assignments, so they don't lose track of what they're doing while they figure out what the question means. In a synchronous session, teachers can and should walk them through a sample assignment using the screen sharing function with the student view in the assignment itself. Teach students what the words of the question mean and how to input the answers.

Often, students in remedial courses need more practice than the average student for changes in long-term memory to occur (i.e., it takes them longer to learn new material). Therefore, teachers should be prepared to repeat instruction on a regular basis. In my preparation for pre-algebra class, I repeat instruction every three to five weeks for the thirty-two weeks of the school year (i.e., I conduct a week of synchronous sessions on decimals at least six times, going a little bit deeper each time).

Furthermore, students with working memory issues are not able to easily re-derive procedures and often don't have good executive functioning to focus through lengthy procedures. They need to be able to just do the work by combining memorized chunks of processes in limited working memory. Teachers need to build in explicit memorization expectations and routines. My preparation for pre-algebra students spend months on independent practice of addition, subtraction, multiplication, and division tables in the computer-adaptive software.

In my experience, successful online teaching of remedial courses involves offline supplemental texts and manipulatives for students who have difficulty with abstract concepts. For example, in my preparation for pre-algebra course, students have a paper workbook, a work-text (a consumable textbook, meant for students to write in), a multiplication card deck, a fraction card deck, and an account on computer-adaptive software. Students work in both books and online every week, as well as play carefully designed math games to reinforce fraction skills.

Teachers in remedial courses should include explicit teaching and practice for parts-to-whole instruction of complicated concepts. For example, during a synchronous session studying the digestive system, ask students to define and label each part individually, from beginning to end, on prepared slides. When students are confident with the vocabulary, use screensharing to show a cued-up animation of the digestive system process. The "pre-training principle" reduces strain on a student's working memory when understanding a complex topic.

Another way to think of this is to start with a concrete example, with something the student can touch. If this is not possible, use a visual display. Then move to a general rule, such as "all triangles have three sides" or "a noun is a person, place, or thing." Apply the abstract rule with multiple examples: "Pencil is a noun because it is a thing." "Fairmont is a noun because it is a place." "Tommy is a noun because he is a person." Do not forget to include non-examples when checking for understanding. "Is 'warmth' a noun?" "Is 'running' a noun?" "Is 'the' a noun?" Then assign independent practice—and keep assigning it. These are never once-and-done activities. A general rule of 80% old material and 20% new material helps etch information into long-term memory.

- Teachers must lead students through years of material.
- If the average tools and techniques worked for these students, they wouldn't be in the class.
- Walk students through sample assignments using the screen sharing function.

- Use offline supplemental texts and manipulatives.
- Spend months on independent practice for memorization.
- Regularly repeat synchronous instruction .
- Include explicit teaching and practice for parts-to-whole instruction of complicated concepts.
- Use the concrete → visual → abstract sequence with examples and non-examples.
- Assign varied, interleaved, interval-spaced independent practice.

Wrapping Up the Lesson

Often this step is overlooked in favor of sending students directly to independent practice, but online teachers should carefully prepare slide decks that include clear summaries of the lesson. If the day's lesson was on a procedure, then teachers should make an easy-to-read flow-chart of the procedure that students can use as a reference when they work on the independent practice. If the day's lesson was on a concept or declarative knowledge, then the teacher should provide students with a completed graphic organizer.

No, this is not "giving students the answer." This is telling students precisely what the teacher wants students to do and telling students exactly how the teacher wants students to do it. Remember, the teacher isn't there when students do independent practice, so it is critical that the lesson wrap-up be explicit. Students need to be able to flip through the PDF of the slide deck and find the definitions of all the vocabulary, an easy-to-follow procedure, and a completed graphic organizer.

My favored method is to create double slides—the first slide has the flow chart or list of steps, but it's blank. The students should be able to fill it in, and the teacher writes the students' answers on the board during the synchronous session. The second slide is the same thing, but neatly typed up for later reference. This double slide set works well with faded, worked examples, too.

At the end of the class, end the recording and then take individual student questions that are not necessarily about the academic content. Offering formal before and after question times limits off-topic question times during the lesson. If students ask an off-topic question, say, "Good question, Austin! Save it until after class; thanks." The recording is automatically made available to the students in the LMS. Many students review the recording later, while completing problem sets.

When It Doesn't Go Well

Sometimes, the idea just doesn't compute for whatever reason and the wrap-up is an unmitigated disaster. What to do? Well, if teachers have assigned problem sets with 80% old material and 20% new, teachers can say, "Skip problems one to ten tonight. We'll get back to this on Wednesday, and you can make them up then." Students can still continue working.

If teachers are leaning heavily on other types of assignments, those can trundle along independently—students don't need to have a refined view of the impacts of the Cold War on non-US-aligned states in order to read a general article about the Cold War and answer discussion questions, or read their textbook and complete their skeleton notes. Come back to it at the next session and get it right then.

Do not harangue students for their failure to learn. As the teacher, it is your responsibility to lead students through understanding. When I flub a lesson, I apologize before beginning a review lesson. "I'm sorry, I didn't teach this well on Wednesday. We need to review this again, and hopefully I'll do a better job. Please stop me if you're confused."

Conduct a lesson with these steps:

- activate prior knowledge
- present learning objective
- present lessons
  - survey class
    - trace components of knowledge
    - subdivide into constituent parts
    - define terms
      - extend term definitions beyond slide
      - use heavily researched background knowledge
    - organize concepts
      - freehand or use diagram for organization
      - use scripted teacher talk to model organization
    - mnemonics
      - issue mnemonics for tricky concepts
      - check for understanding by having students create their own mnemonics

- methods class
  - define underlying concept
    - very short definition
    - present in words and with a visual aid
  - prepare worked examples for "I Do"
    - use high-contrast color coding
    - script teacher talk
  - prepare faded examples for "We Do"
    - include non-examples
    - provide enough examples for fluency
    - script teacher talk
- summarize content
  - flow-chart for procedures
  - graphic organizer for conceptual/declarative knowledge
- independent practice

Independent Practice

When teaching online, teachers have created assignments for each week's content module. These assignments are meant to be done independently. Assignments are for reinforcement, not self-teaching. The teacher's job is to teach, not fob responsibility for learning off on students. Students should always be taught the content during the synchronous lesson or through snippets of asynchronous video.

Each of the assignments should have repetitions of the lesson objectives to help students etch the procedures, knowledge, and skills into their brains. As I explain to students, just like learning a flip-turn in swimming or practicing a backhand in tennis, students need to be able to do their work automatically, without thinking about it. If I come poke them awake at 1:30 in the morning and ask for the definition of meiosis or the steps in adding unlike fractions, they should be able to rattle it off without completely waking up.

Common assignment types were discussed earlier. They include:

- discussion questions
- guided notes

- sketches or diagrams
- videos
- Leitner box
- hands-on activities
- synchronous class discussions
- quizzes
- problem sets

Because the teacher isn't there for the independent practice, students need some way to get support for their assignments. Not all students will need the same support. Research shows that differentiation is successful when it involves computer-adaptive teaching, in which a computer program offers suggestions for individual student instruction based on student performance as assessed by the software. They "positively affect student performance (d = +.290; 95% CI [0.206, 0.373])."[cccxcii]

 Computer-adaptive instruction works well in the online classroom.

Professionally, I use MathXLforSchool software in the online classroom, which offers supplemental per problem instruction based on student performance. In combination with synchronous class sessions, the majority of my students are successful (80% of students successfully earn 80% or above on the problem sets) with MathXLforSchool. Even if I went back to face-to-face instruction, I would continue to use this software. Other, similar software includes MathXL, ALEKS, iReady, Redbird, and Reflex.

Why Is This so Difficult?

As many people found during the pandemic in the spring of 2020, teaching a synchronous session is arguably more difficult than teaching a face-to-face lesson. Part of the reason is that successful online teaching is intensively cognitively fatiguing because teachers are constantly task switching. My algebra students frequently catch me making silly errors. As I explained to them, this is because I am simultaneously:

- reading the chat box
- drawing on the board
- monitoring time
- thinking about the content
- answering student questions aloud
- monitoring student engagement
- gauging needed explanations

- asking student questions
- checking student answers

All of this together for hours at a time is draining. But it's necessary, because students wander far more frequently online than they do in the face-to-face classroom. At least in a face-to-face classroom teachers can demand that students pretend to pay attention, but online teachers must insist on frequent participation. In addition, face-to-face teachers see students roll their eyes or nap, but online teachers only see text or poll participation.

Even when the lesson is not at a point that a check for understanding is appropriate, teachers can always ask students how they're feeling about the content to draw them back in. No, students are not going to be good judges of their learning, but keeping students attentive is worth taking twenty seconds to poll. One of my most-used polls goes like this:

"How are you feeling about _____?"

- "A-OK! Don't worry, be happy."
- "I think I can, I think I can, I think I can."
- "Crying under the dining room table with thirteen-year-old Mrs. Ostaff"

Note that this is a good opportunity to inject a little humor. My students love these polls because I change the answers a little bit every time, and I'm not afraid to admit that I wasn't always a good student. As the year progresses, they become aware of the mismatch between how well they feel they know the material and how well they actually know it when they go to do the work. This sort of meta-cognition of actual skills versus self-assessed skills is a valuable tool.

Tips and Tricks

- Don't let students distract the synchronous class. Off-topic chatting (either text or voice) is the most disliked part of a synchronous class session.
- Don't ask students to do anything other than listen and participate. Focusing is hard enough for them without distracting them with other tasks.
- Expect students to answer frequent (every three minutes, on average) questions, disrupting their web surfing.
- Don't back up and reteach for late students. It's recorded—they can go back and watch it. Late students should slip quietly in.

- Don't insist that all students use their microphone and/or webcam every class. Many students are not comfortable speaking aloud online or have a poor quality connection. Some will only call in and follow along on the PDF of the posted slides.
- Use scripted teacher talk as a transcript for students who need textual reinforcement of the audio-visual presentation.
- Teach English language learners and English as an additional language students to translate scripted teacher talk into their native language using Google Translate or similar. For students with poor literacy skills, team them to use the read aloud function for their native language. This also works for optical character recognition–capable PDF files.
- Expect students of middle school age and up to attend to a synchronous class for a maximum of fifty minutes once or twice a week.
- Do not split student attention from instruction. Teachers should not expect students to turn on their cameras and interact—this is not a fun social engagement.
- Do not allow students to interrupt the class for permission to step away—use a nonverbal signal for that, an "away" message.
- If the lesson is interrupted—the videoconferencing software went down, your power went out, etc.—then make sure to record the lesson by yourself and send students the link for later viewing.
- Do not interrupt students when they are solving a problem and selecting the answer in a poll, or marking their selection on the whiteboard. Keep silent and wait.
- Expect 100% of students to answer questions. To signal the end of the wait period, count down the number of people who have not answered. "Three people have not answered. Two people. Alright, everyone's answered; let's talk about these choices."
- Limit text on slides to five words per line and no more than five lines per slide. Keep all slides high-contrast, black and white if possible. Make sure illustrations are easy to read and understand.

For more about structuring lessons, see *Explicit and Direct Instruction*, edited by Adam Boxer and Tom Bennett, as well as *Explicit Direct Instruction* by John Hollingsworth and Silvia Ybarra.

Chapter Summary

- Think about creating extra sections instead of breakout groups.
- Keep calm, teach on.
- Reassure students, and don't permit discussion derailment.
- Spend time on preparation.
- Set an opening routine that allows students time to hang out, puts an emphasis on attendance, allows time for questions, and handles administrative issues.
- Spend time preparing lessons and slide decks.
- Script teacher talk, down to the minute.
- Expect students to participate every three to five minutes.
- Begin with a review, note the learning objective, and then present material based on the class type.
- Overprepare so teachers can go deep when needed.
- Always wrap up with a review, including flow-charts of procedures or graphic organizers of declarative knowledge.
- Make sure that students have support for their independent practice, including checking for correctness and meaningful per-student feedback.
- Teaching online is hard.

CHAPTER 12
BEST PRACTICES FOR ASYNCHRONOUS LECTURES

When planning to teach online, teachers should be prepared to provide short videos for students to watch on-demand. In this chapter, I review some issues with creating asynchronous videos, as well as best practices.

> **When teaching online, provide students with short videos to watch on demand.**

High-quality content videos have distinctive characteristics and require significant preparation. Much like synchronous sessions, teachers should carefully design a piece of a scripted lesson with a set opening routine, content, and a closing routine followed by independent practice in the content module assignments. The drawback with asynchronous videos is the lack of checks for understanding or guided practice, which makes careful selection of content module assignments that much more important.

Making content videos requires a distinct skill set. For example, Crash Course videos are arguably some of the most famous educational videos freely available on YouTube. John Green notes that he spends about ten hours per episode—and all he does is turn an essay into a draft of the script and host the episode. Other professionals spend over one hundred hours making the Crash Course videos.[cccxciii]

Because there are critical skills that teachers need when designing content videos, before putting in so much effort teachers might want to think about judiciously selecting high-quality videos already available on the internet and referring students to those videos. For example, I maintain a folder in every content module with links to outside simulations and videos that cover that week's content. I almost never create my own content videos because so much high-quality content is already freely available.

However, I don't require students to watch these videos, because not all my students have extensive internet access. In addition, many careful parents and K-12 information technology departments limit students' internet access to pre-approved sites, and YouTube is almost never a permitted site. Therefore, if teachers want to require students to watch videos, then they'll need to find a workaround, which may mean obtaining permission from the video creator to download the video and upload to the LMS. Alternatively, teachers could ask responsible individuals to broaden students' permitted internet access. Note that this does not fix structural issues around internet access for students.

What Works in Making Educational Videos

One of the most influential studies I've seen about creating asynchronous videos for online teaching is "How Video Production Affects Student Engagement: An Empirical Study of MOOC Videos" by Philip Guo (Massachusetts Institute of Technology), Juho Kim (Massachusetts Institute of Technology), and Rob Rubin (edX).[cccxciv] While I temper my understanding of the research with the caveat that I don't think massive open online courses (MOOCs) are models of online education for K-12 students, understanding why a MOOC is popular is worth investigating.

From my experience, I know that many of my students skip watching videos altogether and just tackle the assignments, only searching the videos for help if they feel like they need it—exactly the opposite of the typical MOOC student. However, in both cases, the extent of watching videos and attempting integrated problems makes for a good assessment. Guo, Kim, and Rubin did some other analysis relevant to our interests as online K-12 teachers. They analyzed speaking rate and video types, as well as production style. Luckily for teachers, big bucks doesn't equal better engagement.

The number one factor in whether students watched the videos was length. Essentially, the shorter the video, the more likely students watched it. Videos three minutes or less tended to have the most views. Even if videos were longer than six minutes, if the students watched the videos, they often only watched for about six minutes. Therefore, if teachers want students to know something, they need to plan to explain it in a video of six minutes or less.

Beware, teachers who think, "Oh, I'll just record my normal class and then chop it into six-minute chunks." Even when excellent teachers were recorded in their normal lectures and those lectures were then chopped up into six-minute chunks, students could tell and began to quit watching at the three-minute mark.[cccxcv] Dedicated planning for six-minute chunks matters.

The second most important factor was whether the instructor was visible at their office desk (not behind a podium or in a studio) at certain points in the video. Student engagement is significantly higher when students can see the instructor. Guo, Kim, and Rubin classified videos as being:

- *slides—PowerPoint presentation with a voice-over*
- *code—instructor writing code in a text editor, integrated development environment, or command-line prompt*
- *Khan-style—full-screen video of an instructor drawing freehand on a digital tablet*

- *classroom—recorded classroom lectures*
- *studio—studio with no audience*
- *office desk—close-up of an instructor's head filmed at their desk*

According to the analysis, Khan-style videos are the clear winner for student engagement, keeping students engaged for twice as long. The researchers noted that if teachers want to prepare slides in advance, they should "add emphasis by sketching over the slides and code using a digital tablet."[cccxcvi] I aspire to one day be half as good at this style of tutorial as Sal Khan, and I found Adam Boxer's ResearchEd YouTube video, "Dual Coding for Teachers Who Can't Draw," helpful in this regard.[cccxcvii]

Both Boxer and the researchers point out that Khan-style videos require significant pre-planning. Guo, Kim, and Rubin noted that teachers needed to have "clear handwriting, good drawing skills, and careful layout planning so as not to overcrowd the canvas."[cccxcviii] Students are not going to waste their time with a teacher who hems and haws as they try to figure out what they want to say. If teachers need students to remember key facts or numbers, make sure it's written down on the screen or reference the text that they're using and then illustrate it on the screen. Students are not going to stick around to try to figure out illegible scribbling. I drew this with my mouse as I taught a lesson. This was a blank slide I'd deliberately inserted into my slide deck to work a problem with students.

$$x^2 + 1 = 3x$$

$$(-\tfrac{3}{2})^2 \quad x^2 - 3x = -1$$

$$x^2 - 3x + \frac{9}{4} = -1 + \frac{9}{4}$$

$$\sqrt{(x - \tfrac{3}{2})^2} = -\frac{4}{4} + \frac{9}{4}\sqrt{\frac{5}{4}}$$

$$x - \frac{3}{2} = \sqrt{\frac{5}{4}}$$

$$x = \frac{3}{2} + \sqrt{\frac{5}{4}}$$

1. all x on L, all alone # R
2. (½ of middle)²
3. ans on both sides
4. factor easy b/c #2
5. √ both sdy
6. x =

When teachers prepare slides, try to ensure that each slide works sequentially through the material, answering one question or covering one vocabulary term.

Slides should be high-contrast with few words and a visual illustration of each topic, as well as extensive notes per slide for teacher reference. It's not about being pretty—it's about minimalist, appropriate design.

Organization is important in online teaching, and this includes the asynchronous video. Here's a useful organization pattern:

- Introductory slide
  - school logo
  - teacher name
  - class name
  - week of school number (Week 32)
  - day number (two sessions per week, so Day 1 or Day 2)
- Behind that, a slide with the video's content in a graphic organizer.
- Signal each lesson within a longer video with an introductory black and white text slide (*Lesson 98: Pythagorean Theorem*) so that students reviewing the video have built-in indicators of new topics.
- Each concept should be organized in a linear way within the lesson and have its own slide, which teachers will use for two to five minutes. Each tutorial slide could be its own video segment, used as teachers mark it up.
- Finally, teachers wrap up with a summary slide of the lesson's procedures or concepts.

Khan-style videos work better when the teacher speaks directly into the camera at transition points, or uses a small-to-medium picture-in-picture element.[cccxcix] Because the layers of video are all collapsed in the recording, saving bandwidth and turning off the webcam in the recording is relevant. The Big 3 LMSs all have built-in videoconferencing software that teachers can use to create recordings with picture-in-picture.

Teachers should not allow their nerves to show. Instead, they should work as though they're explaining to a single student or a small group of students. Try planning with an average student in mind, and then deliver the content as though speaking to just one person or a small group of people.

However, there are a couple of caveats. One, the video background shouldn't be distracting. No cluttered rooms, no running children. At one point, I used thumbtacks to hang a white sheet from the ceiling as a background. Second, the audio quality is incredibly important, more so than graphics quality, so invest in a good headset.[cd] The echoing quality of an empty room is distracting.

As anyone knows who has watched a video that Sal Khan made, he's assured but not in a hurry. This is in contrast to the Crash Course videos, which tend to force attentiveness because the hosts speak so fast. Essentially, either one of those speaking styles work well—slow and confident while writing on the board (48 to 130 words per minute) or highly enthusiastic and fast (165+ words per minute). What doesn't work well is a medium-paced, low-energy instructor with lots of "ums" and "ahs."[cdi] Personally, after watching a cringeworthy recording from my first year of synchronous classes, I have consciously worked to remove those "filler" words from my speech patterns.

Finally, students are more tolerant of longer videos when the teacher is lecturing on declarative knowledge like the fall of the Roman Empire or an overview of genetics—they tend to watch for at least six minutes out of a twelve-minute video. On the other hand, students are less tolerant of video length for tutorial videos like dividing polynomials or paragraph composition. In those cases, students tend to quit watching after three minutes, but frequently come back and rewatch.[cdii] As a result, teachers either should script their videos to reflect short tutorials, "This is how you solve this problem," or longer lectures, "Here's a quick rundown."

Making the Most of Asynchronous Videos

Although the LMS is ideal for creating the initial recording, teachers might want to edit their videos. iOS devices have simple drag-and-drop editing built in with apps like Splice, but desktop users might want something more full-featured like Screencast-O-Matic. Don't be carried away with graphic design—remember, simple is best. Always enable captions—on average, captioners need about four minutes of typing to generate captions for one minute of recorded speech.

One advantage of uploading to YouTube is that YouTube can automatically translate and generate captions in other languages, useful for students who are English language learners or English as an additional language learners. The quality of the transcription and translation is not great, so buyer beware. Even though YouTube is mostly free, it may not be worth the trouble of using it. For example, with my distinctively Appalachian accent, transcriptions of my speech are often terrible.

If teachers want to require that students watch videos, they should create assessments for students to incentivize the behavior. TED-Ed does a great job with these kinds of assessments, and teachers might want to review a few to better understand how to set these up. Typically, there are a handful of multiple-choice or fill-in-the-blank questions followed by one or two short-answer essay questions. In the LMS, teachers can upload a video (or link to a recording made in the LMS), and then assign a quiz using the built-in tools. Another alternative is to assign skeleton notes that students complete while watching the video, and then upload to the LMS for the teacher to review and offer feedback on.

Asynchronous videos can be a great way to bring in guest speakers. Many professional organizations have branches dedicated to working with students. For example, NASA has the Educator Resource Center, which employs professionals who are happy to record videos on a given topic for educators to share with their classes. Teachers should check with their local colleges and universities and other major employers to see if there is speaker availability.

Alternatively, teachers can record themselves using a simulation or website that students might not be able to otherwise access, given internet and device limitations. My students call these "field trips," as in, "We're going on a field trip to watch octopuses in the Pacific Ocean today!" Because teachers can offer prompts and questions while at the website, video, or simulation, this can be an easy way to assign a quiz for students. "Turn in your answers to the questions I asked at the 3:28 mark during the video by midnight on Friday."

Chapter Summary:

Dedicate careful planning to make a series of short (three- to six-minutes) videos to cover the topics. Use the LMS to record yourself speaking as you build up legible text on a blank whiteboard, like Sal Khan. Don't be embarrassed by not having perfect hair—the human aspect appeals to students. Edit "ums" and "ahs" out of your speech patterns, and be either quietly focused on the task or fast and enthusiastic. Use slides to label and organize content. Distinguish between brief tutorial videos and longer six-minute rundowns of declarative knowledge. Assess students' watching of asynchronous videos.

CHAPTER 13

SPECIAL EDUCATION

When planning to teach online, teachers should be prepared to provide accommodations and modifications to course assignments, content, and participation for students with special education needs, as per their legal obligation. This chapter covers both, as well as specific ways that online teachers can serve students with specific learning issues in the online class.

> **When teaching online, provide accommodations and modifications to course assignments, content, and participation for students with special education needs.**

Special education is defined under Individuals with Disabilities Education Act as "specially designed instruction, at no cost to the parents, to meet the unique needs of a child with a disability, including—(i) Instruction conducted in the classroom, in the home, in hospitals and institutions, and in other settings."[cdiii] In other words, public school teachers are legally responsible for implementing special education online. In addition, public school teachers cannot legally ask families to buy special equipment or software just because they are teaching an online class.

Public school teachers must also "ensure access of the child to the general curriculum, so that the child can meet the educational standards within the jurisdiction of the public agency that apply to all children."[cdiv] In other words, public school teachers can't legally lower academic standards students with special education needs. Neither can public school teachers legally deny access to any class material for students with special education needs. By law, everything public school teachers provide in the leaning management system (LMS) must be accessible to all students. If public school teachers link to outside material, it should be accessible as well. Furthermore, public school teachers cannot allow students not to turn in work of the same quality.

Accommodations versus Modifications

Even though they are often confused, these are not the same thing. Accommodations are about making the class accessible to students with disabilities—all of the same content is taught to the same standards, just with different ways students access the material.[cdv] For example, a textbook is made available in Braille or audiobook format. Worksheets might be scanned using optical character recognition (OCR) software, so text-to-speech technology like Siri or Cortana can read it aloud to the student. When submitting an assignment, students might receive extra time to complete the work, although the work is still graded like everyone else's. Students with fine motor issues might be allowed to use speech-to-text software or have someone scribe for them.

On the other hand, modifications involve a change in the curriculum.[cdvi] For example, asking a blind student to interpret a map by color differences is not a reasonable request. Similarly, asking a Deaf student without cochlear implants or other assistive technology to listen to a sound and identify the matching waveform is not a sensible assignment. Students with cognitive impairments might be assigned lower-level or shorter texts, as a modification to their curriculum.

Sometimes the difference between a modification and an accommodation can be subtle. For example, vocabulary is a major part of many content classes. A common accommodation for a student with dyslexia is to allow them to use spellcheck when writing an assignment. On the other hand, if a student with dyslexia is being tested on spelling, then assigning fewer words or less complicated words is a modification of the curriculum. If a teacher is confused about whether the change is an accommodation or a modification, keep in mind that an accommodation doesn't change what is learned, and a modification does change the curriculum.

Perhaps the most obvious difference between a modification and an accommodation is in assessment. Accommodations might change *how* a student's learning is assessed but should still require the same quality of work for the same content. For example, I required the student who drew me the illustration to cover the same content as the students who wrote essays, and I required them to illustrate the same depth of knowledge and understanding. Ideally, the same rubric would apply to both ways of assessment. Other common accommodations include extra time, allowing students to take the test in a silent room with fewer distractions, or allowing students to type instead of handwrite.

Alternate assessments are used for students with major cognitive impairments who need significant support and who have modifications to the general education curriculum.[cdvii] According to the US Department of Education, only 1% of students per state per subject are permitted to be tested with an alternate assessment.[cdviii] There are some other technical issues about waivers and so on, but, essentially, alternate assessments are rare.

Special Education Online

There is a long history of students with special education needs moving to online education. In fact, part of special education law requires that students learn in the *least restrictive environment.* However, when the individual education plan committee determines that a student cannot be successful in the *general education environment*, they may be moved to the *special education environment* as their least restrictive environment.[cdix]

If students cannot be successful in the special education environment, then a state-funded boarding school like the West Virginia Schools for the Deaf and Blind in Romney, West Virginia, may accommodate students. However, many parents prefer their child to stay in the home and use online classes. The percentage of students with special education needs who were enrolled in publicly funded virtual (fully online) schools was about the same as face-to-face public schools as of 2016, according to the National Education Policy Center.[cdx] In fact, students with special education needs are more successful than their peers in online classes, according to an analysis conducted by Washington State in 2018.[cdxi]

This is borne out in my experience outside the public education system, where I have observed that non-public students tend to have a higher percentage of students with special education needs. Often, parents withdraw their children because their needs are not met in public schools. While I have been working with the non-public K-12 student population, substantial portions of the students in my online classes have had special education needs. Luckily, I've been able to use my education and certification as a special education teacher to make some accommodations and modifications to my online classes to better suit students with special education needs.

However, not everything that is provided in a face-to-face public school can be provided in an online class. For example, online classes do not provide nursing care such as changing a feeding tube. Neither are online classes suitable for physical therapy such as gait training exercises or occupational therapy like changing pencil grips. Recognizing practical limitations can help students and teachers make the most of online classes.

Successful Online Classes for Students with Special Education Needs

As in so many other areas of life, proper planning and preparation prevents poor performance. As recommended earlier, teachers should structure an online class in a way that is more easily accessible to students with some learning issues—and then use that structure for all students, saving time and effort.

Although all students benefit from structure and routines, these are especially critical for students with special education needs. For example, students with autism often do better with clear guidelines and expectations. Students with attention deficit/hyperactivity disorder often have difficulty with executive functioning, making plans, and goals.[cdxii] "Predictability is very important for anxious children,"[cdxiii] and creating a predictable routine helps them be successful.

Giving students a systematic plan with repetitive daily, weekly, and monthly goals and showing them how to mark work as completed—and then circling back around to check for completion—helps them succeed.[cdxiv] Another benefit is that by limiting the number of assignment types, students focus on the content, not the context. For students who are new to learning online, figuring out how to do a task may take up more of their attention than the content of the task itself.

Accessibility is a major issue for students with special education needs. Fortunately, a good LMS will have a built-in provision for screen readers, including an accessibility checker for instructors. In addition, a good LMS will be available on a wide variety of devices, including via apps optimized for phones and tablets. It should be intuitive, with clear paths and easy-to-read font.

In a good LMS, captions and text chats are saved with recordings, and can be seen in the downloadable file. Captions are helpful for most students, not just students with hearing impairments. In fact, most students watch recordings with the captions on, and 20% use transcripts when available.[cdxv] Captions help students learn to read, help English language learners, boost vocabulary in good readers, and help students attend to videos.[cdxvi]

 Two main rules guide accessibility for an LMS: Section 508 of the Rehabilitation Act issued from the US federal government and the Web Content Accessibility Guidelines (WCAG 2.1) issued by the World Wide Web Consortium (W3C). According to both the US Department of Education and the US Department of Justice,[cdxvii] it is illegal to use public funds to purchase technology (such as e-books) that supplies inaccessible content, both at the collegiate and K-12 level.[cdxviii]

Jennifer Gonzalez's *Student Inventory* is helpful when teaching students with special education needs.[cdxix] Not all students are comfortable demanding their mandated accommodations and modifications, so asking about special needs as part of an introductory survey helps normalize the request. Despite school administration's responsibility for disclosing individual education plan information, not all teachers get that information in advance, so asking students as part of the survey is another way that teachers can plan for accommodations and modifications.

As part of the survey, ask students what the teacher can do to support them outside of special education needs. Brave students often put themselves out there with requests for patience and compassion. Rarely, students will put in a concrete request, like having notes or written directions.

Obtaining feedback about what's working for students and families is useful in tweaking accommodations and modifications for students. About six weeks in and then in again in February, I assign an anonymous survey based on Jennifer Gonzalez's *How's it Going* form.[cdxx] Always leave an open-ended comment box— students might surprise teachers with their insight! Consider adding a response portion for student aides and other responsible adults.

In the same vein, teachers should treat guardian communication about accommodations and modifications with respect. If a discussion takes place via phone, unrecorded videoconferencing, or similar, teachers should always immediately write a follow-up email reviewing the topics discussed during the conversation, the date and time of the conversation, and any agreed-upon future actions. Keeping a paper trail is vitally important for legal repercussions.

That said, your school administration should be in charge of providing information about what is, and isn't, available as accommodations and modifications in online classes. Administration should be on the front line in handling special education needs. Online teachers are already working hard, so they should not bite off more than they can chew in terms of offering accommodations and modifications in their classes. Ultimate responsibility for special education rests with school administration, particularly in using specialized software like Duxbury to encode work into Braille or providing captioners for synchronous session transcripts.

Capable school administrators will reach out to teachers and ask them to make reasonable recommendations about what they are willing and able to do in an online class. Experienced online teachers can often provide a surprising range of support using current technology and good curricula. High-quality curricula can support students with special needs with a clear scope and sequence of instruction, modifiable instructional pacing, and explicit directions for using embedded activities and expectations.

Online Support for Common Special Education Needs

Note that I am a teacher, not a special education subject matter expert. Don't take my writing as the final word on these topics. I encourage teachers and administrators who work with children with special needs to build good working relationships with special education teachers, educational psychologists, psychiatrists, therapists, and other professionals. Monise Seward, a special education teacher in Georgia, has an excellent YouTube video on this topic, made with Common Sense Education, called "How General Ed and Special Ed Teachers Can Partner as Allies."[cdxxi]

Anxiety Disorders

> *People with generalized anxiety disorder (GAD) display excessive anxiety or worry, most days for at least 6 months, about a number of things such as personal health, work, social interactions, and everyday routine life circumstances. The fear and anxiety can cause significant problems in areas of their life, such as social interactions, school, and work.*
>
> –National Institute of Mental Health[cdxxii]

Students with anxiety disorders often do better with online classes when clear goals and expectations are given. They may have significant stress about speaking during synchronous class sessions, so teachers should not put them on the spot. Instead, consider requiring nonverbal participation, such as answering polls or writing on the board.

Orientation is critical for demonstrating expectations during synchronous sessions and for demonstrating appropriate answers in the written discussion questions. When these students know what is expected every week, and feel confident that they can manage the work, they're more likely to succeed. Keep a close eye on their responses on the "how do you feel about this" poll—if they're consistently in the negative, teachers should reach out via email and check in with the responsible individual.

If they have test anxiety, they may need extra time on assessments (easily done in the LMS). Teachers may need to allow them to use their guided notes to help them work through fight-or-flight episodes when testing. Along those lines, students with anxiety do better when teachers let them know how long something should take in the weekly content module, so they know how much effort to apply. Never give them a pop quiz.

Asynchronous videos help students with anxiety disorders because students can watch the videos when they are feeling less stressed. Anxious students are not always shy, so be sure to support their outgoing nature. Frequently, the students have worked up to asking that question in the synchronous session or dropping that email asking for help. Always be warm and supportive when responding to these students.

For more information about working with students with emotional issues, I recommend *The Explosive Child* by Ross Greene.

Attention Deficit/Hyperactivity Disorder

ADHD is a disorder that makes it difficult for a person to pay attention and control impulsive behaviors. He or she may also be restless and almost constantly active.

–National Institute of Mental Health[cdxxiii]

Students with ADHD often have difficulty with executive functioning, or organizing plans and goals and then following through. In an online class, give these students a written step-by-step plan with daily, weekly, and monthly goals, and show them exactly how to mark it off. Teachers can do this by placing the assignments in the LMS calendar, as well as on the front of each content module. Color coding for organization is a useful accommodation, but be sure to adapt for students with red/green or blue/yellow color deficiency. Help students organize the content with guided notes uploaded as part of the weekly content module assignments.

Use the LMS to provide rubrics for assignments, so they have written directions for how to meet expectations. Always break longer assignments into weekly chunks within the content module. Some students with ADHD become overwhelmed when confronted with a long block of text or large question sets, so consider breaking up assessments into smaller pieces—use the LMS option to post only one question at a time in a quiz, for example. When students have trouble staying focused during a synchronous session, consider calling on them more and using more frequent class polling.

A lesser-known issue for students with ADHD is that the impulse control issues apply when speaking—their prefrontal cortexes can be underdeveloped.[cdxxiv] Teachers should keep a close eye on students' written responses and synchronous class chats, and be prepared to head them off at the pass. If needed, mute them during a synchronous session. Often, teachers will need to redirect these students to appropriate questions or times. Usually, these students don't intend to be rude—they're just enthusiastic. Because students with ADHD have social difficulties, they tend to have low self-esteem, so teachers need to emphasize positive reinforcement for good work.

For more information about students with ADHD, I recommend *ADDitude Magazine*.

Autism Spectrum Disorder

a developmental disorder that affects communication and behavior. . . . people with ASD have:

- *Difficulty with communication and interaction with other people*
- *Restricted interests and repetitive behaviors*
- *Symptoms that hurt the person's ability to function properly in school, work, and other areas of life*

–National Institute of Mental Health[cdxxv]

Often one of the most difficult part of the classroom experience for students with autism is reading nonverbal cues and unwritten social rules. Appropriate loudness and tone can also be difficult for them to convey. As a result, students with autism often flourish in online classes where these are not major issues. Because students with autism can be comfortable in their home environment, sensory processing issues are not as prominent as they are in a face-to-face classroom—although teachers should beware of assigning videos that are too loud, noisy, or have bright flashing lights.

Further, students with autism often do not do well with unexpected changes to their routines and plans. Therefore, teachers should give them clear guidelines and expectations. For example, students with autism often appreciate a daily calendar. Because unwritten social rules are difficult, students with autism often want clear concrete examples of good work and a list of assignments to be completed with rubrics. So that they can better plan their time, provide expected times for assignments.

Even in writing, communication by students with autism can be abrupt—don't take it personally. Do monitor their discussion questions carefully, and keep an eye on whether they're dominating the class conversation with communication about their special interest. Help steer students with autism by giving them models of good responses and checking that peers are displaying acceptance of others' differences. Often, students with autism are working hard to craft appropriate replies—be sensitive to their efforts by being upbeat and positive in their feedback. Parents can help support these students in their efforts.

For more information about students with autism, I recommend *Neurotribes: The Legacy of Autism and the Future of Neurodiversity* by Steve Silberman.

Dyscalculia

Dyscalculia is a term used to describe specific learning disabilities that affect a child's ability to understand, learn, and perform math and number-based operations [as well as tell time, measure quantities, understand three-dimensional illustrations, and make change]. . . . it's estimated that between 5 and 7% of elementary school aged children may have dyscalculia. It's also currently thought that dyscalculia occurs equally in both genders.

–Child Mind Institute[cdxxvi]

Dyscalculia is less well known than dyslexia, although chances are good that every teacher has had a student with poor number sense in their classroom. Like many other learning disabilities, good teaching helps students with dyscalculia. Practices such as activating prior knowledge, using teacher talk to model problem solving, teaching students to use flow-charts or diagrams to illustrate concepts, and frequently checking for understanding are critical for students with dyscalculia.

Other math-specific aides include using graph paper to help students line up problems and calculators. Math apps like ModMath are useful for helping students write equations, as well as devices like the ReMarkable that provide unlimited, resizable graph paper. Websites like Geogebra help students understand how graphing equations work and offer virtual drawing tools. Online teachers may want to emphasize the home use of manipulatives like an abacus, Cuisenaire rods, and base-ten blocks. I have been known to provide PDFs with printable copies of Cuisenaire rods for student use.

Other online tips include assigning only one math problem at a time in computer-adaptive software, rather than scanning a non-OCR capable worksheet. Students with dyscalculia often need more time—I worked with a student who took forty-five minutes to calculate what all the other students could do in five minutes. Students may need extra hints and tips, or multiple attempts, which are also readily provided by computer-adaptive software.

For more information about dyscalculia, I recommend Stanislas Dehaene's *The Number Sense: How the Mind Creates Mathematics.*

Dyslexia

- *All children face the same challenges in learning to read, but dyslexics have more difficulty with the essential components. . . .*
- *. . . the child's spoken-language comprehension is within the age-appropriate range.*
- *Dyslexia frequently occurs with other developmental disorders. . . . The most common co-occurring conditions are speech and language disorders, ADHD, and math impairments.*
- *Dyslexia is a language-based disorder. Its origins are anomalies in the development of speech (perception, production) and language (vocabulary, grammar) from birth.*
- *Whether a child falls into the dyslexic spectrum depends on their configuration of strengths and weaknesses.*

–Seidenberg, Mark. *Language at the Speed of Sight: How We Read, Why So Many Can't, and What Can Be Done About It*

Students with dyslexia benefit from visual schedules, such as the ones that I recommend teachers post on the front of their weekly content module. Using repetitive assignments means that students can memorize the directions and names of the assignments, so that reading difficulties don't impair their ability to do the work. Assistive technology such as Bookshare or the screenreader built into iOS devices helps students focus on the content and not be overwhelmed by the task of reading.

Because students with dyslexia have often have difficulty with writing as well as reading, students find speech-to-text software helpful, such as dictating to Siri or Cortana. In severe cases, students may need a scribe to write for them. Quizzes and tests with point-and-click questions and answers are preferable to short-answer essays or fill-in-the-blank questions for these students. A high-quality LMS is accessible to students with dyslexia using text-to-speech software.

Research indicates that students can retain as much from an audio book or a teacher reading aloud as they can from reading it themselves, so do not force students to use low-level texts. Most are perfectly capable of high-level auditory comprehension of complex texts, often at high speed, such as 2× or 3× a normal speaking rate. Because these students are slower readers, they should be given extra time on taking tests.

Lesser known is that dyslexia often includes difficulty with reading and remembering numbers, like phone numbers and zip codes, so teachers in content areas like history and science should provide students with editable document files for guided notes. Students can then complete the notes using speech-to-text software. This way, students can use them as organizers to follow along during a lesson, already exposed to key vocabulary.

Like many other learning disabilities, good teaching during synchronous lessons helps students with dyslexia. Practices such as activating prior knowledge, using teacher talk to model problem solving, teaching students to use flow-charts or diagrams to illustrate concepts, and frequently checking for understanding are critical for students with dyslexia. Avoid unreasonable requests, like handwritten work with good spelling. Online classes should have all typed work anyway, and students should learn how to use spellcheckers and grammar checkers.

For more information about students with dyslexia, I recommend *Language at the Speed of Sight: How We Read, Why So Many Can't, and What Can Be Done About It* by Mark Seidenberg.

Speech or Language Impairment

A speech disorder usually indicates that someone has trouble producing certain sounds accurately. A child with a language disorder may have a difficult time understanding the meaning of what's being said (receptive language issues). Or he may have trouble communicating his own thoughts (expressive language issues).

–Understood For All[cdxxvii]

Students with speech impairments may have difficulty speaking clearly and are often self-conscious about their articulation. Teachers should not require them to use the microphone. Students with expressive language issues may have difficulty formulating their thoughts into verbal form, so let them type slowly in the synchronous text chat. Be prepared to wait patiently while they answer questions.

Typically, oral language skills lag significantly behind receptive skills—students understand far more than they can speak. Allow students to use parts of words or phrases instead of full sentences, whether verbalizing using speech-to-text software or in a synchronous session. In a synchronous session, make good use of nonverbal communication tools, like polling and the "faster" or "slower" indicators.

Students with receptive language difficulties may have difficulty understanding what teachers say aloud or understanding the words on the page, so teachers should provide them with copies of the slide deck in advance and use visual illustrations of the concepts. Teachers should give them a heads up about questions, allowing them to prepare an answer ahead of time.

When using asynchronous videos to reinforce concepts, ensure that the videos cover everything necessary for success in the weekly content module. These students will likely rely heavily on the videos. Ensure that the audio is high quality and that your voice is clear and easy to understand. Use simple sentences and speak slowly.

Teachers should provide rubrics for clear expectations about written assignments and check in with students to see how hard they're working. I had a student who turned in beautiful essays like clockwork, but what I didn't know was that they were spending eight to ten hours per essay. Not until their parent called me, furious at the level of work I was expecting from a student with expressive language disorder, did I become aware of the difficulty. Teachers may need to modify assignments.

Like many other learning disabilities, good teaching during synchronous lessons helps students with speech and language impairments. Practices such as activating prior knowledge, using teacher talk to model problem solving, teaching students to use flow-charts or diagrams to illustrate concepts, and frequently checking for understanding are critical for students with speech and language impairments. Using retrieval practice with interleaved, interval-spaced quizzing is crucial for these students. Teachers should use concrete manipulatives and weekly hands-on projects to reinforce knowledge acquisition for these students.

Allow alternate assignments. Some of the most beautifully illustrated, completely correct concept maps I have ever seen came from allowing a student to draw a comic instead of writing a set of essays. Like students with dyslexia, teachers should allow speech-to-text and text-to-speech software to be used when completing assignments. A high-quality LMS is often more accessible for students with receptive language disorders when they use text-to-speech software.

Auditory Processing Disorder

> *A condition in which a child has trouble accurately processing and interpreting information he hears. Often referred to as APD, this condition makes it difficult to recognize subtle differences in the way words sound.*

–Understood For All[cdxxviii]

Teacher should be sensitive to auditory distractions, like background noise during synchronous sessions and recordings. When teaching a synchronous session, teachers should work in a quiet environment without any distracting background noises, and use a good quality headset to minimize echoing in rooms with hard surfaces. Likewise, all students should be reminded to use headsets when available. During synchronous sessions, teachers should attend to students during the "how do you feel about this" poll—if students are consistently negative, teachers should follow up after the lesson.

Permit the students to opt out of oral participation in the lecture. Use polls and other nonverbal signals to check for student understanding. Make sure all synchronous classes are recorded and that the slide deck is available in each week's assignment folder, so that students who need to listen more than once can go back as often as they need. Using visual aids on slides and repeating information written on slides also helps students with auditory processing disorder (APD).

They may not be able to keep up with the speed of a synchronous class session, so make sure that slides recap all major points. Like many other students, students with APD can make good use of transcripts. By assigning the textbook with skeleton notes first, students can preview the information before attending a synchronous session or watching a recorded video, thus helping their comprehension.

Failure to comply often isn't defiance, but it is instead failure to comprehend. Step-by-step written directions are useful for these students, and teachers should place all the assignments in the LMS calendar, as well as on the front of each content module so that students can easily find the directions. Making a daily and weekly list of assignments is helpful for students.

Visual Impairments

"Low vision" is a medical term that is defined as chronic disabling visual impairments that cannot be corrected with glasses, contact lenses, or medical or surgical treatment. Most people who consider themselves blind would be included in this broad-reaching definition of low vision. An estimated 3.5 million Americans have low vision. Out of that group approximately two million have mild low vision, which mainly affects driving and reading ability, and about one million meet the legal criteria for blindness.

–Robert W. Massof *Low Vision and Blindness: Changing Perspective and Increasing Success*[cdxxix]

Students with visual impairments are less common in classrooms. Together with students who are blind, Deaf, hard of hearing, or who are deafblind, they make up the *low-incidence population* of students with special education needs. These students are typically less than 1% of the student population. Teachers can work their entire career without ever having a blind student in their classroom. I happen to be certified as a teacher of the visually impaired (and yes, that means that I learned Braille).

When teaching online and working with students who are visually impaired, teachers should make sure their weekly content modules are accessible to students who use screen readers. One way to do this is to use a text-based browser, like Lynx, and log in as a student. Teachers often don't realize that students who use screen readers don't use a mouse. So teachers need to double-check that the LMS permits moving around with the tab key, and the CTRL+TAB combination moves between parts of the screen. If there is missing information, then teachers need to fix the issue. All images and videos should have alternative text descriptions where appropriate.

Very few students are completely blind, so when teaching synchronous sessions or making asynchronous recordings, teachers should make sure slides are high contrast (preferably black and white) and have low visual clutter. Teachers should give students copies of the slides in advance so that students can load the slides in the screen enlarging software on their device. All text should be OCR-capable. When creating diagrams and graphic organizers, keep in mind that students will enlarge a small portion of the screen at a time. Students will not be able to easily see an overview, so teachers will have to work hard to provide an overview aloud.

If online teachers have visually impaired students in their class, asynchronous videos should have detailed audio descriptions of what is happening on the screen. The Described and Captioned Media Program, funded by the US Department of Education, is a free service that supports students by providing educational videos with detailed descriptions of what is happening on the screen.

Teachers should work to build a good relationship with the student's responsible individual, whether that is an aide, a parent, or someone else. Teachers will need to work with the responsible individual to ensure that the LMS and handouts provided by the teacher are compatible with the software and technology that the student uses, usually a screen reader.

As anyone who used audio books knows, students will take much longer to listen to a book read aloud. Therefore, teachers should take time to summarize the content of any assigned reading, either in a brief audio recording or in a short text. Students will also take much longer to read the text in Braille. Braille is a set of codes that transcribes text, mathematics, and music, and they are not easy to learn. There are different levels of complexity of Braille. Therefore, teachers should offer OCR-capable text outlines and summaries well in advance—although, if teachers post their weekly content modules two weeks in advance, students will have time to use their software and Brailler to encode the text so that they can read it.

Because students with visual impairments need to use more time-intensive methods of accessing content, they need to have extra time allotted via the LMS, usually doubled time. Another option is to permit alternate assignments by having the assignment read aloud and a responsible individual scribe for the student.

Teachers may need to provide individual synchronous sessions until students settle in. These students are often just as bright and personable as students without visual impairments—don't make the mistake of thinking that impairment equals lack of intelligence.

For more information about working with students with visual impairments in the general education classroom, I recommend *Classroom Collaboration* by Laurel Hudson.

Deaf and Hard of Hearing students

Deafness means a hearing impairment that is so severe that the child is impaired in processing linguistic information through hearing, with or without amplification, that adversely affects a child's educational performance.

–Sec. 300.8 I (3) of the Individuals with Disabilities Education Act

Hearing loss occurs on a spectrum, within a range of sound. For example, a child may have a 30% hearing loss, which seems like less of a concern until it's revealed that the loss is centered in the speaking range. That same child can hear bird song and big bass notes just fine, but may be unable to hear the difference between "d" and "e" in learning to read. Because children with hearing loss often have difficulty hearing sounds, they often have difficulty with clear articulation.

Ensure that all students are aware of the need to minimize background noise when speaking—emphasize using the text chat for this reason. Reiterate that students who use their cameras need to be clear in the webcam and articulate clearly. Because sound is so critical to speech, children who are Deaf or hard of hearing might have difficulty taking notes during synchronous class discussions. I don't recommend students do anything but participate in a synchronous class session, which helps level the playing field for students with hearing issues.

However, participating in synchronous class discussions without proper assistive technology, a skilled captioner, or an American Sign Language interpreter is often dismayingly difficult. Captioning a recording takes time, usually four minutes of typing for every full minute of speech. Difficulty with clear articulation means that presenting material is often a flashpoint for trouble, so teachers should be wary of insisting that students present during synchronous sessions. Teachers might also keep in mind that interveners, communications specialists for students who are both Deaf and blind, might be present in synchronous sessions or might be transcribing for a student.

Therefore, teachers should provide a transcript, preferably in advance. Vocabulary acquisition can be an issue for students who are Deaf or hard of hearing, so teachers should ensure they clearly define all words. Because of the inherent difficulties in synchronous sessions, everything students need to know should be available outside of the synchronous session, written down in the textbook, class links, and so on. Conveying information visually becomes critically important, so teachers need to make slides clear and high contrast, minimizing visual clutter.

Teachers should also know that the Deaf community has its own culture and its own language. Unlike Braille, American Sign Language is a language, with its own grammar, jokes, and idioms. Students constantly switching back and forth from American Sign Language to Standard American English may be tripped up by the different grammar and punctuation requirements. This is not necessarily a sign of poor writing skills.

Teachers may need to provide individual synchronous sessions for extra support until students settle into the rhythm of class, because these students are less likely to pick up conversational asides that convey needed information. These students are often just as bright and personable as students without hearing loss—being Deaf or hard of hearing does not equal lack of intelligence.

For more information about teaching these students, I recommend the short online course *Educating Students Who are Deaf or Hard of Hearing: A Guide for*

Professionals in General Education Settings from the Clerc Center at Gallaudet University, in collaboration with *Education Service Center, Region 20* in Texas.

Gifted and Talented

Students with gifts and talents perform—or have the capability to perform —at higher levels compared to others of the same age, experience, and environment in one or more domains. They require modification(s) to their educational experience(s) to learn and realize their potential.

–National Association for Gifted Children

Although some readers may be surprised to see a section on teaching gifted children in the chapter on special education, gifted children do have special education needs. As discussed earlier, not all gifted children will be successful, and many will not succeed at fulfilling their potential. Though administrative strategies such as universal screening, access to challenging education, and official recognition of children who are both gifted and who have learning issues are beyond the scope of this book, teachers should be aware that gifted students have historically flocked to online education.

Using a back-of-the-envelope calculation based on the average age as revealed by my introductory student survey and the presumed levels of the classes I teach online, I estimate that as many as 25% of my students may fall into the gifted range. Frequently, I have students ranging in age from ten to fifteen in the same class. This is part of why I place such an emphasis on student privacy and explicit instruction of appropriate class communication. What may amuse the average fifteen-year-old may not be appropriate for the average ten-year-old.

Many parents and teachers do not realize that giftedness does not automatically advance a student's knowledge, skills, and abilities across the board. A precocious reader may not have corresponding writing skills. For example, a student who can independently read and appreciate *The Lord of the Rings* trilogy may still be young enough to want to play the characters as make-believe on the living room floor. Often, there are significant differences across skill levels—I know of a student who was working on six different grade levels across six different subjects. Online, teachers may need to accommodate students with varying knowledge, skills, and abilities by modifying assignments, routinely offering students a way to access extensions for interesting topics, and encouraging enthusiasm about special interests.

Within each content module, teachers can make a folder for interesting websites and videos. Whereas other students may use these to supplement assigned reading, gifted students may use these to look at content in more depth, at a more abstract level. In every content module, teachers should include videos from professional organizations, snippets from college lecture courses, and so on. Websites aimed at adults may be useful as well, such as NASA's press release section or the CIA World Factbook. By increasing the level of difficulty of resources, teachers can support their gifted students.

These students often have a wealth of knowledge about their favorite subject area, more so than the teacher. This is part of the reason why I spend so much time researching each week's topics and taking such extensive notes. I'll never forget teaching a high-school level ancient history course, showing a slide with three Egyptian mummies on it, and a student rattling off the names, titles, and dates for each mummy before I even opened my mouth. Be prepared for these students to challenge teachers with incomplete information or strongly held misconceptions about a subject during a synchronous class discussion or in written feedback about work.

While I do not fully subscribe to Dabrowski's theory of overexcitabilities, in my experience gifted students are often emotionally intense and highly sensitive. For example, a young student who learns about the extinction of the dinosaurs may break down in tears in class and have nightmares for months. That student is intellectually capable of understanding the tragedy but does not have the emotional experience or stability to distance themselves from the horror. Teachers need to ensure that while they don't skip tragedies or terror when covering content, teachers don't emphasize it either. Trying to attract students' attention online with amped up intensity about death and destruction may backfire.

Along those lines, gifted students are often perfectionists, to their own detriment. They may have difficulties turning in assignments because they're afraid that it's not their best work. Alternatively, they may be harshly critical of their peers for what they perceive as sloppy thinking or shoddily done work. By offering models of the standard of work within synchronous lessons and in assignment instructions, teachers help gifted students avoid both of those issues.

For more information about teaching gifted children, teachers may want to review the Supporting Emotional Needs of the Gifted website, peruse the National Association for Gifted Children website, and explore the Hoagies' Gifted Education website.

Chapter Summary

Public school teachers are legally obligated to provide specially designed instruction to students with disabilities. Accommodation and modification are the two main avenues for special education. Students with special education needs have been taking online classes for many years and, when given the necessary accommodations and modifications, are just as successful as their peers. Teachers need to plan and prepare materials for special education needs. Rather than do twice the work, teachers should allow all students to take advantage of many accommodations, such as structured classes with repetitive assignments using daily and weekly checklists, and providing resources for students to extend their learning. Captions are helpful for nearly all students, for example. Teachers need to establish a good working relationship with the students' responsible adults. Good teaching during synchronous lessons helps many students with special education needs. Practices such as activating prior knowledge, using teacher talk to model problem solving, teaching students to use flow-charts or diagrams to illustrate concepts, and frequently checking for understanding are all helpful.

CHAPTER 14

ASSESSMENTS—YOURS AND THEIRS

This chapter argues that teachers and students are better served by a focus on formative assessment, as opposed to summative assessments. Part of the rationale is that background content knowledge

> **When teaching online, plan to use formative assessment.**

plays such an outsized role in norm-referenced summative assessments. More practically, assessment plans, writing assessments, and portfolios are all covered, as well as dealing with cheating in online classes. Finally, the chapter ends with a discussion of end-of-the-year surveys.

The Problem with Summative Assessments

At this point in the book, readers may have noticed that I have yet to place much emphasis on grades or testing. This is because, frankly, I don't care much about tests. Tests are a form of *summative* assessment. Summative assessment does just what it sounds like—it sums up everything a student has learned into one neat number, checklist, or letter. The problem is that test results are a purely artificial measure, one that is often highly subjective.

Even IQ tests, often seen as the *sine qua non* for ranking students, have serious issues. I discussed many of those issues in an earlier chapter, but readers might be interested to know that some scientists consider the whole idea of IQ tests to be inherently flawed,[cdxxx] that global IQ increased significantly throughout the twentieth century (the Flynn effect, presumably due to improvements in education),[cdxxxi] and that a person's IQ changes over their lifetime, sometimes significantly.[cdxxxii] In addition, mainstream scientists agree that attributing IQ differences between population groups to genetic factors is junk science boosting racism.[cdxxxiii] If we can't depend on professional psychologists under set conditions with widely agreed upon assessments about such an important topic, how could teachers possibly accurately pigeonhole students with a single handmade test?

The answer is that in many ways, the classroom teacher cannot perfectly assess how much a student knows. In E.D. Hirsch, Jr.'s *The Schools We Need: And Why We Don't Have Them*, he describes a study from 1961 in which Paul Diederich and colleagues had hundreds of student papers assessed by dozens of graders and "more than one third of the papers received every possible grade. That is, 101 of the 300 papers received all nine grades: A, A-, B+, B, B-, C+, C, C-, and D."[cdxxxiv] The results went downhill from there. While the College Board attempts to grade writing, it is well known that the whole process is fraught with difficulty and complications.[cdxxxv] In my home state of West Virginia, students have been subjected to computer-based writing assessment for years, and it is an open secret that the whole process is ineffective.[cdxxxvi] In other words, the gold standard of a final essay is not a reliable assessment of student learning.

Furthermore, as students progress beyond phonics, many summative reading comprehension tests are actually tests of background knowledge. Famously, Recht and Leslie did a reading comprehension study back in the late 1980s that demonstrates this idea. Students who were good readers with lots of knowledge about baseball performed best of all, but surprisingly, students who struggled to read and had lots of knowledge about baseball came in a close second place, well above good readers with little knowledge about baseball.[cdxxxvii] As Dr. Willingham notes in the spring 2006 edition of *American Educator*, the close correspondence between background knowledge and test performance has been replicated many times.[cdxxxviii]

	Good Readers	Struggling Readers
Lots of knowledge about baseball	First place	Second place
Little knowledge about baseball	Third place	Fourth place

As anyone who's tried to teach long division knows, background knowledge is also powerfully important in mathematics. Both students and teachers are frustrated when key background knowledge is missing, making improbable requests of tasks like long division, adding rational expressions with unlike denominators, or calculating probability. In fact, mathematics is so powerfully predicated on previous knowledge that it is one of the few subjects in the United States with a clearly delineated progression of knowledge building. Second languages are usually the other subject.

For example, many of us grew up with pre-algebra, then algebra, then geometry (usually for the knowledge to do well on college admissions tests), then algebra II. Some differences occur at this point (I took algebra III), but most college-bound students will take trigonometry, and then perhaps calculus. Integrated high school mathematics follows a similar progression, albeit with more statistics and less coverage of other topics, such as arithmetic operations on polynomials.[cdxxxix] These are bright line standards for what students should know and when they should know it—and unfortunately, are almost never implemented in other subjects. This leaves our students at a disadvantage in summative assessments.

Summative assessments often test background knowledge.

Because background knowledge is so important in summative assessment, teachers are brought right back around to the importance of a good knowledge-building curriculum. In the United States, we tend to think of any curriculum that says it corresponds to our national standards as a good curriculum; we have already established in Chapter 7 that standards are not actually a curriculum. They're the signposts, not the road. Curriculum is often steered by the standards, but it does not have to be (and absolutely should not be) limited to the standards.

Although this might seem irrational to teachers buckling under the weight of teaching students dozens of standards, going beyond the bare minimum earlier pays high-interest dividends later when students arrive in class well prepared to learn. How much easier might a middle school science teacher's life be if all of her sixth-graders already had knowledge of DNA and RNA? How much easier might life be for a high school literature teacher if he had students who were studying Shakespeare who had more than a passing acquaintance with the Renaissance? Even earlier—what about a fourth-grade teacher with a class of students who could decode the English language on grade level? All of these situations would be less disheartening to both teacher and student when the student is well prepared by earlier years of education.

At this point, I think much credit must be given to our peers across the pond in the United Kingdom for moving this conversation along productively. This summer I picked up a copy of *The Curriculum: An Evidence-Informed Guide for Teachers*, and it contained a series of thoughtful essays from educators about creating a structured curriculum that systematically built knowledge from the earliest years all the way through.[cdxl] Our results on the Program for International Student Assessment indicate this not something at which the United States excels for all of our students.

For instance, as Andreas Schleicher noted in an article in The New York Times, "About a fifth of American 15-year-olds scored so low on the [Program for International Student Assessment] test that it appeared they had not mastered reading skills expected of a 10-year-old."[cdxli] Even by our own standards as set down in the National Assessment of Educational Progress, two-thirds of fourth and eighth graders are not proficient readers.[cdxlii] If we quite reasonably take these kinds of assessments as an indictment of students' background knowledge, we can see that the majority of our students have gaping holes in their knowledge about how the world works.

Students need background knowledge to score well on summative assessments.

School districts with money can buy off-the-shelf curriculum from one of the big companies like Pearson, McGraw-Hill, or Houghton Mifflin Harcourt. Those curricula contain textbooks, teacher's editions, planning guides, workbooks, assessments, Spanish translations, lab manuals, and so on. Basically, the kits include everything a publishing company could possibly sell for teaching the class. Unfortunately, many of these textbooks contain significant issues, like the McGraw-Hill geography textbook that claimed African slaves on American plantations were "workers."[cdxliii] Furthermore, many districts don't buy textbooks regularly or have spent decades pressuring teachers to provide their own materials.[cdxliv] Nevertheless, teachers must do what they can with what they have in terms of summative assessments.

Focus on Formative Assessment Instead

Therefore, as our students come to us with a wide variety of background knowledge, skills, and abilities, and we cannot teach everything, we must attempt to restrict our assessment to the important bits of what we teach, rather than what students already know. Along these lines, I am much less concerned about summative test performance and much more concerned about monitoring how well students can show their learning on a day-to-day basis. There are several ways to tackle this problem, most of which fall under the heading of *formative assessment*—assessment that informs my day-to-day instruction.

Best practice in face-to-face classroom teaching is to design high-quality explicit instruction and then monitor the lesson. Teachers should use checks for understanding throughout the lesson, and perhaps exit tickets to inform the next lesson. Harry Fletcher-Wood's *Responsive Teaching* has a detailed breakdown of the process. As I have suggested in the session on synchronous classes, online teachers can do that too, via whole-class assessment of carefully written guided practice problems or content organization, definitions, and usage.

In asynchronous classes, teachers can require the learning management system (LMS) to issue learning components in sequence, assigning first a video and then a short quiz to as a use check for understanding. If students fail the quiz, the teacher might set the LMS to require them to watch the video again and take the quiz again, until they pass the quiz. Only after students have watched all the assigned video assignments and passed the quizzes would students then be permitted to access the homework assignments. As teachers might be creating these videos and checks for understanding themselves, they must be prepared to quickly respond to student pleas for help when the video or the checks are less than perfect. An analysis of video watching statistics, quiz attempts, and per-question statistics can show areas of difficulty for the class and inform the next video series.

In online classes, teachers can use several asynchronous, ongoing assessments to monitor whole-class understanding. Most experienced online teachers are going to use the online, written discussion questions as ongoing assessments of student knowledge. As teachers gain familiarity with the content, they can anticipate common student misconceptions and be ready to participate with good questions to prompt students to illustrate misunderstandings and bring students to better comprehension.

Computer-adaptive software for problem sets is one of my favorite ways to monitor student progress. Students can receive assistance tailored to their misunderstandings, as well as take advantage of multiple attempts to solve algorithmically generated problems with built-in examples. I'm perfectly content to allow students to work toward mastery, and most do improve their homework scores before I scrape the data from the website every week. Students are capable of understanding their scores without significant individual feedback from me, although I do always provide a way for students to show me their work so we can discuss it.

I use this data to adjust instruction in several ways. For example, I might review the top five most missed question types at the beginning of the next synchronous class session. Alternatively, I might send out helpful emails for a specific difficult problem. Often, I locate a useful outside video and pop it in the content module. For individual students, I might drop a note and ask a student to meet with me one on one, or refer them to tutoring. For small groups, I may offer an extra credit synchronous session.

In classes without significant daily problem sets, teachers can use weekly quizzes to provide a snapshot of student learning. In my experience, the quizzes that are the most useful embed questions about all the tasks in the content module, regardless of whether students were required to turn in the work. For example, if students were to perform a hands-on demonstration (or watch a video of the demonstration), then a useful quiz question might ask students to put the steps of the task in order. For memorization work, cumulative assessment questions might ask students to match the date to its significance, including dates from previous weeks. Vocabulary-intensive classes should have multiple-choice questions with definitions from the vocabulary, for best practice at discriminating definitions.

Although teachers must take into consideration students with special educational needs, LMSs often include the ability to upload an image file, so teachers can ask students to click on a specific place in the image, a "hot spot," useful for identifying processes and diagram pieces. In my astronomy class, I upload images of galaxies as answers to multiple-choice questions, and ask students to correctly identify four galaxy types. Audio files are also able to be included, so teachers could upload audio files for language translation exercises, for example.

Note that these formative assessments are tightly intertwined with the content knowledge in the course. I don't ask questions about what I have not explicitly taught. When creating assessments, I lean on professionally designed questions wherever possible, from the off-the-shelf curriculum or the textbook. One could take an entire college class just on question design, and my master's degree in secondary education didn't include that course. When those questions are not available, I work hard to write good questions that are based solely on information discussed in that content module or, alternately, information discussed in previous content modules.

 Do not assess on what was not taught.

Because all my assessments are based on the class content, when I do ask students to participate in summative assessments, I restrict the summative assessment to material covered within the class. As I tell my students, I'm not interested in tricking them—I just want to know what they know. As per school policy, my students take cumulative final exams each semester, covering all the material learned in the previous sixteen weeks.

In my cumulative final exams in mathematics, I include one question for each learning objective, usually seventy to ninety questions. Often, I provide a study guide, although the textbooks are organized so that students could simply use the table of contents. Predictably, students tend to score well because they already know the content. My students are assigned varied, interleaved, interval-spaced retrieval practice throughout the class, which improves their retention of key information.

While anecdote is not the plural of data, I rarely hear complaints from students about their progression in future classes. In fact, a couple of years back, one of my students let me know that she tested into college algebra based on the strength of my algebra I course. Teaching for knowledge rather than test scores opens up a world of possibilities because learning more than the bare minimum in terms of curriculum depth and rigor makes those big annual standardized tests easy for students.

How to Do It

When teachers make their content module plans, they should also make assessment plans. But the process starts even earlier. When developing a syllabus, teachers should make decisions about what types of assignments they're going to use in the class and how they're going to assess them. Although each teacher will have unique considerations, many assessment types hold true across subjects—math students need to solve problems, geography students need to read maps, literature students need to read texts. In each case, students need to know what to do, how to do it, how it will be assessed, and what work earns a good grade.

 Students need to know: a) what to do, b) how to do it, c) how it will be assessed, and d) what work earns a good grade.

Consider making a chart with assignment types and some notes about each type of assignment. This way, teachers can refer back to it at 8:30 pm on Sunday night when they're designing the upcoming content module and need to help students better understand a concept. Something like the following chart below might be useful to teachers as they go through the year.

Assessment	Feedback	Formative Use	Grading Standards	Summative Use
Discussion Questions	in the DQ responses, with rubric, email if needed	adjust synchronous class, assign other websites, announcements	rubric	% of grade; use Week 3 and 5 as basis for essay test in Week 7
Quizzes	per question, in test results; follow-up email for missing/failing scores; mark up on scratch work if submitted	add most-missed questions to next week's slide deck for synchronous review; individual tutoring as needed; adjust later DQs to review hard topics	objective test questions; completion % for short-answer questions; rubric for essay questions	average assessments and apply as percentage of final grade

Assessment	Feedback	Formative Use	Grading Standards	Summative Use
Journals	by student, in the feedback section, actionable suggestions for next iteration or ask to re-submit; mark-up on essay questions	offer extra practice to students who need it on specific topics; add relevant videos to course module; individual tutoring as needed	complete / incomplete percentage; rubric for essay questions	average assessments and apply as percentage of final grade
Homework	per question; in individualized study plan; follow-up email for missing/failing scores; mark up on scratch work if submitted; ungraded gets no feedback	offer extra practice to students who need it on specific topics; add relevant videos to course module; individual tutoring as needed	objective questions on problem sets (true/false, fill in the blank, multiple choice, etc.); ungraded assumed completion	average assessments and apply as percentage of final grade
Tests	per question with suggestions on where to find key info; mark up on scratch work if submitted; follow-up email for missing/failing scores; mark -up on essay questions with actionable suggestions for future action for improvement	offer extra practice to students who need it on specific topics; add relevant videos to course module; individual/small group tutoring as needed; analyze per question success rate; determine good/ bad questions; adjust next year's slide decks, HW homework as needed	plagiarism detector software; rubric for essays; objective questions (true/ false, fill in the blank, multiple choice, etc.)	average assessments and apply as percentage of final grade

Assessment	Feedback	Formative Use	Grading Standards	Summative Use
Final Exams	per question with suggestions on where to find key info; follow-up email for missing/ failing scores; on scratch work if submitted; mark -up on essay questions with suggestions for future action for improvement	analyze per question success rate; determine good/bad questions; adjust next year's slide decks, homework as needed	plagiarism detector software; rubric for essays; objective questions (true/ false, fill in the blank, multiple choice, etc.)	average assessments and apply as percentage of final grade
Timeline	follow-up email for missing/failing scores	add periodic reminders for completion to class, possibly take up more frequently	complete/ incomplete percentage	% of final grade

Remember that in individual tutoring, teachers need to help students figure out how to make their work better. I recall taking a creative writing class in undergraduate school and on my essays the professor simply wrote, "Develop." If I knew how to develop something, I would have done it! Tell students what they did wrong ("You didn't add enough supporting details to make a convincing scene."). Then, tell them what they need to do next ("You'll need to go back and add more supporting details."). Finally, help them make a plan for getting it done ("Rewrite this with three more supporting details and get it back to me next week by Friday at 5 pm."). Their prefrontal cortexes aren't fully myelinated, so help with that impulse control issue by giving students firm instructions about what to do—these instructions make students more likely to get the work done.

 Tell students a) what they did wrong, b) how to fix it, and c) a plan for getting it done.

Teachers can head off confusion by being very clear about assignment expectations. The assignment name should be listed in the content module task list, on the calendar on the front of the module, in the LMS calendar, and within the content module. When students click on that link, the assignment itself should load, along with specific directions, including the due date. Students should be able to easily understand how the teacher will assess the assignment, and where and when the teacher will leave feedback. Remember to issue all feedback within a reasonable period (e.g. a week).

Concurrent with this kind of feedback is building a relationship with students by couching this in warm praise. For example, "Julio, I can see you worked really hard on this, and I appreciate it." But never give false praise—students can smell that stink a mile off. If you have a student whom you feel quite sure didn't put much effort into it, you could say something like, "James, can you tell me how you worked on this? I really want to help, and the more I know about how you did this, the better I can help you." Reframing the issue as offering support instead of judgment is more likely to lead to a positive reaction from the student.

One of my favorite ways to build a relationship with students is to ask them to write the test questions, with suggested model answers. An ideal way to do this is in the discussion questions, with the responses to another student as the sample model answers. This helps students practice thinking about the class content and elaborate on their knowledge. While I don't always use those exam questions, I frequently save one or two for the next year's class. Most students get some satisfaction from knowing that they are contributing to the course design.

Another key way to build relationships is to normalize revisions. In my math classes, I tell students that I offer these seemingly infinite opportunities to work until they get the problem right because I want them to master the material. Similarly, I'll closely monitor discussion questions to catch errors in a positive way. "Sarah, that's really interesting. How do you know that? This link might help you with some information." In addition, when I assign writing, I tell students about my husband, who is a professional writer, and how he works closely with his editors to ensure that his writing is what is needed. Therefore, I expect them to need revisions on their writing and I build that process into the class. Trying over and over doesn't make them a bad student—it makes them a hard worker.

Teachers should also provide written descriptions of each assignment for students, as well how much each assignment is worth in the class. This helps students know what to expect, and helps them plan their time. Synchronous sessions should be required, but they should not be a key part of students' grades due to inequity in access. Remember, all information reviewed in live class sessions should be available in writing in the course module, and students should be taught how to find the information during orientation. Teachers should be sure to periodically review this with students, and remind them via LMS announcements.

Here is a sample from our hypothetical class:

Written Assignments:

- *Journal:* Students will write about their learning experience on a regular basis. 5% of final grade
- *Weekly Discussion Questions:* Discussion questions will be drawn from the text. Each student must write a meaningful reply to a question by midnight, EST, Monday, and meaningfully respond to two other students' responses by midnight, EST, on Wednesday. See the Assignment policies for more information about meaningful participation. 15% of final grade

Quizzes and Tests:

- *Weekly Quizzes:* Students will complete problems drawn from the text as well as non-text material. 20% of final grade
- *Tests:* Students will complete problems drawn from the text as well as non-text material. 20% of final grade
- *Comprehensive Exams:* There will be two comprehensive exams. 10% of final grade.

Other Assignments/Requirements:

- *Homework:* Students will complete a variety of tasks and exercises. 20% of final grade, total
- *Timeline:* Students will maintain a historical timeline of major scientific discoveries. 10% of final grade

Grading Breakdown:

Course Work	Percentage
Homework	20
Weekly quizzes	20
Tests	20
Discussion questions	15
Journal	5
Timeline	10
Comprehensive final exams—2	10
Total	100

Once teachers have decided what they what to assign, they can decide when they want to assign it. Remember, this pacing guide should exist for the entire school year at this point, including a rough idea of how teachers going to assign each component. For example, I know that the essay writing will take six weeks for students, and nine weeks for me. From earlier chapters, here is a tentative schedule for the first part of our hypothetical science class:

Week	Chapter	Assignment	Topic
0	--	Introduction	Orientation
1	1	DQs HW/Quiz	Scientific Method
2	7	DQs HW/Quiz	Evolution
3	8	DQs HW/Quiz	History of Life
4	13	DQs HW/Quiz	Plant Processes
5	14	DQs HW/Quiz	Animals and Behavior writing: topic selection
6	18	DQs HW/Quiz	Interactions of Living Things writing: note taking
7	19	DQs HW/Quiz	Natural Cycles writing: thesis statement begin lab: nitrogen cycle
8	20	DQs HW/Quiz	Ecosystems writing: introduction/conclusion continue lab: nitrogen cycle
9	21	DQs HW/Quiz	Environmental Challenges writing: rough draft due continue lab: nitrogen cycle
10	--	DQs Test	Review writing: final draft due lab: lab report due, with growth chart

Scheduling the work is easier when teachers have a weekly calendar with tentative times. By estimating times for each assignment (and remember, assignments will take longer when students are working independently from home), teachers can avoid assigning too much work. Teachers should work with colleagues and parents to get a rough estimate about how much time students are spending on their class, as well as on their other classes. Often, I ask students about work time as part of the anonymous How's It Going survey at the six-week mark, but teachers shouldn't hesitate to poll parents and students earlier and with more frequency. Teachers might even consider making it an extra credit question on each week's quiz.

Week 2: Understanding How Evolution Works

1) At the end of Week 2, students will have:

- Attended the video conference session
- Answered the Discussion Question (ten minutes)
- Responded to 2 other students (fifteen minutes)
- Completed the Sedimentary Rock diagram (fifteen minutes)
- Read and summarized the *Origin of the Species* excerpt (twenty minutes)
- Completed the *Galapagos Islands* lab (twenty minutes per day/sixty minutes)
- Read Chapter 7 and completed the Guided Notes (twenty minutes per day/sixty minutes)
- Added *adaptation, evolution, natural selection* to your Leitner box (five minutes)
- Added dates to your timeline (ten minutes)
- Completed the quiz in the LMS (thirty minutes)

2) Your calendar for Week 2 is below.

Monday	Tuesday	Wednesday	Thursday	Friday
Day 1	**Day 2**	**Day 3**	**Day 4**	**Day 5**
Aug 26	**Aug 27**	**Aug 28**	**Aug 29**	**Aug 30**
DQ Due (ten minutes)	Lecture 1 pm	**Two DQ Responses Due (fifteen minutes)**	Lecture 1 pm	**Quiz (thirty minutes)**
Read Chapter 7, Section 1 and completed the Guided Notes (twenty minutes)	Read Chapter 7, Section 2 and complete the Guided Notes (twenty minutes)	Read Chapter 7, Section 3 and complete the Guided Notes (twenty minutes)	Read and summarize the *Origin of the Species* excerpt (twenty minutes)	
Add adaptation, evolution, natural selection to your Leitner box (five minutes)	Complete Part A of the *Galapagos Islands* lab (twenty minutes)	Complete Part B of the *Galapagos Islands* lab (twenty minutes)	Complete Part C of the *Galapagos Islands* lab (twenty minutes) Add dates to your timeline (ten minutes)	
Complete the Sedimentary Rock diagram (twenty minutes) fifty-five minutes	Review Memory Work (five minutes) Complete the Sedimentary Rock diagram (fifteen minutes) sixty minutes + class session	Review Memory Work (five minutes) sixty minutes	Review Memory Work (five minutes) fifty-five minutes + class session	

Assessing Writing

I am not a writing teacher. I have never been trained on teaching writing, and I am not certified as an English teacher. However, what I do have is significant experience in academia, including hundreds of college credits. I use that experience to inform my academic writing instruction.

Typically, when I want students to write something, I will tell them exactly what I want, and how I want them to do it, as per Chapter 7, "Putting It All Together." Many of my older students are confident writers, but some are not. For those students, I offer a generic outline, useful in all sorts of non-English classes.

Although many writing teachers will scoff, I find that students are often terribly grateful for this minimal assistance. A teacher should of course use their best judgment, but some teachers may find the idea useful. Enforcing the citations and transitions depends on the age and previous writing experience of the student. This outline may already be familiar to some readers:

1) thesis sentence

    a) first concept
    b) second concept
    c) third concept; transition

2) transition; first concept restatement

    a) first supporting fact(s) (cited)
    b) second supporting fact(s) (cited)
    c) third supporting fact(s) (cited); transition

3) transition; second concept restatement

    a) first supporting fact(s) (cited)
    b) second supporting fact(s) (cited)
    c) third supporting fact(s) (cited); transition

4) transition; third concept restatement

    a) first supporting fact(s) (cited)
    b) second supporting fact(s) (cited)
    c) third supporting fact(s) (cited); transition

5) concluding statement

    a) first concept restatement
    b) second concept restatement

c) third concept restatement

d) conclusion/thesis restatement

Typically, I grade essays with a rubric that looks something like the following. Keep in mind that this is the most complex version of the rubric. However, I strip out sections with younger students to focus on the most important parts, like supporting the student's position and linking the argument to relevant examples.

Criteria	Novice	Competent	Proficient
Content and Development: Key Elements	**1 Points** Student attempts key elements of the assignment.	**2 Points** Some key elements of the assignment are covered in a substantive way.	**4 Points** All key elements of the assignment are covered in a substantive way.
Content and Development: Good Reasons	**6 Points** One good reason is given in support of the student's position	**12 Points** Two good reasons are given in support of the student's position	**18 Points** At least three good reasons are given in support of the student's position
Content and Development: Issue Identification	**0 Points** No issues related to the question are identified.	**3 Points** Some issues related to question are somewhat identified.	**6 Points** The issues related to question are identified.
Content and Development: Length	**0 Points** The paper is minimal.	**3 Points** The paper is significantly shorter than six pages in length or is significantly longer.	**6 Points** The paper is six pages in length.
Content and Development: Persuasiveness	**0 Points** The content is not comprehensive, accurate, and/or persuasive.	**3 Points** The content is somewhat comprehensive, accurate, and/or persuasive.	**6 Points** The content is comprehensive, accurate, and/or persuasive.

Criteria	Novice	Competent	Proficient
Content and Development: Theme Development	**0 Points** The paper does not develop a central theme or idea, directed toward the appropriate audience.	**3 Points** The paper somewhat develops a central theme or idea, directed toward the appropriate audience.	**6 Points** The paper does develop a central theme or idea, directed toward the appropriate audience.
Content and Development: Vocabulary Use and Text Linkage	**0 Points** The paper does not link theory to relevant examples from the text and does not use the vocabulary of the theory correctly.	**3 Points** The paper may link theory to relevant examples from the text and sometimes uses the vocabulary of the theory correctly.	**6 Points** The paper does link theory to relevant examples from the text and does use the vocabulary of the theory correctly.
Content and Development: Support, Analysis, and Logic	**0 Points** Major points are not stated clearly; are not supported by specific details, examples, or analysis; or are not organized logically.	**3 Points** Major points are sometimes stated clearly; may be supported by specific details, examples, or analysis; and are sometimes organized logically.	**6 Points** Major points are stated clearly; are supported by specific details, examples, or analysis; and are organized logically.
Content and Development: Introduction	**0 Points** The introduction does not provide sufficient background on the topic and does not preview major points.	**3 Points** The introduction may provide sufficient background on the topic and may preview major points.	**6 Points** The introduction does provide sufficient background on the topic and does preview major points.
Content and Development: Conclusion	**0 Points** The conclusion is logical, flows from the body of the paper, and/or does not review the major points.	**3 Points** The conclusion may be logical, may flows from the body of the paper, and may review the major points.	**6 Points** The conclusion is logical, flows from the body of the paper, and does review the major points.

Criteria	Novice	Competent	Proficient
Readability and Style: Paragraph Transitions	**0 Points** Paragraph transitions are not present and logical and do not maintain the flow throughout the paper.	**1.5 Points** Paragraph transitions may be present and logical and may maintain the flow throughout the paper.	**3 Points** Paragraph transitions are present and logical and do maintain the flow throughout the paper.
Readability and Style: Tone	**0 Points** The tone is not appropriate to the content and assignment.	**1.5 Points** The tone may be appropriate to the content and assignment.	**3 Points** The tone is appropriate to the content and assignment.
Readability and Style: Sentence Structure	**0 Points** Sentences are not complete, clear, and concise.	**1.5 Points** Sentences may be complete, clear, and concise.	**3 Points** Sentences are complete, clear, and concise.
Readability and Style: Sentence Construction	**0 Points** Sentences are not well constructed, without consistently strong, varied sentences.	**1.5 Points** Sentences are somewhat well constructed, with inconsistently strong, varied sentences.	**3 Points** Sentences are well constructed, with consistently strong, varied sentences.
Readability and Style: Sentence Transitions	**0 Points** Sentence transitions are not present and do not maintain the flow of thought.	**1.5 Points** Sentence transitions are sometimes present and sometimes maintain the flow of thought.	**3 Points** Sentence transitions are present and maintain the flow of thought.
Mechanics: APA guidelines for format	**0 Points** The paper does *not* follow APA guidelines for format.	**1.5 Points** The paper sometimes follows APA guidelines for format.	**3 Points** The paper does follow APA guidelines for format.

Criteria	Novice	Competent	Proficient
Mechanics: APA guidelines for citations	**0 Points** Citations of original works within the body of the paper do not follow APA guidelines.	**1.5 Points** Citations of original works within the body of the paper sometimes follow APA guidelines.	**3 Points** Citations of original works within the body of the paper do follow APA guidelines.
Mechanics: Layout	**0 Points** The paper is not laid out with effective use of headings, font styles, and white space.	**1.5 Points** The paper is sometimes laid out with effective use of headings, font styles, and white space.	**3 Points** The paper is laid out with effective use of headings, font styles, and white space.
Mechanics: Grammar, Usage, and Punctuation	**0 Points** Rules of grammar, usage, and punctuation are *not* followed.	**1.5 Points** Rules of grammar, usage, and punctuation are sometimes followed.	**3 Points** Rules of grammar, usage, and punctuation are always followed.
Mechanics: Spelling	**0 Points** Spelling is often incorrect.	**1.5 Points** Spelling is mostly correct.	**3 Points** Spelling is correct.

In addition, the Big 3 LMSs all have content mark up tools, allowing teachers to use a digital pen to mark up student's papers. This is particularly helpful for illustrating organization issues, allowing teachers to draw linkages between topics.

Portfolios

In one sense, LMSs are fantastic ways to create a portfolio of student work. Barring software failure, all the previously assessed work is archived. Alternatively, teachers can assign a portfolio as an assignment, complete with software-created templates. Teachers can offer text feedback, use a rubric, or both.

However, getting the portfolio offline is a little trickier. Students or teachers have to download a .ZIP package (file compression software) and then extract the files (Windows has this built in). Finally, the results are in HTML format—basically, what is downloaded is a mini-website.

Because not all students are easily able to access the LMS and upload large files like videos, sound recordings, and image files of drawings, using portfolios as a main part of the class assessment can be an equity issue. Not all students will complain about it, because they often don't realize how poor their internet connection is when compared to other students. Be cautious when assigning portfolios.

Cheating

Although the research is inconclusive, my experience tends to align with the research that suggests that cheating is no more likely online than it is face to face.[cdxlv] In fact, I am frequently surprised by the obvious lack of cheating on some assessments. Part of this is due to integrity—I make it clear that I expect students to act with integrity, and many do their best live up to my expectations. Another part is that students of a certain age are frequently overconfident.

> When I was a boy of 14, my father was so ignorant I could hardly stand to have the old man around. But when I got to be 21, I was astonished at how much the old man had learned in seven years.

–often attributed to Mark Twain[cdxlvi]

In my experience, this quote is spot on with a certain group of students. This sort of thinking also applies to many terrible attempts at plagiarism, like copying and pasting direct from Wikipedia, complete with hyperlinks. Those assignments I assign a zero to and contact the parent, asking them to work with the student to resubmit properly done work.

Another kind of student simply can't be bothered to cheat—it's easier to click the first answer or write something sloppy and vague than it is to do the work. Or perhaps they're like a student I once knew who no longer wanted to participate in the class and turned in blank sheets of paper with their name on them for an entire semester. Those students often benefit from concerned emails home and the arrangement of some individual synchronous sessions to help engage them in the class.

Finally, despite the hand waving about digital natives, many students are merely bad at using the internet to cheat. They don't know how to Google things properly, and they're not good at adapting items they copy and paste. Although some students can search for YouTube videos, those are not good for cheating on essays. That kind of cheating stands out. Letting students know that cheating will not be tolerated, with a note home to parents, tends to sort that out.

Many parents are resistant to the idea that their child cheated, so using software like Turnitin offers mathematical support to the teacher's argument. Remember, never blame and shame. Just be matter of fact, stating the issue and the solution. Typically, I send an email that looks like thing like this:

> *Good evening,*
>
> *I have been reviewing ___'s report, and I couldn't help but notice that ___ copied and pasted most of it from Wikipedia, including the html links. Please see the included screenshot of the originality report: over half is a direct copy. In addition, students were all warned that Wikipedia was not an acceptable source for the paper.*
>
> *Please review the concept of plagiarism with ____, and have him revise as per the attached template for the final draft next Friday.*

Generally, parents are responsive to this kind of request. However, the youngest students may not have been exposed to the concept of plagiarism. Generally, this can be solved with a quick one-to-one lesson and a gentle referral back to the parent. Teachers should clearly define plagiarism the syllabus and explain exactly how they want students to cite their work (and provide models!). In addition, teachers should explain why it matters. I often refer to apocryphal duels with swords over correct citations. A syllabus quiz can assist in ensuring that all students are clear on what is acceptable in the course.

As a matter of policy, I inform my supervisor about all instances of cheating, although I can often deal with it by myself. School administration never wants an unexpected phone call from an angry parent about an email accusing their child of plagiarism. Making a habit of BCCing one's supervisor on all emails that might provoke an angry response is a good idea. In practice, this means that I BCC my boss on any email that isn't a normal question. That way, she's never caught by surprise.

"Out of sight, out of mind" means that students might cheat because they perceive no consequences for it. This is why I have a policy about cheating in my syllabus, which refers to the school honor code. Reviewing the policy in the class orientation makes intolerance for cheating clear to all students in advance.

Because I offer so many low-stakes assessments, each assessment is worth a small part of the overall grade. I work through the calculations with the students to show them that each homework problem is a small fraction of a percent of the final grade, that each quiz problem is a slightly larger fraction of a percent of the final grade, and so on. Research shows that low-stakes assessments reduce the likelihood of student cheating.[cdxlvii]

Parents often inappropriately offer help. One parent contacted me to ask for an answer key to their child's test, because they were checking every problem and making their child correct the work before their child turned it in to me. I had to gently explain to the parent that the child was capable of learning from the feedback given in the course, and that learning to self-check their work was a valuable life skill. A teacher might want to request that school administration create parent coaching guides—how much help is appropriate? When should parents help? With what, exactly?

Other preventative measures are easy to apply. In my math courses, because I use web-based computer adaptive software (Pearson's MathXL for School), each student is assigned a unique problem set for every homework, quiz, and test. This means that every student has their own, separate assignments—no two are alike. In addition, plagiarism-checking software is easily enabled in any of the Big 3 LMSs. Teachers can use drafts and revisions for major written assignments, so students cannot easily outsource any given essay.

Another often-overlooked problem is when a teacher assigns more difficult questions on the exam than the students had been grappling with in the course. Students find it unfair and feel justified in cheating because they feel that the teacher cheated them. I find it difficult to argue with students on this point, and so I do my best to ensure that students always know what I expect of them. There are never any surprises on my assessments. I tell students that I'm not there to make their life difficult, that I just want to see how much they know— that the point of the assessment is determine how much they've learned.

Less common online is when students feel obligated to assist their peers succeed on exams and other assignments. Reducing the point value of any one assignment helps reduce the temptation to ask for assistance. In addition, having a clear policy helps draw a bright line rule for acceptable and unacceptable assistance.

Some students cheat out of desperation. They feel overwhelmed by the demands of the class. This is where providing emotional support and reassurance helps prevent poor behavior. "Yes, this course demands sixty-eight minutes per day of study, on average. You can do this!" Offering one-to-one tutoring sessions, referring students to additional academic support, and facilitating peer study groups all help students feel less helpless. In addition, offering clear daily schedules breaks down what seems like an insurmountable task into bite-sized parts. What Lemov refers to as "dipsticking" or quick, anonymous checks for understanding[cdxlviii] helps teachers track students who might feel overwhelmed and offer support as needed.

I have taken courses graded on a curve, and no one enjoyed the experience. My students are usually horrified when I explain how it works: in a class of twelve students, one student will get an A, three students will get a B, four students will get a C, three students will get a D, and one student will get an F. The F student could obtain a 90%, but if it's the lowest grade in the class, they'll fail. Obviously, this sort of high-stakes grading practically compels students to cheat, which is why I don't use it. I use criterion-referenced grading, instead. If students meet the standard, they earn the grade.

End -of -Year Wrap-Up

At the end of the school year, use those last few days to seek feedback from students and parents. An anonymous survey from both is helpful. Teachers could recycle their How's It Going survey again. However, at the end of the year, teachers might look for a different kind of feedback as parents and students reflect on the school year as a whole.

When surveying parents, teachers might want to ask questions like, "Would you recommend this teacher to others?" and "Did your student get better at ____?" Especially important are questions around clear guidance, such as "My student learned from feedback on their work" or "My student knew what to do to get a good grade." In terms of building community, ask parents about whether you "used examples of different cultures, backgrounds, and families to connect with students" and "My child's teacher respected students from different cultures or backgrounds." Make sure to get feedback on your online classroom management skills with questions such as, "My student felt that most students were on-task and completed their work" and "My student wanted to attend synchronous class sessions." The answers may be painful, but they are useful for identifying areas for self-improvement.

Although many students are often happy at the end of the school year and tend to give positive answers when asked about their classes, I find that asking students what advice they'd give next year's students is often revealing about areas in which I can improve. This is easily done in a discussion question for the last week of class. For example, here are some collated answers from my 2019/2020 math students:

- Take screenshots .
- Ask questions.

- Come to class.
- Re-watch the lectures.
- Taking handwritten notes during the lectures is very helpful..
- If you need help, email .
- Don't procrastinate.
- Try and get a day or so ahead .
- Read the textbook.
- Take good notes.
- Take breaks.
- Don't give up.
- Memorize formulas.
- Copy and paste your discussion question answer.
- It's not a race.
- Stay organized.

Taking notes came up twice, both in the context of lectures and in the context of reading the textbook. While I do provide copies of my slide deck, I have not provided notes nor have I assigned notes for most of my math students. An area of improvement could be making weekly notes assignments for students.

Finally, the last item in each of my classes is the goodbye email. In that email, I thank parents for entrusting me with their child's education that year, let them know that the final report card notes are available, and wish their child well in their future educational endeavors. Always end the class on a high note—teachers want students to finish with a positive feeling about the class so students will be more willing to attend school next autumn.

Chapter Summary

Summative assessments are often not useful in ensuring student learning. Instead, teachers should focus on formative assessment. One way to make formative assessment useful is to create a formal plan, including how feedback will be given, how teachers will use that feedback, what kind of grading standards a teacher will use, and how it contributes to summative assessment. Once that plan is in place, teachers can use it to help schedule work, both by the content module and inside the module. Other kinds of assessment include writing assignments, often graded with a rubric. Likewise, portfolios can be made online, although that requires digitizing content. There are specific ways that teachers can avoid student cheating, although teachers shouldn't worry too much about online cheating. At the end of the year, teachers should self-assess by surveying students and parents and using the results to inform next year's teaching.

APPENDIX A
SUGGESTED RESOURCES

Books:

A Mathematician's Lament by Lockhart

Bringing Words to Life by Beck, McKeown, and Kucan

Classroom Collaboration by Laurel Hudson

Culturally Responsive Teaching and the Brain by Hammond

Dual Coding with Teachers by Caviglioli

e-Learning and the Science of Instruction by Clark and Mayer

Explicit and Direct Instruction, edited by Boxer and Bennett

Explicit Direct Instruction by Hollingsworth and Ybarra

How Learning Happens by Kirschner and Hendrick

Language at the Speed of Sight by Seidenberg

Make It Stick by Brown, Roediger, and McDaniel.

Making Kids Cleverer by Didau

Neurotribes by Silberman

Other People's Children by Delpit

Reader, Come Home by Wolf

Reading in the Brain by Dehaene

Reading Reconsidered by Lemov, Driggs, and Woolway

Responsive Teaching by Fletcher-Wood

Small Teaching Online by Darby and Lang

Teach Like a Champion by Lemov

Teach Your Child to Read in 100 Easy Lessons by Engelman

Teachers vs. Tech by Christodoulou

The Checklist Manifesto by Gawande

The Curriculum, edited by Sealy and Bennett

The Explosive Child by Greene

The Knowledge Deficit by Hirsch, Jr.

The Math Gene by Keith Devlin

The Number Sense by Dehaene

The Schools We Need by Hirsch, Jr.

The Teenage Brain by Jensen and Nutt

The Writing Revolution by Hochman and Wexler

Thinking, Fast and Slow by Kahneman

What's Going on in There? by Eliot

When Can You Trust the Experts? by Willingham

Why Don't Students Like School? by Willingham

Websites, Apps, and Documents:

- "Educating Students Who are Deaf or Hard of Hearing: A Guide for Professionals in General Education Settings" by the Clerc Center at Gallaudet University, in collaboration with Educational Regional Center 20 in Texas
- "How General Ed and Special Ed Teachers Can Partner as Allies," YouTube video by Common Sense Education and Monise Seward
- *ADDitude Magazine*
- Anki
- Canva
- EdReports
- Evidence for ESSA (Every Student Succeeds Act)
- Hoagies' Gifted Education website
- Jennifer Gonzalez's Student Inventory
- Memrise

- National Association for Gifted Children
- Rosenshine's Principles of Instruction
- Supporting Emotional Needs of the Gifted
- The Noun Project
- Tinycards
- What Works Clearinghouse

BIBLIOGRAPHY

The Aspen Institute Education & Society Program. (2018). Pursuing Social and Emotional Development Through a Racial Equity Lens: A Call to Action. Retrieved June 2, 2020 from https://assets.aspeninstitute.org/content/uploads/2018/05/Aspen-Institute_Framing-Doc_Call-to-Action.pdf

(PTAC), P. T. (2014, February). Protecting Student Privacy While Using Online Educational Services: Requirements and Best Practices. Retrieved May 28, 2020, from tech.ed.gov: https://tech.ed.gov/wp-content/uploads/2014/09/Student-Privacy-and-Online-Educational-Services-February-2014.pdf

@dylanwiliam. (2020, May 29). Agreed. But if you explain the "hypercorrection effect" to them, they might see that making mistakes and being corrected is better for long-term learning than getting the correct answer by guesswork . . . *Twitter*, 9:57 AM.

Aaronson, T., & O'Connor, J. (2012, September 16). In K12 Courses, 275 Students to a Single Teacher. Retrieved April 6, 2020, from https://stateimpact.npr.org/florida/2012/09/16/in-k12-courses-275-students-to-a-single-teacher/

ABC News. (2010, April 9). What Kids Know: McDonald's, Toyota, Disney. Retrieved June 15, 2020, from https://abcnews.go.com/Business/kids-mcdonalds-toyota-disney/story?id=10333145

Adelman, H. S., & Taylor, L. (2005). *The Implementation Guide to Student Learning Supports in the Classroom and Schoolwide*. Thousand Oaks, CA: Corwin Press.

ADHD Editorial Board. (n.d.). 12 Ways to Make Instructions Sink In. Retrieved June 8, 2020, from https://www.additudemag.com/teaching-students-to-follow-directions/

American Psychological Association. (2006, July 15). Stereotype Threat Widens Achievement Gap. Retrieved July 2, 2020, from https://www.apa.org/research/action/stereotype

Anderson, M. (2019, June 13). Mobile Technology and Home Broadband 2019. Retrieved June 24, 2020, from https://www.pewresearch.org/internet/2019/06/13/mobile-technology-and-home-broadband-2019/

Arbaugh, J., Godfrey, M., Johnson, M., Pollack, B. N., & Wresch, W. (2009). Research in Online and Blended Learning in the Business Disciplines: Key Findings and Possible Future Directions. *Internet and Higher Education*, 71–87.

Arnstein, A. F. (2009). The Emerging Neurobiology of Attention Deficit Hyperactivity Disorder: The Key Role of the Prefrontal Association Cortex. *The Journal of Pediatrics*, 154–59.

Associated Press. (2020, April 8). Teen Arrested after "Zoom Bombing" High School Classes. Retrieved June 1, 2020, from https://nypost.com/2020/04/08/teen-arrested-after-zoom-bombing-high-school-classes/

Auwarter, A. E., & Aruguete, M. S. (2010). Effects of Student Gender and Socioeconomic Status on Teacher Perceptions. *The Journal of Educational Research*, 242–46.

Babb, K. A., & Ross, C. (2009). The Timing of Online Lecture Slide Availability and Its Effect on Attendance, Participation, and Exam Performance. *Computers & Education*, 868–881.

Balf, T. (2014, March 6). The Story Behind the SAT Overhaul. Retrieved July 10, 2020, from https://www.nytimes.com/2014/03/09/magazine/the-story-behind-the-sat-overhaul.html

Bartlett, J. D., Griffin, J., & Thomson, D. (2020, March 19). Resources for Supporting Children's Emotional Well-being during the COVID-19 Pandemic. Retrieved May 27, 2020, from https://www.childtrends.org/publications/resources-for-supporting-childrens-emotional-well-being-during-the-covid-19-pandemic

Bauer, J. F., & Anderson, R. S. (2000). Evaluating Students' Written Performance in the Online Classroom. *New Directions for Teaching and Learning*, 65–71.

Bauer, S. W., & Wise, J. (2016). *The Well-Trained Mind*. New York, NY: W.W. Norton & Company, Inc.

Beck, I. L., McKeown, M. G., & Kucan, L. (2013). *Bringing Words to Life: Robust Vocabulary Instruction*. New York: Guilford Press.

Bernard, R. M., Abrami, P. C., Borokhovski, E., Wade, C. A., Tamim, R. M., Surkes, M. A., et al. (2009). A Meta-Analysis of Three Types of Interaction Treatments in Distance Education. *Review of Educational Research*, 1243–1289.

Blackboard. (n.d.). Video. Retrieved June 2, 2020, from https://help.blackboard.com/Collaborate/v12/Moderator/Configure_Your_Session/Video

Board, A. E., & Barkely, R. (2019, October 3). What Is Executive Function? 7 Deficits Tied to ADHD. Retrieved May 27, 2020, from https://www.additudemag.com/7-executive-function-deficits-linked-to-adhd/

Bowles, N., & Keller, M. H. (2019, December 7). Video Games and Online Chats Are "Hunting Grounds" for Sexual Predators. Retrieved June 30, 2020, from https://www.nytimes.com/interactive/2019/12/07/us/video-games-child-sex-abuse.html

Boxer, A. (2020, April 21). Dual Coding for Teachers Who Can't Draw. Retrieved June 17, 2020, from https://www.youtube.com/watch?v=16SBht2iF_k

Boxer, A. (2019, April 11). Planning Smarter: Rethinking the Short, Medium and Long Term. Retrieved May 27, 2020, from https://achemicalorthodoxy.wordpress.com/2019/04/11/planning-smarter-rethinking-the-short-medium-and-long-term/

Brann, A. (2011). Captioning to Support Literacy. Retrieved May 20, 2020, from https://www.readingrockets.org/article/captioning-support-literacy-0

Bratsberg, B., & Rogeberg, O. (2018). Flynn Effect and Its Reversal are Both Environmentally Caused. *PNAS*, 6674–78.

Brown, P. C., Roediger III, H. L., & McDaniel, M. A. (2014). *Make It Stick: The Science of Successful Learning*. Boston, MA: Belknap Press.

Burgess, D. (2012). *Teach Like a PIRATE: Increase Student Engagement, Boost Your Creativity, and Transform Your Life as an Educator*. Dave Burgess Consulting, Inc.

Bush, G. W. (2000, July 10). George W. Bush's Speech to the NAACP. Retrieved June 9, 2020, from https://www.washingtonpost.com/wp-srv/onpolitics/elections/bushtext071000.htm

Butler, A., Marsh, E., & Godbole, N. (2013). Explanation Feedback is Better Than Correct Answer Feedback for Promoting Transfer of Learning. *Journal of Educational Psychology*, 290–98.

Cantor, C. (2019, November 6). Why Being Bored Can Be Hazardous to Your Health. Retrieved May 21, 2020, from https://science.fas.columbia.edu/news/why-being-bored-can-be-hazardous-to-your-health/

Carey, B. (2013, September 25). Language Gap between Rich and Poor Children Begins in Infancy, Stanford Psychologists Find. Retrieved June 15, 2020, from https://news.stanford.edu/news/2013/september/toddler-language-gap-091213.html

Carnegie Foundation. (2014, August 4). What is the Carnegie Unit? Retrieved June 15, 2020, from https://www.carnegiefoundation.org/faqs/carnegie-unit/

Carpenter, S., & Toftness, A. (2017). The Effect of Prequestions on Learning from Video Presentations. *Journal of Applied Research in Memory and Cognition*, 313–36.

Carr, J. M. (2019, July 10). Two Tips to Increase Students' Use of Office Hours. Retrieved June 3, 2020, from https://www.facultyfocus.com/articles/effective-classroom-management/increase-office-hours/

Carr, J. M. (2019, July 10). Two Tips to Increase Students' Use of Office Hours. Retrieved July 6, 2020, from https://www.facultyfocus.com/articles/effective-classroom-management/increase-office-hours/

Carter, C. E., & Grahn, J. A. (2016). Optimizing Music Learning: Exploring How Blocked and Interleaved Practice Schedules Affect Advanced Performance. *Frontiers in Psychology*, 1251.

Caviglioli, O. (2019). *Dual Coding with Teachers*. Melton, Woodbridge, UK: John Catt Educational Ltd.

Chatmon, L. R., & Osta, K. (2018, August 17). 5 Steps for Liberating Public Education From Its Deep Racial Bias. Retrieved June 2, 2020, from https://www.edweek.org/ew/articles/2018/08/22/5-steps-for-liberating-public-education-from.html

Cho, K., & MacArthur, C. (2011). Learning by Reviewing. *Journal of Educational Psychology*, 73–84.

Christodoulou, D. (2020). *Teachers vs Tech: The Case for an Ed Tech Revolution*. Oxford: Oxford University Press.

Clark, D. (2020, April 11). *Nass & Reeves – Computers are Seen as Human*. Retrieved July 7, 2020, from Donald Clark Plan B: https://donaldclarkplanb.blogspot.com/2020/04/nass-reeves-computers-are-seen-as-human.html

Clark, R. C., & Mayer, R. E. (2016). *E-learning and the Science of Instruction*. Hoboken, NJ: John Wiley & Sons, Inc.

Classroom Accommodations for Dysgraphia. (n.d.). Retrieved May 20, 2020, from https://www.understood.org/en/school-learning/partnering-with-childs-school/instructional-strategies/at-a-glance-classroom-accommodations-for-dysgraphia

Common Core State Standards Initiative. (2020). Grade 4 » Operations & Algebraic Thinking » Generate and analyze patterns. » 5. Retrieved June 14, 2020, from http://www.corestandards.org/Math/Content/4/OA/C/5/

Conradt, S. (2016, February 26). Why No One Wanted A&W's Third-Pound Burger. Retrieved June 24, 2020, from https://www.mentalfloss.com/article/76144/why-no-one-wanted-aws-third-pound-burger

Copyright Law of the United States (Title 17) Chapter 1: Section 110(2)(A). (n.d.). Retrieved May 27, 2020, from https://www.copyright.gov/title17/92chap1.html#110?loclr=blogcop

Curators of the University of Missouri. (2011). Visual Schedules. Retrieved June 8, 2020, from http://ebi.missouri.edu/?p=1503

Darby, F. (n.d.). How to Be a Better Online Teacher. Retrieved May 28, 2020, from https://www.chronicle.com/interactives/advice-online-teaching

Darby, F., & Lang, J. M. (2019). *Small Teaching Online*. San Francisco, CA: Jossey-Bass.

Darling-Hammond, L., Flook, L., Cook-Harvey, C., Barron, B., & Osher, D. (2020). Implications for Educational Practice of the Science of Learning and Development. *Applied Developmental Science*, 97–140.

Dehaene, S. (2011). *The Number Sense: How the Mind Creates Mathematics*. New York: Oxford University Press.

Deunk, M. I., Smale-Jacobse, A. E., de Boer, H., Doolaard, S., & Bosker, R. J. (2018). Effective Differentiation Practices: A Systematic Review and Metaanalysis of Studies on the Cognitive Effects of Differentiation Practices in Primary Education. *Educational Research Review*, 31–54.

Didau, D. (2019). *Making Kids Cleverer*. Williston, VT: Crown House Publishing Company.

Dixson, M. D. (2010). Creating Effective Student Engagement in Online Courses: What do Students Find Engaging? *Journal of the Scholarship of Teaching and Learning*, 1–13.

DO-IT, University of Washington (2019, April 30). What is the Difference between Accommodation and Modification for a Student with a Disability? Retrieved July 8, 2020, from https://www.washington.edu/doit/what-difference-between-accommodation-and-modification-student-disability

Dougherty, E. (2012, September). Why Assignments Matter. Retrieved June 8, 2020, from http://www.ascd.org/publications/books/112048/chapters/Why-Assignments-Matter.aspx

Draeger, K. J. (2013). *Draw the USA*. CreateSpace Independent Publishing Platform.

Draus, P. J., Curran, M. J., & Trempus, M. S. (2014). The Influence of Instructor-Generated Video Content on Student Satisfaction with and Engagement in Asynchronous Online Classes. *MERLOT Journal of Online Learning and Teaching*, 240–54.

Eberly Center for Teaching Excellence and Educational Innovation. (2020). My Students Cheat on Assignments and Exams. Retrieved June 18, 2020, from https://www.cmu.edu/teaching/solveproblem/strat-cheating/cheating-05.html

Emanuel, G. (2013, September 3). Time Poverty. Retrieved June 2, 2020, from State of Opportunity: https://stateofopportunity.michiganradio.org/post/time-poverty

eMarketer. (2007). Data: How Many People Own a Printer. Retrieved July 3, 2020, from http://adverlab.blogspot.com/2009/05/data-how-many-people-own-printer.html

Fagell, P. L. (2019, July 1). Teachers and Social Media: A Cautionary Tale about the Risks. Retrieved June 2, 2020, from https://kappanonline.org/fagell-teachers-social-media-risks-compliance-specialist-corruption/

Feldstein, M. (2018, July 6). Canvas Surpasses Blackboard Learn in US Market Share. Retrieved May 28, 2020, from https://eliterate.us/canvas-surpasses-blackboard-learn-in-us-market-share/

Fenton, W. (2017, June 21). Google Classroom Absent From College Courses. Retrieved May 28, 2020, from https://www.insidehighered.com/digital-learning/article/2017/06/21/google-classroom-not-college-classroom

Fernandez, M., & Hauser, C. (2015, October 5). Texas Mother Teaches Textbook Company a Lesson on Accuracy. Retrieved July 13, 2020, from https://www.nytimes.com/2015/10/06/us/publisher-promises-revisions-after-textbook-refers-to-african-slaves-as-workers.html

Ferris, R. (2017, March 8). Scientists Show How Anyone can Improve Memory. Retrieved June 15, 2020, from https://www.cnbc.com/2017/03/08/scientists-taught-normal-people-to-become-extremely-good-at-memorization.html

Finn Jr., C. E. (2014, Winter). Gifted, Talented, and Underserved. Retrieved June 9, 2020, from https://www.nationalaffairs.com/publications/detail/gifted-talented-and-underserved

Fleming, M. B., Harmon-Cooley, A., & Mcfadden-Wade, G. (2009). Morals Clauses for Educators in Secondary and Postsecondary Schools: Legal Applications and Constitutional Concerns. *Brigham Young University Education and Law Journal*, 67–102.

Fletcher-Wood, H. (2019, January 13). Forming Good Habits, Breaking Bad Habits: What Works? Retrieved May 19, 2020, from https://improvingteaching.co.uk/2019/01/13/forming-good-habits-breaking-bad-habits-what-works/

Franceschini, S., Trevisan, P., Ronconi, L., et al. (2017). Action Video Games Improve Reading Abilities and Visual-to-Auditory Attentional Shifting in English-speaking Children with Dyslexia. *Scientific Reports*.

Gernsbacher, M. A. (2015). Video Captions Benefit Everyone. *Policy Insights from the Behavioral and Brain Sciences*, 195–202.

Goldstein, D. (2018, December 5). "It Just Isn't Working": PISA Test Scores Cast Doubt on U.S. Education Efforts. Retrieved July 13, 2020, from https://www.nytimes.com/2019/12/03/us/us-students-international-test-scores.html

Gonzalez, J. (2016, July 10). A 4-Part System for Getting to Know Your Students. Retrieved June 23, 2020, from https://www.cultofpedagogy.com/relationship-building/

Gonzalez, J. (2018, September 9). Note-taking: A Research Roundup. Retrieved June 8, 2020, from https://www.cultofpedagogy.com/note-taking/Cult of Pedagogy.

Gorman, N. (2017, February 7). Survey Finds Teachers Spend 7 Hours Per Week Searching for Instructional Materials. Retrieved June 22, 2020, from https://www.educationworld.com/a_news/survey-finds-teachers-spend-7-hours-week-searching-instructional-materials-490526015

Gormley, H. (2020, March 17). TEACHing from a Distance and Copyright Considerations. Retrieved May 27, 2020, from https://blogs.loc.gov/copyright/2020/03/teaching-from-a-distance-and-copyright-considerations/

Green, E. L., & Goldstein, D. (2019, October 30). Reading Scores on National Exam Decline in Half the States. Retrieved July 13, 2020, from https://www.nytimes.com/2019/10/30/us/reading-scores-national-exam.html

Green, J. (2016, January 8). How Long on Average does John Green Take to Produce One of His Online Course Videos? Retrieved July 7, 2020, from https://www.quora.com/How-long-on-average-does-John-Green-take-to-produce-one-of-his-online-course-videos

Greene, P. (2018, July 2). Automated Essay Scoring Remains An Empty Dream. Retrieved July 10, 2020, from https://www.forbes.com/sites/petergreene/2018/07/02/automated-essay-scoring-remains-an-empty-dream/

Grose, J. (2020, April 1). 4 Ways to Help Your Anxious Kid. Retrieved May 27, 2020, from https://www.nytimes.com/2020/04/01/parenting/coronavirus-help-anxious-kid.html

Gryvatz Copquin, C. (2013, February 5). Life Is What Happens While We're Not Checking Facts. Retrieved July 1, 2020, from https://www.huffpost.com/entry/gilda-radner_b_2231040

Guo, P. J., Kim, J., & Rubin, R. (2014). How Video Production Affects Student Engagement: An Empirical Study of MOOC Videos. Retrieved July 7, 2020, from http://up.csail.mit.edu/other-pubs/las2014-pguo-engagement.pdf

Gustafson, J. (2020, June 11). Habits for Lifelong Learning: Applying Behavioral Insights to Education. Retrieved June 19, 2020, from https://mrgmpls.wordpress.com/2020/06/11/habits-for-life-long-learning-applying-behavioral-insights-to-education/

Gustafson, J. (2019, June 26). On Curriculum: How Pinterest and TpT Exacerbate Inequity. Retrieved May 27, 2020, from https://achievethecore.org/aligned/curriculum-pinterest-tpt-exacerbate-inequity/

Hampshire, A., Highfield, R. R., Parkin, B. L., & Owen, A. M. (2012). Fractionating Human Intelligence. *Neuron*, 1225–37.

Hanover Research. (2017, November). Best Practices in Math Course Sequencing and Integrated Math. Retrieved July 13, 2020, from https://www.birmingham.k12.mi.us/cms/lib/MI01908619/Centricity/Domain/84/Staceys%20Uploads/Best%20Practices%20in%20Math%20Course%20Sequencing.pdf

Harris, E. A. (2020, April 27). "It Was Just Too Much": How Remote Learning Is Breaking Parents. Retrieved June 1, 2020, from https://www.nytimes.com/2020/04/27/nyregion/coronavirus-homeschooling-parents.html

Harvard, B. (2019, March 13). Brain – Book – Buddy: A Strategy for Assessment. Retrieved June 18, 2020, from https://theeffortfuleducator.com/2019/03/13/brain-book-buddy-a-strategy-for-assessment/

Harvard, B. (2020, June 14). Multiple-Choice Questioning as a Valuable Learning Opportunity. Retrieved July 9, 2020, from https://theeffortfuleducator.com/2020/06/14/multiple-choice-questioning-as-a-valuable-learning-opportunity/

Haydon, T., Mancil, R., Kroeger, S., Mcleskey, J., & Lin, W.-Y. (2011). A Review of the Effectiveness of Guided Notes for Students who Struggle Learning Academic Content. *Preventing School Failure: Alternative Education for Children and Youth*, 226–31.

Hirsch Jr., E. (1996). *The Schools We Need: And Why We Don't Have Them.* New York: Anchor Books.

Hui, C. S., Hoe, N. L., & Lee, P. K. (2017). Teaching and Learning with Concrete-Pictorial-Abstract Sequence – A Proposed Model. *The Mathematics Educator*, 1–28.

Humble, K. (2017, August 7). Gifted vs Gifted. Retrieved May 20, 2020, from https://yellowreadis.com/2017/08/gifted-vs-gifted.html

Hummer, R. A., & Hernandez, E. M. (2013, July 18). The Effect of Educational Attainment on Adult Mortality in the U.S. Retrieved July 1, 2020, from https://www.prb.org/us-educational-attainment-mortality/

Is Progress Being Made Toward Closing the Achievement Gap in Special Education? (2017, October 5). Retrieved June 9, 2020, from https://degree.utpb.edu/articles/education/achievement-gap-special-education.aspx

Jacobson, R. (n.d.). How to Spot Dyscalculia. Retrieved July 8, 2020, from https://childmind.org/article/how-to-spot-dyscalculia/

James, W. (1890). *The Principles of Psychology, Vol. 1.* New York: Dover Press.

Jensen, F. E., & Nutt, A. E. (2015). *The Teenage Brain: A Neuroscientist's Survival Guide to Raising Adolescents and Young Adults.* New York: HarperCollins: New York.

Johnson, J. R. (2015, May 17). Teacher Perceptions of Students in Poverty. *Student Research Submissions*, p. 217.

Kamenetz, A. (2020, June 17). 5 Radical Schooling Ideas For An Uncertain Fall And Beyond. Retrieved June 24, 2020, from https://www.npr.org/2020/06/17/878205853/5-radical-schooling-ideas-for-an-uncertain-fall-and-beyond

Kardas, M., & O'Brien, E. (2018). Easier Seen than Done: Merely Watching Others Perform can Foster an Illusion of Skill Aquisition. *Psychological Science*, 521–36.

Katusic, S., Colligan, R., Barbaresi, W., Schaid, D., & Jacobsen, S. (2001). Incidence of Reading Disability in a Population-based Birth Cohort, 1976-1982, Rochester, Minn. *Mayo Clin Proc*, 1081-10–92.

Kentner, D. (2013, January 11). The Readers' Writers: Educator, Author and Professor Siegfried Engelmann. Retrieved June 24, 2020, from https://www.pekintimes.com/article/20130111/NEWS/301119910

Kim, R., Sheridan, D., & Holcomb, S. (2009). *A Report on the Status of Gay, Lesbian, Bisexual and Transgender People in Education*. Washington, DC: National Education Association of the United States.

Kirschner, P. A., & Hendrick, C. (2020). *How Learning Happens*. New York: Routledge.

Kluger, A., & DeNisi, A. (1996). The Effects of Feedback Interventions on Performance: A Historical Review, a Meta-analysis and a Preliminary Feedback Intervention Theory. *Psychological Bulletin* , 254–84.

Konrad, M., Joseph, L., & Eveleigh, E. (2009). A Meta-Analytic Review of Guided Notes. *Education and Treatment of Children*, 421–44.

Koslo, E. (n.d.). What's the Difference Between a Speech Impairment and a Language Disorder? Retrieved July 8, 2020, from https://www.understood.org/en/learning-thinking-differences/child-learning-disabilities/communication-disorders/difference-between-speech-impairment-and-language-disorder

Kruger, J., & Dunning, D. (1999). Unskilled and Unaware of It: How Difficulties in Recognizing One's Own Incompetence Lead to Inflated Self-assessments. *Journal of Personality and Social Psychology*.

Kruger, L. G. (2017). *Defining Broadband: Minimum Threshold Speeds and Broadband Policy*. Washington, DC: Congressional Research Service.

Kuznekoff, J., Munz, S., & Titsworth, S. (2015). Mobile Phones in the Classrom: Examining the Effects of Texting, Twitter, and Message Content on Student Learning. *Communication Education*, 344-3–65.

Landau, E. (2011, October 19). Why Teens are Wired for Risk. Retrieved June 30, 2020, from https://www.cnn.com/2011/10/19/health/mental-health/teen-brain-impulses/index.html

Lemov, D. (2018). *Teach Like A Champion: 49 Techniques that Put Students on the Path to College*. San Francisco, CA: Jossey-Bass.

Lemov, D., Driggs, C., & Woolway, E. (2016). *Reading Reconsidered: A Practical Guide to Rigorous Literacy Instruction*. San Francisco, CA: Jossey-Bass.

Li, J., Klahr, D., & Siler, S. (2006, Spring). What Lies Beneath the Science Achievement Gap: The Challenges of Aligning Science Instruction With Standards and Tests. *Science Educator*, 15 (1), pp. 1–12.

Lin, C.-H. (2019). Auto-grading versus Instructor Grading in Online English Courses. Retrieved June 8, 2020, from https://michiganvirtual.org/research/publications/auto-grading-versus-instructor-grading-in-online-english-courses/

Linder, K. (2016). *Student Uses and Perceptions of Closed Captions and Transcripts: Results from a National Study*. Corvallis, OR: Oregon State University Ecampus Research Unit.

Little, J. L., Bjork, E. L., Bjork, R. A., & Angello, G. (2012). Multiple-Choice Tests Exonerated, at Least of Some Charges: Fostering Test-Induced Learning and Avoiding Test-Induced Forgetting. *Psychological Science*, 1337–44.

Loewus, L. (2017, August 15). The Nation's Teaching Force Is Still Mostly White and Female. Retrieved July 3, 2020, from https://www.edweek.org/ew/articles/2017/08/15/the-nations-teaching-force-is-still-mostly.html

LoGerfo, L., Nicholas, A., & Reardon, S. F. (2006). *Achievement Gains in Elementary and High School*. Washington, DC: Urban Institute.

Mahnken, K. (2018, December 5). National Poll on Education Attitudes Finds Majority of Teachers Down on Profession, Lack Trust in Parents. Retrieved July 3, 2020, from https://www.the74million.org/teachers-down-on-profession-lack-trust-in-parents-poll-finds/

Marsh, E., & Sink, H. (2009). Access to Handouts of Presentation Slides during Lecture: Consequences for Learning. *Applied Cognitive Psychology*, 691–706.

Massof, R. W. (2006, November). Low Vision and Blindness: Changing Perspective and Increasing Success. Retrieved July 8, 2020, from https://www.nfb.org/sites/www.nfb.org/files/images/nfb/publications/bm/bm06/bm0610/bm061005.htm

Mayer, R., & Anderson, R. (1991). Animations Need Narrations: An Experimental Test of a Dual-Coding Hypothesis. *Journal of Educational Psychology*, 484-4–90.

McHale, S. M., Updegraff, K. A., & Whiteman, S. D. (2012). Sibling Relationships and Influences in Childhood and Adolescence. *Journal of Marriage and Family*, 913–30.

Meckler, L., & Rabinowitz, K. (2019, December 27). *America's Schools are More Diverse Than.* Retrieved July 3, 2020, from https://www.washingtonpost.com/graphics/2019/local/education/teacher-diversity/

Metcalfe, J., & Miele, D. B. (2014). Hypercorrection of High Confidence Errors: Prior Testing Both Enhances Delayed Performance and Blocks the Return of the Errors. *Journal of Applied Research in Memory and Cognition*, 189-1–97.

Miron, G., Shank, C., & Davidson, C. (2018). *Full-Time Virtual and Blended Schools: Enrollment, Student Characteristics, and Performance.* Boulder, CO: National Education Policy Center.

Morin, A. (n.d.). Classroom Accommodations for ADHD. Retrieved May 27, 2020, from https://www.understood.org/en/school-learning/partnering-with-childs-school/instructional-strategies/classroom-accommodations-for-adhd

Morin, A. (n.d.). Least Restrictive Environment (LRE): What You Need to Know. Retrieved July 8, 2020, from https://www.understood.org/en/school-learning/special-services/special-education-basics/least-restrictive-environment-lre-what-you-need-to-know

myViewBoard. (2019, November 5). Adobe Flash End of Life & the Threat to Education. Retrieved June 24, 2020, from https://myviewboard.com/blog/education/adobe-flash-end-of-life-the-threat-to-education/

Nancekivell, S. (2019, May 30). Belief in Learning Styles Myth May Be Detrimental. Retrieved June 17, 2020, from https://www.apa.org/news/press/releases/2019/05/learning-styles-myth

National Center for Education Statistics. (2018, September). Table 702.15. Percentage of Children Ages 3 to 18 who Use the Internet from Home, by Selected Child and Family Characteristics: Selected Years, 2010 through 2017. Retrieved June 24, 2020, from https://nces.ed.gov/programs/digest/d18/tables/dt18_702.15.asp?current=yes

National Center for Education Statistics. (2020, May). English Language Learners in Public Schools. Retrieved May 20, 2020, from https://nces.ed.gov/programs/coe/indicator_cgf.asp: https://nces.ed.gov/programs/coe/indicator_cgf.asp

National Center for Education Statistics. (2020). National Assessment of Educational Progress (NAEP): Reading Performance. *The Condition of Education 2020*, 2.

National Center for Homeless Education . (2019). *Federal Data Summary School Years 2014-15 to 2016-17.* Browns Summit, NC: National Center for Homeless Education .

National Council on Disability. (2004). *Improving Educational Outcomes for Students with Disabilities.* Washington, D.C: National Council on Disability.

National Education Association. (2006). The Twice-Exceptional Dilemma. Retrieved May 20, 2020, from http://www.nea.org/assets/docs/twiceexceptional.pdf

National Institute of Mental Health. (2018, July). Anxiety Disorders. Retrieved July 8, 2020, from https://www.nimh.nih.gov/health/topics/anxiety-disorders/index.shtml

National Institute of Mental Health. (2016). Attention-Deficit/Hyperactivity Disorder (ADHD): The Basics. Retrieved July 8, 2020, from https://www.nimh.nih.gov/health/publications/attention-deficit-hyperactivity-disorder-adhd-the-basics/index.shtml

National Institute of Mental Health Information Resource Center. (2018, March). Autism Spectrum Disorder. Retrieved July 8, 2020, from https://www.nimh.nih.gov/health/topics/autism-spectrum-disorders-asd/index.shtml

National Restaurant Association Educational Foundation. (2017, January 26). High School ProStart I Curriculum. Retrieved June 17, 2020, from https://www.parkhill.k12.mo.us/UserFiles/Servers/Server_62416/File/Academic%20Services/Board%20Approved%20Curriculum/Family%20and%20Consumer%20Science/Revisions%20Spring%202017/HighSchoolProStartI%20Board%20Approved--January%2026,%202017.pdf

NCS Pearson, Inc. (2015). WISC-V Interpretetive Report Sample. Retrieved June 15, 2020, from https://images.pearsonclinical.com/images/assets/wisc-v/WISC-VInterpretiveReportSample-1.pdf

Nelson, R., & González, N. S. (2018). *Update: Online Learning.* Olympia, WA: Office of Superintendent of Public Instruction.

NGSS Lead States. (2013). MS-LS2-2 Ecosystems: Interactions, Energy, and Dynamics. Retrieved June 22, 2020, from https://www.nextgenscience.org/pe/ms-ls2-2-ecosystems-interactions-energy-and-dynamics

Olson, D. R. (2020). Writing. In *Encyclopædia Britannica*.

Oral Comprehension Sets the Ceiling on Reading Comprehension. (2003, Spring). Retrieved May 20, 2020, from https://www.aft.org/periodical/american-educator/spring-2003/oral-comprehension-sets-ceiling-reading

Ounce of Prevention Fund. (2017). *The Language of Babies, Toddlers and Preschoolers: Connecting Research to Practice*. Chicago, IL: Ounce of Prevention Fund.

Paas, F., Renkl, A., & Sweller, J. (2004). Cognitive Load Theory: Instructional Implications of the Interaction between Information Structures and Cognitive Architecture. *Instructional Science*, 1–8.

Page, A., & Abbott, M. (2020, February 3). A Discussion About Online Discussion. Retrieved June 3, 2020, from https://www.facultyfocus.com/articles/online-education/discussion-about-online-discussion/

Perino, M., Kiersz, A., & Hoff, M. (2020, May 5). Here's How Much Every US State Pays Its Teachers and How Much They Spend on Each Student. Retrieved June 22, 2020, from https://www.businessinsider.com/teacher-salary-in-every-state-2018-4

Perrin, A. (2019, September 25). One-in-Five Americans now Listen to Audiobooks. Retrieved May 21, 2020, from https://www.pewresearch.org/fact-tank/2019/09/25/one-in-five-americans-now-listen-to-audiobooks/

Pew Research Center. (2019, June 12). Internet/Broadband Fact Sheet. Retrieved July 3, 2020, from https://www.pewresearch.org/internet/fact-sheet/internet-broadband/

Pew Research Center. (2019, June 12). Mobile Fact Sheet. Retrieved July 3, 2020, from https://www.pewresearch.org/internet/fact-sheet/mobile/

Pi, Z., Hong, J., & Yang, J. (2017). Does Instructor's Image Size in Video Lectures Affect Learning Outcomes?: Image size. *Journal of Computer Assisted Learning*, 33 (4).

Pianta, R. C., Hamre, B. K., & Allen, J. P. (2012). Teacher-Student Relationships and Engagement: Conceptualizing, Measuring, and Improving the Capacity of Classroom Interactions. In S. C. (eds.), *Handbook of Research on Student Engagement* (pp. 365–386). Berlin: Springer Science+Business Media, LLC.

Pilgrim, C., & Scanlon, C. (2018, July 27). Don't Assume Online Students are More Likely to Cheat. The Evidence is Murky. Retrieved June 18, 2020, from The Conversation: https://phys.org/news/2018-07-dont-assume-online-students-evidence.html

Platt, S. (Ed.). (1993). *Respectfully Quoted: A Dictionary of Quotations*. Barnes & Noble Books.

Polikoff, M., & Dean, J. (2019). *The Supplemental Curriculum Bazaar: Is What's Online Any Good?* Washington, D.C.: Thomas B. Fordham Institute.

Pondiscio, R. (2016, May 6). Education's Dirty Little Secret. Retrieved May 21, 2020, from https://www.usnews.com/opinion/articles/2016-05-06/why-teachers-rely-on-google-and-pinterest-for-course-materials

prenner. (2015, November 11). Tech: Online OCR. Retrieved June 8, 2020, from http://dyslexiahelp.umich.edu/latest/tech-online-ocr

Rampell, C. (2009, September 11). Class Size Around the World. Retrieved May 20, 2020, from https://economix.blogs.nytimes.com/2009/09/11/class-size-around-the-world/

Raver, S. A., & Maydosz, A. (2010). Impact of the Provision and Timing of Instructor-Provided Notes on University Students' *Learning. Active Learning in Higher Education*, 189-–200.

Rebora, A. (2011, October 12). Keeping Special Ed in Proportion. Retrieved June 9, 2020, from https://www.edweek.org/tsb/articles/2011/10/13/01disproportion.h05.html

researchED. (2019). *Explicit & Direct Instruction*. Melton, Woodbridge, United Kingdom: John Catt Educational Ltd.

Ringen, J. (2015, January 8). How Lego Became The Apple of Toys. Retrieved June 15, 2020, from https://www.fastcompany.com/3040223/when-it-clicks-it-clicks

Robertson, K. (2020). Distance Learning for ELLs: Planning Instruction. Retrieved June 8, 2020, from https://www.colorincolorado.org/article/distance-learning-ells-instruction

Rodríguez-Naveiras, E., Verche, E., Hernández-Lastiri, P., Montero, R., & Borges, Á. (2019). Differences in Working Memory between Gifted or Talented Students and Community Samples: A Meta-analysis. *Psicothema*, 255–62.

Roediger III, H., & Karpicke, J. (2006). Test-Enhanced Learning: Taking Memory Tests Improves Long-Term Retention. *Psychological Science*, 249-2–55.

Rosen, P. (n.d.). Classroom Accommodations for Auditory Processing Disorder. Retrieved July 8, 2020, from https://www.understood.org/en/school-learning/partnering-with-childs-school/instructional-strategies/classroom-accommodations-for-auditory-processing-disorder

Rosenshine, B. (2012). Principles of Instruction. *American Educator*, pp. 12–-39.

Royce, C. A. (2020, January). Teaching Through Trade Books: Understanding Chemical and Physical Changes. Retrieved June 15, 2020, from https://www.nsta.org/science-and-children/science-and-children-january-2020/understanding-chemical-and-physical-changes

Ryder, R. E., & Rooney, P. (2017, May 16). Requirements for the Cap on the Percentage of Students who may be Assessed with an Alternate Assessment Aligned with Alternate Academic Achievement Standards. Retrieved July 8, 2020, from https://www2.ed.gov/admins/lead/account/saa/onepercentcapmemo51617.pdf

Sacks, V. (2016, August 22). The Other Achievement Gap: Poverty and Academic Success. Retrieved June 9, 2020, from https://www.childtrends.org/the-other-achievement-gap-poverty-and-academic-success

Schmitt, B. D. (2014). Attention Deficit/Hyperactivity Disorder (ADHD): How to Help Your Child. Retrieved June 15, 2020, from https://www.summitmedicalgroup.com/library/pediatric_health/pa-hhgbeh_attention/: https://www.summitmedicalgroup.com/library/pediatric_health/pa-hhgbeh_attention/

Schoenberger, J. (n.d.). Bending Light. Retrieved June 17, 2020, from https://ngss.nsta.org/Resource.aspx?ResourceID=866

Schuberth, E., & Kuettel, N. (2014). *Geometry Lessons in the Waldorf School Grades 4 & 5: Freehand Form Drawing and Basic Geometric Construction in Grades 4 and 5*. Grapevine, TX: Waldorf Publications.

Schwartz, S. (2018, December 19). On "Teachers Pay Teachers," Some Sellers are Profiting from Stolen Work. Retrieved May 27, 2020, from https://www.edweek.org/ew/articles/2018/12/19/on-teachers-pay-teachers-some-sellers-are.html

Sealy, C., Bennett, T., Young, M., Ashbee, R., Reid, A., Thompson, S., et al. (2020). *The researchEd Guide to The Curriculum: An Evidence-Informed Guide for Teachers*. Melton, Woodbridge, United Kingdom: John Catt Educational Ltd.

Sedgwick, J. (2018, April 16). 25-Year-Old Textbooks and Holes in the Ceiling: Inside America's Public Schools. Retrieved July 13, 2020, from https://www.nytimes.com/2018/04/16/reader-center/us-public-schools-conditions.html

Seward, M. (2020, July 10). How General Ed and Special Ed Teachers Can Partner as Allies. (J. Ehehalt, Interviewer)

Shammas, B. (2015, October 17). Broward's Gifted Programs Getting More Diverse. Retrieved May 20, 2020, from https://www.sun-sentinel.com/local/broward/fl-broward-gifted-universal-test-20151015-story.html

Shaughnessy, M. F. (2013, July 29). An Interview with Robert Pondisco: Civic Education in A Time of Turmoil. Retrieved June 15, 2020, from https://www.educationviews.org/an-interview-with-robert-pondisco-civic-education-in-a-time-of-turmoil/

Sherrington, T. (2020, April 20). The next edu-revolution*: Textbooks! Retrieved May 27, 2020, from https://teacherhead.com/2020/04/20/the-next-edu-revolution-textbooks/

Sherrington, T., & Caviglioli, O. (2020). Teaching Walkthrus. Melton, Woodbridge, UK: John Catt Educational Ltd.

Siegel, R. (2019, October 29). Tweens, Teens and Screens: The Average Time Kids Spend Watching Online Videos has Doubled in 4 Years. Retrieved July 3, 2020, from https://www.washingtonpost.com/technology/2019/10/29/survey-average-time-young-people-spend-watching-videos-mostly-youtube-has-doubled-since/

Simply Charlotte Mason. (n.d.). Scripture Memory System. Retrieved June 17, 2020, from https://simplycharlottemason.com/timesavers/memorysys/

Startz, D. (2019, June 12). Do Teachers Work Long Hours? Retrieved June 22, 2020, from https://www.brookings.edu/blog/brown-center-chalkboard/2019/06/12/do-teachers-work-long-hours/

Steiner, D. (2017). *Curriculum Research: What We Know and Where We Need to Go*. Baltimore, MD: Johns Hopkins Institute for Education Policy.

Sundararajan, N., & Adesope, O. (2020). Keep It Coherent: A Meta-Analysis of the Seductive Details Effect. *Educational Psychology Review*.

Swanson, H. L., & Sachse-Lee, C. (2001). Mathematical Problem Solving and Working Memory in Children with Learning Disabilities: Both Executive and Phonological Processes Are Important. *Journal of Experimental Child Psychology*, 294–321.

Tall Poppy Syndrome. (n.d.). Retrieved June 9, 2020, from https://tvtropes.org/pmwiki/pmwiki.php/Main/TallPoppySyndrome

Taylor, K., & Rohrere, D. (2009). The Effects of Interleaved Practice. *Applied Cognitive Psychology*, 837–848.

The Annie E. Casey Foundation. (2019, September). Data Center. Retrieved June 9, 2020, from https://datacenter.kidscount.org/data/tables/44-children-in-poverty-by-race-and-ethnicit

The Writing Revolution. (2017). *The Writing Revolution*. San Francisco, CA: Jossey-Bass.

Thorne, G. (2006). 10 Strategies to Enhance Students' Memory. Retrieved May 27, 2020, from https://www.readingrockets.org/article/10-strategies-enhance-students-memory

Thurlow, M. L., Larson, E. D., Albus, D. A., Liu, K. K., & Kwong, E. (2017). *Alternate Assessments for Students with Significant Cognitive Disabilities: Participation Guidelines and Definitions (NCEO Report 406)*. Minneapolis, MN: National Center on Education.

Too Little Sleep Lowers IQ: Report. (1999, March 20). Retrieved June 30, 2020, from https://www.cbc.ca/news/technology/too-little-sleep-lowers-iq-report-1.168864

Turkheimer, E., Harden, K. P., & Nisbett, R. E. (2017, January 17). There's Still no Good Reason to Believe Black-White IQ Differences are Due to Genes. Retrieved July 13, 2020, from https://www.vox.com/the-big-idea/2017/6/15/15797120/race-black-white-iq-response-critics

Turner, C. A. (2020, April 11). "There's A Huge Disparity": What Teaching Looks Like During Coronavirus. Retrieved June 2, 2020, from https://www.npr.org/2020/04/11/830856140/teaching-without-schools-grief-then-a-free-for-all

U.S. Department of Education. (2011, May 26). Frequently Asked Questions About the June 29, 2010, Dear Colleague Letter. Retrieved June 3, 2020, from https://www2.ed.gov/about/offices/list/ocr/docs/dcl-ebook-faq-201105.pdf

U.S. Department of Education. (2018, May). Percentage of Elementary and Secondary School Students who do Homework, Average Time Spent Doing Homework, Percentage Whose Parents Check that Homework is Done, and Percentage Whose Parents Help with Homework, by Frequency and Selected Characteristics: 20. Retrieved July 3, 2020, from National Center for https://nces.ed.gov/programs/digest/d17/tables/dt17_227.40.asp

US Bureau of Labor Statistics. (2020, April 21). Employment Characteristics of Families Summary. Retrieved June 24, 2020, from https://www.bls.gov/news.release/famee.nr0.htm

US Census Bureau. (2016, November 17). The Majority of Children Live With Two Parents, Census Bureau Reports. Retrieved June 24, 2020, from https://www.census.gov/newsroom/press-releases/2016/cb16-192.html

US Department of Education. (2018). Early Literacy Activities. Retrieved July 3, 2020, from National Center for https://nces.ed.gov/fastfacts/display.asp?id=56

US Department of Education. (2017, May 2). Sec. 300.39 Special Education. Retrieved July 8, 2020, from https://sites.ed.gov/idea/regs/b/a/300.39

US Department of Education. (2017, May 2). Sec. 300.39 (a) (1). Retrieved July 8, 2020, from https://sites.ed.gov/idea/regs/b/a/300.39/a/1

US Department of Justice & US Department of Education. (2010, June 29). Dear College or University President. Retrieved June 3, 2020, from https://www.ada.gov/kindle_ltr_eddoj.htm

Varao-Sousa, L., T., & Kingstone, A. (2015). Memory for Lectures: How Lecture Format Impacts the Learning Experience. *PLoS ONE*.

Vaughn, S., Danielson, L., Zumeta, R., & Holdheide, L. (2015). *Deeper Learning for Students with Disabilities*. Cincinnati, OH: Jobs for the Future: Students at the Center.

Walker, R. (2018, 8 16). E. Coli and Quality First Teaching. Retrieved May 20, 2020, from https://rosalindwalker.wordpress.com/2018/08/16/e-coli-and-quality-first-teaching/

Walker, T. (n.d.). Legal Controversy Over Lesson Plans. Retrieved May 27, 2020, from http://www.nea.org/home/37583.htm

Walvoord, B. E., & Johnson Anderson, V. (2009). *Effective Grading: A Tool for Learning and Assessment in College*. San Francisco, CA: John Wiley & Sons, Inc.

Webb, J. T., Amend, E. R., Webb, N. E., Goerss, J., Beljan, P., & Olenchak, F. R. (2019, January 10). Misdiagnosis and Dual Diagnosis of Gifted Children. Retrieved June 9, 2020, from https://www.sengifted.org/post/misdiagnosis-and-dual-diagnosis-of-gifted-children

Weisberg, D. (2019, November 5). To Help Students Who are Behind, Find Out if Their Assignments Match Their Goals. Retrieved May 21, 2020, from https://fordhaminstitute.org/national/commentary/help-students-who-are-behind-find-out-if-their-assignments-match-their-goals

West Virginia Department of Education. (n.d.). Science – Grade-6 Standards. Retrieved June 22, 2020, from https://wvde.us/tree/middlesecondary-learning/science/science-grade-6-standards/

Wexler, N. (2020, May 17). Achievement Gaps Increase The Longer Kids Stay In School. Here's Why. Retrieved May 18, 2020, from https://www.forbes.com/sites/nataliewexler/2020/05/17/achievement-gaps-increase-the-longer-kids-stay-in-school-heres-why/

Willingham, D. (n.d.). Learning Styles FAQ. Retrieved June 14, 2020, from http://www.danielwillingham.com/learning-styles-faq.html

Willingham, D. T. (2002, Summer). Ask the Cognitive Scientist: Allocating Student Study Time: "Massed" versus "Distributed" Practice. *American Educator.*

Willingham, D. T. (2002). Ask the Cognitive Scientist: Inflexible Knowledge: The First Step to Expertise. Retrieved May 21, 2020, from https://www.aft.org/periodical/american-educator/winter-2002/ask-cognitive-scientist-inflexible-knowledge

Willingham, D. T. (2003, Summer). Ask the Cognitive Scientist: Remember . . . What They Think About. *American Educator.*

Willingham, D. T. (2006, Spring). How Knowledge Helps. Retrieved July 13, 2020, from https://www.aft.org/periodical/american-educator/spring-2006/how-knowledge-helps

Willingham, D. T. (2012). *When Can You Trust the Experts: How to Tell Good Science from Bad in Education.* San Francisco, CA: Jossey-Bass.

Willingham, D. (2009). *Why Don't Students Like School?* San Francisco, CA: Jossey-Bass.

Willis, J. (2007). Brain-Friendly Strategies for the Inclusion Classroom. Retrieved May 27, 2020, from http://www.ascd.org/publications/books/107040/chapters/Success-for-all-Students-in-Inclusion-Classes.aspx

ENDNOTES

i   (Dehaene, 2009)

ii   (Willingham, *When Can You Trust the Experts: How to Tell Good Science from Bad in Education*, 2012)

iii   (Willingham, *When Can You Trust the Experts: How to Tell Good Science from Bad in Education*, 2012)

iv   (Willingham, *When Can You Trust the Experts: How to Tell Good Science from Bad in Education*, 2012)

v   (John Wiley & Sons, Inc., 2009)

vi   (Hirsch, 2006)

vii   (Delisle, 2015)

viii   (Tomlinson, 2015)

ix   (Williams, 2012)

x   (Rojo, 2013)

xi   (Bloom, 1987)

xii   (Deresiewicz, 2015)

xiii   (Center on Education Policy, 2007)

xiv   (Jesuit High School of New Orleans)

xv   (Martin-Chang, Gould, & Meuse, 2011)

xvi   (Brown, Roediger III, & McDaniel, 2014)

xvii   (Brown, Roediger III, & McDaniel, 2014)

xviii   (Literacy Minnesota, 2010)

xix   (Reeves & Nass, 1996)

xx   (Harris, 2020)

xxi   (Soffer & Nachmias, 2018)

xxii   (Salter, Douglas, & Kember, 2016)

xxiii   (Pytash & Ferdig, 2017)

xxiv   (Grison, Luke, Shigeto, & Watson, 2011, November)

xxv   (Bowers & Kumar, 2015)

xxvi   (Auxier & Anderson, 2020)

xxvii   (Guskin, 2018)

xxviii   (Bayeck, 2016)

xxix   (Lederman, 2019)

xxx   (Topolovec, 2018)

xxxi   (Aaronson & O'Connor, 2012)

xxxii   (Bedortha, 2014)

xxxiii   (EducationSuperHighway, 2019)

xxxiv   (West Virginia Library Commission, 2017)

xxxv   (West Virginia Library Commission)

xxxvi   (Biola, 2019)

xxxvii   (The West Virginia Virtual School (WVVS))

xxxviii   (Nguyen, 2018)

xxxix   (Banna, Meng-Fen, Stewart, & Fialkowski, 2015)

xl   (National Center for Education Statistics, 2018)

xli   (Pew Research Center, 2015)

xlii   Techniques 8, 11, 15, 26, 27, 28, 31, 32, 33, 34, 36, and 38. (Devos, 2018)

xliii   (Lederman, 2019)

xliv   (Kirsch, 2017)

xlv   (Arias, Swinton, & Anderson, 2018)

xlvi   (Soffer & Nachmias, 2018)

xlvii   (Korbey, 2014)

xlviii   (Willingham, Students Remember . . . What They Think About, 2003)

xlix   (Groshek, Cutino, & Walsh, 2016)

l   (Desmos)

li   (Sangwin & Budd, 2000)

lii   (Peace Hill Press, 2006)

liii   (Koenig, 2019)

liv   (Devos, 2018)

lv   (Guskin, 2018)

lvi   (Bowers & Kumar, 2015)

lvii   (Pew Research Center, 2019)

lviii   (Kirsch, 2017)

lix   (Devos, 2018)

lx   (Kirsch, 2017)

lxi   (Strauss, 2015)

lxii   (Wexler, The Knowledge Gap, 2019)

lxiii   (Bauer & Wise, 2016)

lxiv   (Brown, Roediger III, & McDaniel, 2014)

lxv   (Brown, Roediger III, & McDaniel, 2014)

lxvi   (Willingham D. T., 2012)

lxvii   (Willingham, 2002)

lxviii   (Willingham, 2002)

lxix   (Gustafson, 2019)

lxx   (Hui, Hoe, & Lee, 2017)

lxxi   (Weisberg, 2019)

lxxii   (Cantor, 2019)

lxxiii   (Chatmon & Osta, 2018)

lxxiv   (Pondiscio, 2016)

lxxv   (Perrin, 2019)

lxxvi   (Sherrington, 2020)

lxxvii   (Steiner, 2017)

lxxviii   (Education Commission of the States, 2018)

lxxix   (Schwartz, 2018)

lxxx   (Walker T.)

lxxxi   (Gormley, 2020)

lxxxii   (Copyright Law of the United States (Title 17) Chapter 1: Section 110(2) (A))

lxxxiii   (Gormley, 2020)

lxxxiv   (Polikoff & Dean, 2019)

lxxxv   (Polikoff & Dean, 2019)

lxxxvi   (U.S. Department of Education, 2010)

lxxxvii   (Emanuel, 2013)

lxxxviii   (Varao-Sousa, L., & Kingstone, 2015)

lxxxix   (Wasser, 2015)

xc   (National Center for Education Statistics, 2018)

xci   (Pew Research Center, 2015)

xcii   (Devos, 2018)

xciii   (Fletcher-Wood, 2019)

xciv   (Fletcher-Wood, 2019)

xcv   (Fletcher-Wood, 2019)

xcvi   (Fletcher-Wood, 2019)

xcvii   (Sherrington & Caviglioli, Teaching Walkthrus, 2020)

xcviii   (Board & Barkely, 2019)

xcix   (Morin)

c   (Bartlett, Griffin, & Thomson, 2020)

ci   (Grose, 2020)

cii   (Willingham, Students Remember . . . What They Think About, 2003)

ciii   (Boxer, 2019)

civ   (Boxer, 2019)

cv   (Willis, 2007)

cvi   (Falchikov & Boud, 1989)

cvii   (Thorne, 2006)

cviii   (Ferdman, 2015)

cix   (Wexler, 2020)

cx   (LoGerfo, Nicholas, & Reardon, 2006)

cxi   (Li, Klahr, & Siler, 2006)

cxii   (Mathewson, 2019)

cxiii   (Darby)

cxiv   (Pianta, Hamre, & Allen, 2012)

cxv   (The Aspen Institute Education & Society Program, 2018)

cxvi   (Dixson, 2010)

cxvii   (Feldstein, 2018)

cxviii   (Feldstein, 2018)

cxix   (Fenton, 2017)

cxx   (Harris, 2020)

cxxi   (Justice & Education, 2010)

cxxii   (U.S. Department of Education, 2011)

cxxiii   (Fleming, Harmon-Cooley, & Mcfadden-Wade, 2009)

cxxiv   (Fagell, 2019)

cxxv   (Arbaugh, Godfrey, Johnson, Pollack, & Wresch, 2009)

cxxvi   (Blackboard)

cxxvii   (Kruger & Dunning, 1999)

cxxviii   (Kardas & O'Brien, 2018)

cxxix   (Roediger III & Karpicke, 2006)

cxxx   (Kluger & DeNisi, 1996)

cxxxi   (Blackboard)

cxxxii   (Kuznekoff, Munz, & Titsworth, 2015)

cxxxiii   (Christodoulou, 2020)

cxxxiv   (Turner, 2020)

cxxxv   (The Aspen Institute Education & Society Program, 2018)

cxxxvi   (Pi, Hong, & Yang, 2017)

cxxxvii   (Draus, Curran, & Trempus, 2014)

cxxxviii   (Blackboard)

cxxxix   (Linder, 2016)

cxl   (Gernsbacher, 2015)

cxli   (Carr, 2019)

cxlii   (Cho & MacArthur, 2011)

cxliii   (Page & Abbott, 2020)

cxliv   ((PTAC), 2014)

cxlv   ((PTAC), 2014)

cxlvi   (Aaronson & O'Connor, 2012)

cxlvii   (Associated Press, 2020)

cxlviii   (Deunk, Smale-Jacobse, de Boer, Doolaard, & Bosker, 2018)

cxlix   (Deunk, Smale-Jacobse, de Boer, Doolaard, & Bosker, 2018)

cl   (The Aspen Institute Education & Society Program, 2018)

cli   (Auwarter & Aruguete, 2010)

clii   (Deunk, Smale-Jacobse, de Boer, Doolaard, & Bosker, 2018)

cliii   (Humble, 2017)

cliv   (Tall Poppy Syndrome)

clv   (Humble, 2017)

clvi   (Webb, Amend, Webb, Goerss, Beljan, & Olenchak, 2019)

clvii   (National Education Association, 2006)

clviii   (Is Progress Being Made Toward Closing the Achievement Gap in Special Education?, 2017)

clix   (National Council on Disability, 2004)

clx   (Johnson, 2015)

clxi   (Sacks, 2016)

clxii   (The Annie E. Casey Foundation, 2019)

clxiii   (Rebora, 2011)

clxiv   (Bush, 2000)

clxv   (Kim, Sheridan, & Holcomb, 2009)

clxvi   (Shammas, 2015)

clxvii   (Finn Jr., 2014)

clxviii   (Deunk, Smale-Jacobse, de Boer, Doolaard, & Bosker, 2018)

clxix   (Deunk, Smale-Jacobse, de Boer, Doolaard, & Bosker, 2018)

clxx   (Deunk, Smale-Jacobse, de Boer, Doolaard, & Bosker, 2018)

clxxi   (Wexler, 2020)

clxxii   (Walker, 2018)

clxxiii   (National Center for Education Statistics, 2020)

clxxiv   (Katusic, Colligan, Barbaresi, Schaid, & Jacobsen, 2001)

clxxv   (National Center for Education Statistics, 2020)

clxxvi   (Rampell, 2009)

clxxvii   (Curators of the University of Missouri, 2011)

clxxviii   (prenner, 2015)

clxxix   (Oral Comprehension Sets the Ceiling on Reading Comprehension, 2003)

clxxx   (Raver & Maydosz, 2010)

clxxxi   (Babb & Ross, 2009)

clxxxii   (Marsh & Sink, 2009)

clxxxiii   (Robertson, 2020)

clxxxiv   (Dougherty, 2012)

clxxxv   (Sherrington & Caviglioli, Teaching Walkthrus, 2020) clxxxvi   (ADHD Editorial Board, n.d.)

clxxxvii   (Adelman & Taylor, 2005)

clxxxviii   (researchED, 2019)

clxxxix   (Sherrington & Caviglioli, Teaching Walkthrus, 2020)

cxc   (The Writing Revolution, 2017)

cxci   (Brown, Roediger III, & McDaniel, 2014)

cxcii   (Rosenshine, 2012)

cxciii   (Walvoord & Johnson Anderson, 2009)

cxciv   (Bauer & Anderson, 2000)

cxcv   (Lin, 2019)

cxcvi   (Caviglioli, 2019)

cxcvii   (Darby & Lang, Small Teaching Online, 2019)

cxcviii   (Brann, 2011)

cxcix   (Christodoulou, Teachers vs Tech, 2020)

cc   (The Writing Revolution, 2017)

cci   (Gonzalez, 2018)

ccii   (Willingham D. T., 2002)

cciii   (Board & Barkely, 2019)

cciv   (Morin)

ccv   (Bartlett, Griffin, & Thomson, 2020)

ccvi   (Grose, 2020)

ccvii   (Sherrington & Caviglioli, Teaching Walkthrus, 2020)

ccviii   (Darling-Hammond, Flook, Cook-Harvey, Barron, & Osher, 2020)

ccix   (Paas, Renkl, & Sweller, 2004)

ccx   (Darby & Lang, Small Teaching Online, 2019)

ccxi   (Clark & Mayer, 2016)

ccxii   (Willingham D. T., Ask the Cognitive Scientist: Remember . . . What They Think About, 2003)

ccxiii   (Willingham D. T., Ask the Cognitive Scientist: Allocating Student Study Time: "Massed" versus "Distributed" Practice, 2002)

ccxiv   (Clark & Mayer, 2016)

ccxv   (Brown, Roediger III, & McDaniel, 2014)

ccxvi   (Brown, Roediger III, & McDaniel, 2014)

ccxvii   (Vaughn, Danielson, Zumeta, & Holdheide, 2015)

ccxviii   (Willingham D. , Learning Styles FAQ)

ccxix   (Kirschner & Hendrick, 2020)

ccxx   (Kirschner & Hendrick, 2020)

ccxxi   (Mayer & Anderson, 1991)

ccxxii   (Carpenter & Toftness, 2017)

ccxxiii   (Kirschner & Hendrick, 2020)

ccxxiv   (Brown, Roediger III, & McDaniel, 2014)

ccxxv   (Willingham D. , 2009)

ccxxvi   (Devos, 2018)

ccxxvii   (Kirschner & Hendrick, 2020)

ccxxviii   (Little, Bjork, Bjork, & Angello, 2012)

ccxxix   (Stenger, 2014)

ccxxx   (Anderman & Murdock, 2007)

ccxxxi   (Bernard, et al., 2009)

ccxxxii   (Clark & Mayer, 2016)

ccxxxiii   (Brown, Roediger III, & McDaniel, 2014)

ccxxxiv   (Clark & Mayer, 2016)

ccxxxv   (Shaughnessy, 2013)

ccxxxvi   (The Aspen Institute Education & Society Program, 2018)

ccxxxvii   (Clark & Mayer, 2016)

ccxxxviii   (Clark & Mayer, 2016)

ccxxxix   (Darby & Lang, Small Teaching Online, 2019)

ccxl   (Darby & Lang, Small Teaching Online, 2019)

ccxli   (Clark & Mayer, 2016)

ccxlii   (Clark & Mayer, 2016)

ccxliii   (Rosenshine, 2012)

ccxliv   (Kirschner & Hendrick, 2020)

ccxlv   (The Writing Revolution, 2017)

ccxlvi   (Beck, McKeown, & Kucan, 2013)

ccxlvii   (Beck, McKeown, & Kucan, 2013)

ccxlviii   (Lemov, Driggs, & Woolway, 2016)

ccxlix   (Darby, How to Be a Better Online Teacher)

ccl   (Chatmon & Osta, 2018)

ccli   (Clark & Mayer, 2016)

cclii   (Konrad, Joseph, & Eveleigh, 2009)

ccliii   (Haydon, Mancil, Kroeger, Mcleskey, & Lin, 2011)

ccliv   (Gonzalez, 2018)

cclv   (Brown, Roediger III, & McDaniel, 2014)

cclvi   (Beck, McKeown, & Kucan, 2013)

cclvii   (Clark & Mayer, 2016)

cclviii   (Clark & Mayer, 2016)

cclix   (Clark & Mayer, 2016)

cclx   (Clark & Mayer, 2016)

cclxi   (Clark & Mayer, 2016)

cclxii   (Clark & Mayer, 2016)

cclxiii   (Willingham D. T., Ask the Cognitive Scientist: Remember...What They Think About, 2003)

cclxiv   (Harvard, Multiple-Choice Questioning as a Valuable Learning Opportunity, 2020)

cclxv   (Clark & Mayer, 2016)

cclxvi   (Rosenshine, 2012)

cclxvii   (Kirschner & Hendrick, 2020)

cclxviii   (Clark & Mayer, 2016)

cclxix   (Carnegie Foundation, 2014)

cclxx   (Schmitt, 2014)

cclxxi   (Kirschner & Hendrick, 2020)

cclxxii   (Christodoulou, Teachers vs Tech, 2020)

cclxxiii   (Rosenshine, 2012)

cclxxiv   (Kirschner & Hendrick, 2020)

cclxxv   (Kirschner & Hendrick, 2020)

cclxxvi   (Rodríguez-Naveiras, Verche, Hernández-Lastiri, Montero, & Borges, 2019)

cclxxvii   (Swanson & Sachse-Lee, 2001)

cclxxviii   (Kirschner & Hendrick, 2020)

cclxxix   (Swanson & Sachse-Lee, 2001)

cclxxx   (ABC News, 2010)

cclxxxi   (Dehaene, 2011)

cclxxxii   (Didau, 2019)

cclxxxiii   (NCS Pearson, Inc, 2015)

cclxxxiv   (Carey, 2013)

cclxxxv   (NCS Pearson, Inc, 2015)

cclxxxvi   (Ringen, 2015)

cclxxxvii   (NCS Pearson, Inc, 2015)

cclxxxviii   (NCS Pearson, Inc, 2015)

cclxxxix   (Common Core State Standards Initiative, 2020)

ccxc   (NCS Pearson, Inc, 2015)

ccxci   (Royce, 2020)

ccxcii   (NCS Pearson, Inc, 2015)

ccxciii   (Ferris, 2017)

ccxciv   (Brown, Roediger III, & McDaniel, 2014)

ccxcv   (Franceschini, Trevisan, Ronconi, et al, 2017)

ccxcvi   (NCS Pearson, Inc, 2015)

ccxcvii   (Kirschner & Hendrick, 2020)

ccxcviii   (Brown, Roediger III, & McDaniel, 2014)

ccxcix   (Simply Charlotte Mason)

ccc   (Brown, Roediger III, & McDaniel, 2014)

ccci   (Kirschner & Hendrick, 2020)

cccii   (Willingham D., Learning Styles FAQ)

ccciii   (Nancekivell, 2019)

ccciv   (Olson, 2020)

cccv   (Kirschner & Hendrick, 2020)

cccvi   (Kirschner & Hendrick, 2020)

cccvii   (Burgess, 2012)

cccviii   (Kirschner & Hendrick, 2020)

cccix   (Hui, Hoe, & Lee, 2017)

cccx   (National Center for Homeless Education, 2019)

cccxi   (Sangwin & Budd, 2000)

cccxii   (Peace Hill Press, 2006)

cccxiii   (Gustafson, Habits for Lifelong Learning: Applying Behavioral Insights to Education, 2020)

cccxiv   (Boxer, Dual Coding for Teachers Who Can't Draw, 2020)

cccxv   (Brown, Roediger III, & McDaniel, 2014)

cccxvi   (Gonzalez, A 4-Part System for Getting to Know Your Students, 2016)

cccxvii   (Darby & Lang, Small Teaching Online, 2019)

cccxviii   (Butler, Marsh, & Godbole, 2013)

cccxix   (Rosenshine, 2012)

cccxx   (Harvard, 2019)

cccxxi   (Brown, Roediger III, & McDaniel, 2014)

cccxxii   (Brown, Roediger III, & McDaniel, 2014)

cccxxiii   (Brown, Roediger III, & McDaniel, 2014)

cccxxiv   (Taylor & Rohrere, 2009)

cccxxv   (Carter & Grahn, 2016)

cccxxvi   (@dylanwiliam, 2020)

cccxxvii   (Metcalfe & Miele, 2014)

cccxxviii   (Gonzalez, A 4-Part System for Getting to Know Your Students, 2016)

cccxxix   (Gonzalez, A 4-Part System for Getting to Know Your Students, 2016)

cccxxx   (Conradt, 2016)

cccxxxi   (Common Core State Standards Initiative, 2020)

cccxxxii   (West Virginia Department of Education)

cccxxxiii   (NGSS Lead States, 2013)

cccxxxiv   (West Virginia Department of Education)

cccxxxv   (West Virginia Department of Education)

cccxxxvi   (Gorman, 2017)

cccxxxvii   (Perino, Kiersz, & Hoff, 2020)

cccxxxviii   (Startz, 2019)

cccxxxix   (Sherrington & Caviglioli, Teaching Walkthrus, 2020)

cccxl   (National Center for Education Statistics, 2018)

cccxli   (Anderson, 2019)

cccxlii   (Kruger L. G., 2017)

cccxliii   (myViewBoard, 2019)

cccxliv   (Literacy Minnesota, 2010)

cccxlv   (Reeves & Nass, 1996)

cccxlvi   (Harris, 2020)

cccxlvii   (Justice & Education, 2010)

cccxlviii   U.S. Department of Education, 2011)

cccxlix   (Willingham D. T., Ask the Cognitive Scientist: Remember . . . What They Think About, 2003)

cccl   (Board & Barkely, 2019)

cccli   (Morin)

ccclii   (Bartlett, Griffin, & Thomson, 2020)

cccliii   (Grose, 2020)

cccliv   (Willingham, Students Remember . . . What They Think About, 2003)

ccclv   (Christodoulou, Teachers vs Tech, 2020)

ccclvi   (Sundararajan & Adesope, 2020)

ccclvii   (NGSS Lead States, 2013)

ccclviii   (NGSS Lead States, 2013)

ccclix   (Ounce of Prevention Fund, 2017)

ccclx   (James, 1890)

ccclxi   (McHale, Updegraff, & Whiteman, 2012)

ccclxii   (US Census Bureau, 2016)

ccclxiii   (US Bureau of Labor Statistics, 2020)

ccclxiv   (US Census Bureau, 2016)

ccclxv   (US Bureau of Labor Statistics, 2020)

ccclxvi   (Kamenetz, 2020)

ccclxvii   (Gonzalez, A 4-Part System for Getting to Know Your Students, 2016)

ccclxviii   (Landau, 2011)

ccclxix   (Too little sleep lowers IQ: report, 1999)

ccclxx   (Bowles & Keller, 2019)

ccclxxi   (Carr J. M., 2019)

ccclxxii   (Hummer & Hernandez, 2013)

ccclxxiii   (Gryvatz Copquin, 2013)

ccclxxiv (Varao-Sousa, L., & Kingstone, 2015)

ccclxxv (American Psychological Association, 2006)

ccclxxvi (The Aspen Institute Education & Society Program, 2018)

ccclxxvii (Mahnken, 2018)

ccclxxviii (Loewus, 2017)

ccclxxix (Pew Research Center, 2019)

ccclxxx (US Department of Education, 2018)

ccclxxxi (Wasser, 2015)

ccclxxxii (Pew Research Center, 2019)

ccclxxxiii (eMarketer, 2007)

ccclxxxiv (Siegel, 2019)

ccclxxxv (US Department of Education, 2018)

ccclxxxvi (US Department of Education, 2018)

ccclxxxvii (US Department of Education, 2010)

ccclxxxviii (Rosenshine, 2012)

ccclxxxix (Guo, Kim, & Rubin, 2014)

cccxc (Rodríguez-Naveiras, Verche, Hernández-Lastiri, Montero, & Borges, 2019)

cccxci (Swanson & Sachse-Lee, 2001)

cccxcii (Deunk, Smale-Jacobse, de Boer, Doolaard, & Bosker, 2018)

cccxciii (Green, 2016)

cccxciv (Guo, Kim, & Rubin, 2014)

cccxcv (Guo, Kim, & Rubin, 2014)

cccxcvi (Guo, Kim, & Rubin, 2014)

cccxcvii (Boxer, Dual Coding for Teachers Who Can't Draw, 2020)

cccxcviii (Guo, Kim, & Rubin, 2014)

cccxcix (Guo, Kim, & Rubin, 2014)

cd (Clark D. , 2020)

cdi (Guo, Kim, & Rubin, 2014)

cdii (Guo, Kim, & Rubin, 2014)

cdiii (US Dept of Education, 2017)

cdiv (US Department of Education, 2017)

cdv (DO-IT, University of Washington (UW), 2019)

cdvi   (DO-IT, University of Washington (UW), 2019)

cdvii   (Thurlow, Larson, Albus, Liu, & Kwong, 2017)

cdviii   (Ryder & Rooney, 2017)

cdix   (Morin, Least Restrictive Environment (LRE): What You Need to Know)

cdx   (Miron, Shank, & Davidson, 2018)

cdxi   (Nelson & González, 2018)

cdxii   (Board & Barkely, 2019)

cdxiii   (Grose, 2020)

cdxiv   (Morin)

cdxv   (Linder, 2016)

cdxvi   (Gernsbacher, 2015)

cdxvii   (Justice & Education, 2010)

cdxviii   (U.S. Department of Education, 2011)

cdxix   (Gonzalez, A 4-Part System for Getting to Know Your Students, 2016)

cdxx   (Gonzalez, A 4-Part System for Getting to Know Your Students, 2016)

cdxxi   (Seward, 2020)

cdxxii   (National Institute of Mental Health, 2018)

cdxxiii   (National Institute of Mental Health, 2016)

cdxxiv   (Arnstein, 2009)

cdxxv   (National Institute of Mental Health Information Resource Center, 2018)

cdxxvi   (Jacobson)

cdxxvii   (Koslo)

cdxxviii   (Rosen)

cdxxix   (Massof, 2006)

cdxxx   (Hampshire, Highfield, Parkin, & Owen, 2012)

cdxxxi   (Bratsberg & Rogeberg, 2018)

cdxxxii   (Jensen & Nutt, 2015)

cdxxxiii   (Turkheimer, Harden, & Nisbett, 2017)

cdxxxiv   (Hirsch Jr., 1996)

cdxxxv   (Balf, 2014)

cdxxxvi   (Greene, 2018)

cdxxxvii   (Kirschner & Hendrick, 2020, p. 228)

cdxxxviii   (Willingham D. T., *How Knowledge Helps*, 2006)

cdxxxix   (Hanover Research, 2017)

cdxl   (Sealy, et al., 2020)

cdxli   (Goldstein, 2018)

cdxlii   (Green & Goldstein, 2019)

cdxliii   (Fernandez & Hauser, 2015)

cdxliv   (Sedgwick, 2018)

cdxlv   (Pilgrim & Scanlon, 2018)

cdxlvi   (Platt, 1993)

cdxlvii   (Eberly Center for Teaching Excellence and Educational Innovation, 2020)

cdxlviii   (Devos, 2018)

CPSIA information can be obtained
at www.ICGtesting.com
Printed in the USA
JSHW031155041120
9299JS00004B/8